The Tailor-King

Also by Anthony Arthur

Deliverance at Los Baños
Bushmasters

The ✝ailor-King

The Rise and Fall of the Anabaptist Kingdom of Münster

ANTHONY ARTHUR

ST. MARTIN'S PRESS
NEW YORK

THOMAS DUNNE BOOKS.
An imprint of St. Martin's Press.

Design by Nancy Resnick

ISBN 0-312-20515-5

First Edition: September 1999

10   9   8   7   6   5   4   3   2   1

Dedicated to the memory of my sister, Helen Wishart

ACKNOWLEDGMENTS

I am pleasantly indebted to Rosemary Zahn and Susanne Fröhnel for their advice on the use of German names and grammar; to Alasdair Heron for his wise counsel concerning the Reformation; and to Barbara Kelly for her sensitive editorial suggestions on style. I am also grateful to Karl-Heinz Kirchhoff for personally sharing some of his vast knowledge of the Anabaptists with me during my visit to Münster. Finally, thanks again to my wife, Carolyn, for her patience and her good humor.

CONTENTS

Introduction   1

1. A New Dawn   5
2. The Godless Expelled   29
3. A Mighty Fortress   44
4. Death of a Prophet   59
5. The Bishop and the Maiden   74
6. Counterrevolution   91
7. King Jan   103
8. The Return of Henry Graes   118
9. Restitution and Revenge   130
10. Flight   143
11. Attack   156
12. Punishment   170
13. The Legacy of the Tailor-King   179

Cast of Characters   202
Chronology   205
Notes   209
Sources and Writings about the Anabaptists   222
Bibliography   230
Index   235

NOTES FOR THE ILLUSTRATIONS

Illustrations follow page 116.

ANABAPTISTS BATHING. Copper engraving by Virgil Solis (1514–1562) after Heinrich Aldegrever. Mid-sixteenth century. Courtesy Westfälisches Landesmuseum für Kunst und Kulturgeschichte, Münster.

FRANZ VON WALDECK. Unsigned and undated oil painting, probably mid-seventeenth century. Münster Catalog #46, p. 111. Courtesy Land Niedersachsen, Polizeiausbildungstätte, Bad Iburg.

KING JAN. Copper etched portrait by Heinrich Aldegrever, 1536. Courtesy Stadtmuseum Münster. Authorities differ as to whether Aldegrever's celebrated portrait of Jan van Leyden was begun as a crayon sketch during the last months of the young king's reign or initiated after his capture, at the command of the Prince-Bishop. We know that the artist's father was arrested and tortured in a nearby city in 1522 for protesting the execution of some religious dissidents, and that the artist was sympathetic to the Anabaptists' cause. Certainly the richly detailed symbolism of Jan's kingly regalia and his look of dignified determination convey a more favorable image than his deeds would justify.

THE SIEGE OF MÜNSTER, 1534. Woodcut by Erhard Schoen, 1535. Catalog #149, p. 207. Courtesy Stadtmuseum Münster; on loan from a private source.

BERNARD KNIPPERDOLLING. Portrait by Heinrich Aldegrever. Catalog #122, p. 186. Courtesy Stadtmuseum Münster. In *Das Graphische Werk Heinrich Aldegrevers: Ein Beitrag zu seinem Stil im Rahmen der Deutschen Stilentwicklung* (The Graphic Work of Heinrich Aldegrever: A Contribution to His Style in the Context of German Stylistic Development; Heitz: Strassburg, 1933), the German art critic Herbert Zschelletzschky offers instructive comments on the painting: "The coat of arms, in the upper right corner of the engraving, describes a knotty, muscular fist holding the sword of judgment, surrounded by a laurel wreath. Note also the brilliantly opposed black and white stripes of the coat and the elaborately worked collar, contrasted with the bland background into which the head emerges, comparatively small, but one that deeply impresses the observer with its suggestion of energy and movement. There is a piercing sensation, a sense of looking into the distance, and a certain suggestion of uneasy tension. More than in the coolly detailed and reserved, unapproachable majesty of Jan's picture is it possible with Knipperdolling's, behind the stiff mien with the arched eyebrows, to read the character of this remarkable man, of . . . his head full of strange thoughts and impulses, a man noble in appearance, respected by the common man for his conduct, and his wise counsel in practical affairs, dignified and commanding, inclined to reject authority over him with courage, in quieter times certainly a man who could lead other men in powerful ways. . . ."

KNIPPERDOLLING CAPERING BEFORE KING JAN. An illustration by the Dutch artist Lambertus Hortensius, Amsterdam, 1694. Catalog #193A, p. 235. Courtesy Stadtmuseum Münster.

THE MOLLENHECK REBELLION. Unsigned and undated illustration, early eighteenth century. Catalog #105, p. 164. *Libri picturait* A 96, Bl. 45. Courtesy Staatsbibliothek Preußicher Kulturbesitz, Berlin.

KING JAN EXECUTES ELIZABETH WANDSCHEER and THE KING AND HIS OTHER WIVES CELEBRATE THE DEATH. Both illustrations by Lambertus Hortensius. Catalog #192, B and C. Courtesy Stadtmuseum Münster.

Introduction

We have two choices when we learn about extraordinary events and people. They can be taken as typical and representative of human nature and history, or they can be seen as aberrant exceptions to the norm. This is a story about a group of religious enthusiasts called Anabaptists who took over a north-German city nearly five centuries ago, turned it into a militant theocracy, and held it for over a year against overwhelming military odds, until they died. The sequence of actions is so strange, and its participants so apparently bizarre, that the Anabaptists have long been viewed as belonging to the second group—to the one characterized by a Victorian writer as "freaks of fanaticism."

My own view is that the Anabaptists in Münster, though certainly "fanatical" in many ways, were not "freaks," if by freaks we mean barely imaginable distortions of the norm; and that, for good or for evil, they were far more representative than not of human nature and history. My reason for telling their story is that I think it provides insight into our own time as well as theirs.

Late-medieval Germany, however, differed so radically from modern Europe and America that a few introductory reminders are in order. The most important point is that if you were born in Europe prior to 1517, you were probably a Roman Catholic. This was not a matter of choice, any more than susceptibility to gravity or to the autonomic nervous system is a choice. It was natural to believe in the Holy Trinity as it was explained by the Church; it was unnatural not to. To go against the Church was to violate both God and nature.

Yet the Church had become undeniably corrupt. In Fyodor

Dostoevsky's last novel, *The Brothers Karamazov* (1880), he imagines Jesus returning to earth during the time of the Spanish Inquisition in Seville, at the end of the sixteenth century. The "Grand Inquisitor" recognizes Jesus and immediately has him thrown into a dungeon. He visits Jesus in his cell and demands to know why he has returned. Jesus never answers, merely gazing with compassion at the aged Inquisitor. The priest says that Jesus erred in his original insistence that man must be free to choose whether to follow God or Satan; what men want, the priest says, is not freedom but bread. They want comfort, security, and the certainty of being saved if they follow the dictates of the Church.

Jesus, by returning, threatens the elaborate structure that has taken the Church many centuries to construct, the priest says. That hierarchy is based upon three critical concepts that all must accept, or die in the flames of the Inquisition. The first of these is Miracle; the second is Mystery; the third, and most important, is Authority. A challenge to any of these is pernicious; a challenge to all three is deadly. Because he personifies the purity of the original faith, before the structure of Miracle, Mystery, and Authority had replaced it, Jesus must now die again. In parting, the Inquisitor reveals that he belongs not to the party of God but to that of Satan, and that he and Jesus are therefore mortal antagonists; then, despite himself, he relents and orders Jesus to leave the dungeon.

Martin Luther shook the structure that Dostoevsky's Inquisitor described, but, according to the Anabaptists, he did not go far enough—he insisted on obedience to the state while trying to work out a satisfactory compromise. The Anabaptists held that, in particular, Authority had to be denied and defied, if necessary, because it was often an agent of Satan. Luther saw the Anabaptists' intransigence as endangering the survival of the Reformation itself, and denounced them as bitterly as did the Catholics. Emperor Charles V ordered their extermination. Within a decade after their first appearance, in 1523, most of the responsible leaders of the Anabaptists, who essentially asked merely to be left alone so that they could re-create the purity of the original Christian Church, had been killed or, like Menno Simons, virtually silenced. But some of the most radical and dangerous leaders had survived, generally by going underground and forming secret cells of true believers.

The insistence on the integrity of the primitive Church survives today in the United States among the placid descendants of Menno Simons, the Mennonites, as well as among other denominations. So also, in different groups, does the belief in a coming Last Judgment survive. The Anabaptists of the sixteenth century believed more strongly than any group today that the time was imminent for the apocalyptic final battle between God and Satan. It would occur in the years 1534–1535; the place would be in northern Germany, in the small Westphalian city of Münster. They began to gather there by the thousands in 1533, invited and encouraged by some of the natives of the city. By early 1534 they had displaced the elected council, composed of Lutherans and Catholics who had managed to establish a peaceful relationship. They evicted all "unbelievers" from the city and dared the Prince-Bishop in whose domain it lay to attack. When he did, they regarded it as confirmation that they, the Anabaptists, had been specially ordained by God to engage in the final battle between good and evil.

The Anabaptists were so badly treated during the years preceding this battle that, despite the irrationality of their beliefs and their self-righteous stubbornness, they attracted many sympathizers to their ranks. In the nineteenth and twentieth centuries they would be praised by communist ideologues as the first proletarian revolutionaries, precursors to the French revolution of 1789 and the Russian revolution of 1917. Unhappily, as in Russia and France, the revolution in Münster was soon taken over by terrorists and tyrants.

The story of the Anabaptists is, then, an archetype, not an exception or an anomaly, despite the apparent remoteness of the time and place. But what allowed them to survive for so long, in the face of overwhelming military power available to be used against them? It is true that Münster was a heavily fortified walled city, with ample supplies of water and food, but the Bishop had thousands of men at his disposal, as well as heavy cannon capable of lofting "solid shot" stones and iron balls weighing up to thirty pounds for hundreds of yards.

The essential answer is provided by an incident that occurred much later in southern Germany, during the Napoleonic Wars. Napoleon's progress was blocked by an immense stone fort high on a mountain near Passau; it had withstood any number of solid-shot cannon sieges during the Middle Ages. Napoleon informed the defending commander that he could destroy his mighty fortress within a matter of hours, but that he preferred not to. The fortress was surrendered intact, and remains so today. The signal difference between 1534 and 1800 is in firepower—if the Bishop's soldiers had had Napoleon's array of explosive projectiles available to them, they could have obliterated the city walls within hours, and the story of the Anabaptist rebels in Münster would have remained merely an anecdote, instead of becoming a saga.

Thus both the religious attitudes and the military technology of the early sixteenth century differ radically from those of our day. But the aspects of human character that impel people to do strange and terrible things, as well as to seek their causes and explain their meaning, remain much the same. Many scholars have addressed themselves to this particular story both in Europe and in America, but there have been few successful efforts to reach a wide audience with a readable, yet reliable narrative. What follows is such an attempt.*

---

*A cast of characters (page 202) and a chronology of events (page 205) follow the conclusion of the text.

1

A New Dawn

And the same hour was there a great earthquake, and the tenth part of the city fell, and in the earthquake were slain of men seven thousand; and the remnant were affrighted, and gave glory to the God of heaven.

—Revelation 11:13

HERMAN KERSSENBRÜCK WAS destined for life as a theologian and a schoolmaster but he was also blessed with an eye for lively detail and a keen dramatic sense. The story that he would experience and, unlike many others, live to tell about, began long before the night of February 8, 1534, but it was then that it reached its first critical point. From those frantic early-morning hours in the cobblestoned streets of his temporary home in northern Germany until the conclusion of the drama nearly two years later, a handful of men would lead thousands of devoted followers not to God, as they promised to do, but to their destruction.

It was unclear to the young Latin scholar, only thirteen on this fateful night, whether he was witnessing a comedy or a tragedy, but he had a secure sense even then of the stage and of the characters who would dominate it. The place was the north German city called Münster in Westphalia. Secure from attack behind its double walls and double moat, its ten gates were guarded by small stone bastions or "roundels"; wealthy from commerce and farming, proud of its independence as a powerful city-state on the far fringes of the Holy Roman Empire, it had perhaps grown arrogant in its presumption that

God thought it especially worthy of his concern. The time was that of the early Renaissance and the Protestant Reformation, still deeply rooted in the Middle Ages but bursting with energetic demands for change, for justice, for freedom of choice in all matters both secular and religious. The characters on the crowded world stage included John Calvin in Geneva, Henry VIII in England, and the young Emperor Charles V in Germany—and, transcending borders of language and national identity, towering above all of them in terms of his ultimate importance, the apostate German priest, Martin Luther.

The small city of Münster had its own important men. Foremost among them was the merchant-prince Bernard Knipperdolling; fifty years old, tall and burly, with a thick beard, square-cut in the fashion of the day, always soberly dressed in heavy gray robes, Knipperdolling was a cloth merchant who had warehouses and offices in several cities besides Münster, including Lübeck and Amsterdam. He had two grown daughters and, after the death of his first wife, had recently married a wealthy widow. He was a prominent member of the city council, a man who spoke seldom but always with weight and point to his remarks. The most visible symbol of his success was the magnificent three-story gabled house that stood on the Market Square, at an angle to the stately St. Lambert's Church and a block away from the renowned City Hall.

Now, as the young Herman (who was not only a devout Catholic but, like most adolescent boys, a confirmed cynic) tells it, this dignified and respectable man appeared in the doorway of his grand house, arm in arm with a much younger, slighter man, a newcomer from Leyden called Jan Bockelson, a "bastard Dutch tailor and bawdy-house keeper." Both men were screaming and pointing to the sky, shouting, "Repent! Repent! For the hour of the Lord is now upon us!" They were not alone in their frenzy: the Market Square, lit by torchlight reflected against the low clouds, was like a Witches' Sabbath to Herman and two schoolmates as they crouched fearfully in a doorway to watch. It was a carnival of madness, a gathering of demons, who in the light of day wore the familiar faces of carpenters, blacksmiths, and merchants, of schoolchildren and nuns, even of the august members of the city council. Among these moved a dark-robed, stocky figure, the third of Kerssenbrück's lead players, the hot-tempered and brilliant young Anabaptist preacher Bernard Rothmann. A few years earlier Rothmann had been an earnest intellectual who had studied with the great Melanchthon, Luther's disciple. Now he thrust his short, broad-chested figure through the crowd, his eyes rolling, demanding that "all repent!"

The mob surged around the preacher, terrified and exhilarated. Many, like Knipperdolling, were hysterical, with a slather of foam issuing from their mouths. The shrill voice of an impassioned young woman standing on the steps of St. Lambert's Church cut through the clamor; the daughter of the tailor Jurgen tom Berg was calling for repentance so effectively that her father, inspired by her passion, raised his arms to the flame-reddened heavens and cried, "I see the majesty of God and Jesus, who bears the flag of victory in His hands. Beware, you Godless ones! Repent! God will reap His harvest and let the chaff burn in the all-consuming fires. Cease from sinning! Repent!" He leaped into the air as though he might fly, then threw himself on his face in the dirt and dung in the shape of a cross.

Everywhere Herman Kerssenbrück looked he saw similar small dramas of ecstatic possession. The blind Scottish beggar who had somehow ended up in Münster, dressed in a motley assortment of colored rags, his great gaunt frame made even taller by high-heeled boots, ran about in circles crying that he could see, he could see again. A crowd gathered around him as he turned the corner into King Street, shouting that the heavens were about to fall on their heads, at which moment he tripped and fell into a pile of dung, and the crowd deserted him in search of more reliable visionaries. The miller Jodokus Culenberg galloped around the square on a borrowed white stallion, calling for all to repent. An old woman who had lost her voice in the excitement raced through the crowd, shaking a bell. Although fires of such heat usually burn themselves out quickly, the midnight tumult seemed to go on and on. When, young Herman must have wondered, would it end? And how, later generations would ask, had it all begun?

The immediate cause of this night's revelries lay in what had *not* happened at midnight, as foretold by Pastor Bernard Rothmann. That was the hour, he had announced two days earlier, for the Catholic Convent next to the river Aa to crumble before the might of the

Lord, taking with it the bodies and souls of the scores of nuns it so invidiously sheltered. This improbable event was announced by Rothmann after he marched into the Overwater Church, as it was called, at the head of a mob of guildsmen and farmers and forced the Abbess, Ida von Merveldt, to assemble her trembling charges. This convent, Rothmann told the women, was an offense in the eyes of God. "It is your holy duty," he admonished them, "not to withhold your bodies for Christ but to go forth and multiply. You must have men, you must marry, you must bear children."

In fact, this would not have been an unpleasant injunction for some of Rothmann's listeners—young women were often dispatched by their families to convents for other than religious reasons, and some of them might even have set their caps for the handsome preacher had he not recently married a wealthy young widow. Others, like the Abbess, were devout Catholics and horrified by Rothmann's presumptuous attack. Devout or inclined to stray, each of the nuns heard Rothmann explain how he had come by the information that she was in danger of losing her life. This "salutary announcement has been made to me," the pastor said, "by one of the prophets now present in this city, and the Heavenly Father has also favored me with a direct and special revelation to the same effect."

Twenty years earlier Bernard Rothmann's attempt to frighten the nuns would have been met with laughter or blank stares of incomprehension. That he could succeed now derived in part from his compelling personality and his undoubted moral intensity, but even more from the example set earlier by a man whom Rothmann resembled in some ways, Martin Luther.

The critical event of the sixteenth century occurred near its beginning, in 1517; it was then, as every schoolboy and -girl has learned ever since, that the young Catholic priest Martin Luther challenged the Church of Rome to reform itself. Private protests having proved futile, Luther took the irreversible step of publicly announcing an invitation to discuss his objections and demands, nailing them, as tradition has it, to the door of the Cathedral in Wittenberg. This and later acts of protest and defiance led the Pope to order Luther to Rome for "examination." Justly fearing that he would not live to leave

Rome, where far more powerful men than he, including popes and princes, were routinely murdered, Luther refused to budge from Germany or to recant. In 1520 he was excommunicated, and central Germany became the throbbing heart of the most profoundly divisive and destructive, yet at the same time creative and energizing movement in Western history—the Protestant Reformation.

Albrecht Dürer, Luther's contemporary then living in Nuremberg, perfectly captured the destructive aspects of their time in his famous *Four Horsemen of the Apocalypse,* which depicts the scourges of famine, fire, pestilence, and war riding over the land. Within a few years of Luther's defiance of the Pope, Rome itself was sacked and destroyed, in 1527. At almost the same time, in 1525, starving farmers in Germany had formed themselves into a vast army, attacking land owners, the Church, and the Emperor's armies until they were slaughtered; more than a hundred thousand farmers and their urban allies in the trade guilds died in what came to be called the Peasants' War. Thus within two turbulent years the two great pillars of the western world, those of the Church and of the state, were severely shaken; the so-called Holy Roman Empire was in danger of imminent collapse.

In the midst of this chaos arose a new group that caused great alarm among both religious and civil authorities. They were called the Anabaptists, and they provided Catholics and Protestants with a rare common cause: their extermination. The original concept of Anabaptism, as first formulated by a Swiss reformer, Conrad Grebel, in 1523, sounds reasonable enough to modern sensibilities, shaped by a heritage of democracy and a belief in a degree of free will. The true faith, Grebel said, is not a matter of being born into a belief because of what your parents profess, or of having it imposed upon you because you happen to live in a certain place. It is a voluntary community of believers who have freely entered it as responsible, thinking adults through the symbolic act of baptism. Thus, infant baptism is meaningless; the only true baptism has to come later, when the act can be understood as a conversion and as a true commitment to God.

Grebel and later believers never referred to "re-baptism," because they did not believe a first baptism had ever actually occurred. They usually called themselves "the brethren" or, as in Münster, "the company of Christ." Nevertheless, they became notorious throughout Europe as the "Wiedertäufer" or "Ana-baptists" (the prefix coming from the Greek for "again") because their Catholic enemies could then condemn them to death for violating a key church law against second baptisms of any kind.

By 1529 Charles V had become so concerned that the dangerous doctrines of Anabaptism were "getting the upper hand" that he ordered the wholesale extermination of "every anabaptist and rebaptized man and woman of the age of reason. [They] shall be condemned and brought from natural life into death by fire, sword, and the like, according to the person, without proceeding by the inquisition of the spiritual judges; and let the same [punishment be inflicted on the] pseudo-preachers, instigators, vagabonds, and tumultuous inciters of the said vice of anabaptism."

From Switzerland in the south, throughout central Europe and Germany, and as far north and west as England, where Henry VIII burned a dozen Anabaptists at the stake, thousands of men and women were subjected to the most terrible persecution. Many of the more moderate leaders who abjured violence were martyred, leaving a gap in the leadership that was often filled by men of little education but much passion. In some parts of northern Germany and Holland a few princes offered the Anabaptists a degree of protection, but even there they were severely restricted. Many Anabaptists accordingly began to meet in small, secret cells, known only to themselves—thus adding another reason for the authorities to fear them and to hunt them down.

Luther himself detested the Anabaptists. A radical only in the religious sense, he depended on the goodwill of princes to keep him from the fires that punished heretics, and he declared that a good Christian must obey the secular laws of the state. Church and state should be separate, but people owed obligations to both. The Anabaptists denied any such obligation. As the self-proclaimed Elect of God, they acknowledged allegiance to no authority but their own: not to the city, not to the state, and certainly not to any established Church, be it Roman or Lutheran.

Even Ulrich Zwingli, the radical Swiss reformer whose follower Conrad Grebel had once been and whom Luther thought too extreme, denounced the Anabaptists. He said infant baptism was a traditional ritual of immense value to the adults and older children who participated in it. He said the denial of public obligation to city and state was not only impractical but arrogant—the Anabaptists claimed that the whole world except for themselves was damned; that they were, as Norman Cohn later put it, "small islands in a sea of iniquity." Yet because they sinned as much as anyone else, Zwingli said, the Anabaptists were not only impossibly self-righteous but hypocrites as well. Their emotional indulgence in religious ecstasy led them to ranting demonstrations of babbling idiocy. Finally, their belief that all property and goods should be held in common—their primitive communism—led when put into practice to all kinds of economic dislocation and abuse.

In short, their opponents of whatever persuasion agreed, the Anabaptists threatened the unity of the family, the stability of the state, the structure of all religious institutions, and the divine injunctions of God. But what made the Anabaptists particularly dangerous was their unshakable conviction that the world was about to end soon in the bloody Second Coming of Christ, as foretold in the Book of Revelation. All the signs indicated that this miraculous event, the most significant since the birth of Christ, was going to happen very soon, not just as an allegory, as in Dürer's representation, but as a literal series of events.

Ideas of all sorts, both useful and crackbrained, require gifted advocates for them to come alive, and Münster was to suffer the presence of more than one of these. But before these men had come the eloquent Melchior Hoffman, a gentle soul who must bear the blame for much of what was to happen in Münster, though he never set foot in the city. Born in southern Germany in 1495, the son of a furrier, Hoffman was first a Catholic, then a Lutheran, then a follower of Zwingli, and finally the "Anabaptist Apostle of the North." He wandered for years through northern Europe, from Frisia to Scandinavia, trading furs and preaching that Christ would soon return to begin his thousand-year reign on earth.

Hoffman thought of himself as the new Elijah, the storied prophet of Gilead who heard in a cave the "still, small voice" of God and went forth to save his people. Only those who had been properly baptized would be saved, so Hoffman devoted his energies in the tumultuous decade of the 1520s to making converts to Anabaptism. He found his richest soil in Holland, where he brought a semiliterate baker called Jan Matthias, who would later figure prominently in the story of the Anabaptists in Münster, into his fold.

Barefoot and humble, like the holy fathers of the early primitive Church, Hoffman himself renounced the initiation of violence but was sure it would soon arrive in the form of terrible oppression. The designated year was 1534, the place Strasbourg. At that time, Hoffman proposed to gather with the rest of the 140,000 messengers of world regeneration described in Revelation 14:1. He and they would suffer a bloody siege of the chosen city, but would then recover their strength and destroy the ungodly. With the victory of the Chosen Ones, the Second Coming would be at hand.

The city fathers of Strasbourg, impressed with Hoffman's piety though worried about the unrest his message inspired, treated him gently when he returned there in 1533 to await the end, along with hundreds of his followers. The true believers were chased out of town and some of their leaders executed. Hoffman was spared, his integrity shining through his probable madness, but he was clearly too danger-ous to leave at large; he was locked in a cage within a tower, his hoarse voice drifting to the street below where the people could hear him chanting psalms and crying, "Woe, ye godless scribes of Strasbourg!" There he remained until his death a decade later. In the meantime, his followers changed the designated site of the Second Coming from Strasbourg to Münster, over two hundred miles to the north, near the Dutch border, and the year from 1534 to 1535.

Like Strasbourg, most of the cities where the Anabaptists gathered were governed by prudent and, if need be, ruthless men who either evicted or executed their antagonists when they became troublesome. However, many of these same cities were essentially sympathetic to the goals of religious freedom and economic justice for which the Anabaptists seemed willing to die. The more radical Lutherans, who were becoming increasingly strong during the decade after Luther's defiance in Wittenberg, viewed the Anabaptists as eccentric allies rather than dangerous heretics. Individualistic and scattered in small groups throughout northern Europe, the Anabaptists were generally committed to non-violence, and they had been stripped of their leadership by bloody governmental and religious persecution. They were dangerous not so much for their numbers as for the power of their message, with its vision of a pure restoration of the original Church and its vision of Jesus Christ welcoming them to a certain future in Heaven. Among these long-suffering true believers, however, were some men who believed in the redeeming power of revenge, retribution, and violence. Where they appeared, Anabaptism began to justify the fears of those who saw it as a disruptive, indeed a satanic, force.

Such would be the case in Münster, for a variety of reasons. Shortly after the Reformation started, Münster had become in many ways both a model of the conditions against which Luther protested and an example of how opposing Catholics and Protestants could live together peacefully—but the tensions remained severe. The name of the city came from the Latin word for "monastery," and it had been a bishopric for half the lifetime of the Church itself, beginning in A.D. 805. Now, though, the humble traditions of the early monks were belied by the sumptuous splendor of the Church. This small city of slightly more than nine thousand people supported not only the magnificent St. Paul's Cathedral, but also ten churches, five of them grander than those found in much larger cities, plus seven convents, four charitable foundations, and four monasteries. Lovers of religious art and architecture crossing the plains as they approached Münster were thrilled by the sight of dozens of spires ascending toward the heavens; but the citizens whose taxes paid for much of it could not be blamed for regarding the Church architecture as a testimony to ecclesiastical indifference to their welfare.

Following long-established tradition, the Church paid no property taxes to the city. It contributed no men to the periodic military levies enacted by the Prince-Bishop. The monasteries and convents farmed their own plots and thus bought little from the local farmers; on the contrary, they sold their surplus on the open market or gave it away, failing to support, if not actively undermining, the tax-paying farmers of the region. They engaged in active competition with the businessmen and artisans of the city: the nuns were busy at their looms, weaving tapestries and fabrics, and the brothers made furniture and tools in their shops. In sum, as all Protestants and not a few Catholics agreed, the Church contributed little to, and took much from, the local economy.

Until Luther, all this was as it had been for centuries, and the peasants and tradesmen and artisans on whose weary backs the Church rested had voiced few audible complaints. Mostly illiterate in Latin, they depended as Roman Catholics on their priests to explain what the Latin Bible meant to them, and they learned that complaints against the Church would earn them eternal damnation. But when Luther translated the Latin Bible into everyday German, the first version of the New Testament appearing in 1522, he released millions from dependence on the priests for their instruction. Within a few years of Luther's translation, hundreds of his followers had spread through central Europe with what they called the original word of God, as opposed to what Rome claimed it was.

The inevitable result of millions of people being encouraged to think for themselves was resistance to arbitrary authority, slow and hesitant at first, then insistent, and finally violent. Luther himself, the very father of the Reformation, not only advised against violent revolt against either Church or state, he counseled rulers to hang and burn without mercy renegades like Thomas Müntzer, who had incited the peasants to violence in 1525. The Peasants' War, however, did prompt the authorities in many places to grant more self-rule, as happened in Münster. There the then–Prince-Bishop, Frederick von Wiede, felt compelled to grant the city, in 1525, a considerable degree of the independence from Church authority that it had lost in recent decades. The city was now to be ruled by a council of twenty-four men, two of whom acted as co-mayors. The men, Catholics as well as Lutherans, were members of the crafts guilds (smiths, tailors, furriers), merchants, and property holders. Housed in the splendid City Hall whose ornate facade rose a hundred feet above the Market Square, the council achieved for a few years a tenuous equanimity.

Like Martin Luther, Bernard Rothmann had not intended to rebel against the Church, which had some reason to expect gratitude from him. The son of a blacksmith, Rothmann had been raised in poverty and could easily have died poor, ignorant, and unknown. His gifts were too obvious, however, to remain unnoticed; his uncle, a vicar in Münster, had recognized the boy's potential and rescued him, first sending him to school, then securing for him a position as chaplain of the church of St. Mauritz, just outside the city gate. By 1525 the energy, intelligence, and personal charm of the blacksmith's son had won him a sinecure for life.

But the events of the decade when he came to his maturity, particularly the Peasants' War, stirred the young priest's social conscience. He began to challenge the Church for its failure to support the farmers, and finally to accuse it of conspiring with the civil authorities to murder its own followers. He feared that Luther was right, that the Church was irretrievably corrupt. By 1530 Rothmann had earned such a reputation as a radical Catholic dissident that his uncle handed him a bag of gold coins and sent him to Cologne, about forty miles south of Münster, for further religious study and devotional exercises. Rothmann signed a promissory note for the money and vanished for months, never even appearing in Cologne. He returned in 1531 not as a Catholic priest but as a declared Lutheran and soon led a mob through his former church, St. Mauritz, in a rampage of idol-smashing. The altar was toppled, the silver communion chalice was crushed, and paintings of the Virgin were torn from the walls and burned in the church courtyard.

Rothmann left Münster again in some haste after this episode to visit Luther and the famous theologian Philip Melanchthon in Wittenberg. Whatever his faults, Rothmann was hardly the fool the later chroniclers of the Kingdom of Münster would make him out to be, for he impressed these two brilliant men profoundly, much though Luther disapproved of his actions then and later. Melanchthon, for his part, had even greater doubts about the young convert, fearing that he was mentally unstable; he remarked to Luther that Rothmann had great potential, but it was a toss-up whether he would turn out to be "extraordinarily good or extraordinarily bad."

Herman Kerssenbrück had no difficulty determining which course Rothmann had chosen by the time he returned to Münster early in 1532, this time to stay: all the "poisonous beliefs that had been festering in him" finally broke out in a series of frenzied denunciations of the Catholic Church. Although still nominally a Lutheran, it seems clear in retrospect that Rothmann had crossed the thin line dividing radical Lutherans from the Anabaptists. He did not make a public pronouncement to this effect, since to do so would mean immediate imprisonment, if not death, but his sermons began to include disparaging references to infant baptism and to the holding of private property, two Anabaptist bugbears. He found his message increasingly well received by growing crowds of eager supporters in the city streets, including not only Lutherans but a number of Catholics. Ignoring the protestations of the Catholic hierarchy and of the mostly Lutheran city council, which he had begun to frighten as well, Rothmann finally acceded for a few weeks to an order from Bishop von Wiede to desist from public preaching, but then reconsidered. In a letter to von Wiede, he challenged the Bishop not to let his "godless oppressors escape the deserved punishment of heaven. Because my conscience is clear, I have no doubt that I can rely on God's mercy. He will protect me and rescue me from danger, when my enemies fall upon me like the lion. I know that at this moment I am surrounded by a pack of dogs and a horde of evildoers." He signed this remarkable appeal, "From the humble servant of the merciful Bishop, his soldier in Christ, BR."

The Bishop responded by ordering the bailiff of the Cathedral, Dirk von Merveldt, to pressure the council to expel Rothmann from the city. Rothmann refused to leave, asserting that God had protected him with His heavenly wings and the council's commands were hollow: God only was to be obeyed, not the mere men who tried to deprive the people of the word of God that he was bringing them. Some of the key council members broke away to support the radical preacher, chief among them the merchant Bernard Knipperdolling.

Knipperdolling, like Rothmann, had by 1532 become a convert to the doctrine of radical resistance proposed by the Dutch Anabaptist Jan Matthias and his followers. Again, this conversion was kept from his fellow council members, who still considered him a Lutheran. Meeting in Knipperdolling's house in February 1532, a group of prominent citizens signed a pact that in its brave idealism seems to foreshadow the American Founding Fathers' words two centuries later: they swore to devote their personal fortunes, their reputations, and even their lives to the cause of freedom from oppression that Rothmann now symbolized to them.

Their subsequent actions were, however, less high-minded. Led by Knipperdolling, the men now marched with Rothmann and with scores of shouting followers to St. Lambert's Church, forced their way in, and destroyed the stone coffins holding the ashes of long-dead bishops and priests. The crowd became a mob that raged through the city for a full day, sparing from attack only the Cathedral itself, not out of a lingering sense of piety but because it was too securely barred and defended. Huge fires consumed wax votive candles, priestly vestments, paintings, and tapestries. A massive book-burning took place in the market square: Latin Bibles, devotional texts, as well as secular works from personal libraries—the philosophical works of Boethius and Thomas Aquinas, the poetry of Horace and Chaucer, and the engravings of Heinrich Aldegrever and the paintings of Ludger tom Ring, both well-known local artists—all fed the swirling flames. Rothmann even consigned his own sermons to the bonfire: "The truth of Holy Scripture shall triumph!" he proclaimed, and it alone was exempt from destruction.

The conflict between the radical Protestants and the ruling Catholic authorities had now moved beyond words into action, the gauntlet insultingly tossed at the feet of Prince-Bishop Frederick von Wiede. The city waited anxiously for his response.

Many of the dozens of late-medieval "prince-bishops" scattered throughout the German-speaking areas of central Europe were really feudal lords, not ecclesiastical figures. They acquired their possessions by means of marriage, political connections, armed conquest, and sometimes by simply purchasing them from the current owners. Powerful by virtue of the money, arms, and soldiers that they could command from lesser lords, the prince-bishops had nearly unrestrained power to do as they wished with even the most prominent of their subjects. One reason for Bernard Knipperdolling's devotion to Rothmann was that a few years earlier von Wiede had kidnapped him while he was en route to Lübeck on a business trip. The respected merchant was thrown into jail and kept there for six months, until his brothers ransomed him. When he was released, according to some accounts, he walked with a crooked gait and in obvious pain: his toes, it was said, had been crushed in iron boots. He had been forced to agree not to engage in religious agitation. Instead, he went literally underground, churning out pamphlets based on Rothmann's sermons on a printing press in his basement. Thus the Bishop turned the merchant from an opponent whose stated cause—the independence of his city—was respectable, into a revolutionary who would finally destroy it.

There was little room for compromise or negotiation between opponents who both detested and disdained each other as godless: to the Catholics, Knipperdolling and Rothmann seemed to be crazed fanatics, resistant to reason or to compromise. The merchant and the renegade priest, for their part, charged that the Church and its minions were exploiters, thieves, and tyrants. Armed conflict seemed inevitable in 1532. Both sides, surprisingly, took heart when the ailing and frustrated Bishop von Wiede chose to retire early that year rather than pursue the fight with Rothmann and was succeeded by the nobleman Franz von Waldeck. The Catholics were encouraged because they saw in von Waldeck a "brave and righteous knight," endowed with new authority from Emperor Charles V to quell this troubling source of unrest in his realm. The Lutherans for their part regarded von Waldeck as anything but "righteous": he was not even an ordained priest but a typical lusty baron who lived for the hunt, for drink, and for women—in addition to his wife he had an official mistress who had borne him a son. He owed his power to family connections with Philip of Hesse, himself a Lutheran, and insofar as he had any religious leanings, he was inclined to sympathize more with the Lutherans than with the Church of Rome. The radicals in Münster thus saw von Waldeck as a greedy, lascivious political hack, utterly lacking in conviction and most unlikely to kill the golden goose, the city that was the commercial heart of his domain.

A painting of Franz von Waldeck by a later artist reveals a different man from either the "righteous knight" or the corrupt wastrel. In it we see a broad-chested man in bishop's regalia. His hands are enormous, with fingers the thickness of fat sausages. The left hand loosely supports the symbol of the Church, the shepherd's crook. His right hand clasps firmly the hilt of a heavy sword, the symbol of the state. The sword is at the ready, opposed to and dominant over the passive shepherd's crook. Heavily lidded eyes gaze from under bushy eye-brows past the sword; the nose is thick and prominent, the lips full and sensuous. The curled side-whiskers and down-turning mustache accentuate the deeply threatening aspect of his presence. Franz von Waldeck's potential for ruthless force is obvious through a centuries-old painting; how much more so it must have been to his contemporaries who saw him in the flesh.

But the rebels seemed for now to have taken von Waldeck's measure: Münster was formidably defended and would cost a fortune to subdue. The new Bishop was forced by his own prudence and by his advisers to tell the city council that he would delay an action against Rothmann until he had received guidance from Emperor Charles V; as he and they both knew, Münster was by no means unique in its religious disputation, and a decree was due soon from the Emperor concerning methods of resolving these matters peacefully, if that was possible.

This unexpected passivity in the face of aggression encouraged the rebels to further demands. Knipperdolling openly challenged the new Bishop by appointing an armed guard to protect Rothmann, himself, and their allies. Even more significantly, he forced the council to impose a code of sixteen articles that virtually denied Roman Catholics the right to practice their faith in Münster. Chief among these articles was a complete proscription of the Catholic Mass, of communion, of prayers for the dead, of the use of Latin in any form, of the worship of Mary, of "smearing oil" on the dying to ease the departure of the soul to Heaven, and of various other Catholic habits of "disgusting idolatry."

Rothmann justified these attacks on Catholic doctrine and practice at every opportunity. As was often the case with the Anabaptists, then and later, many of his explanations have seemed soundly reasoned to later theologians. The Holy Communion supper, he said, should be kept only as a reminder of Jesus and a way of expanding their fellowship, not as a religious sacrament—the belief that the wafer and the wine were literally the body and blood of Christ was wrong, for these were symbolic, not literal. In addition, human delight in food and sex were God-given and divine, and not to be denied by foolish fasting or priestly chastity, which were seldom observed in any event. Rothmann's own religious services were enlivened by song and by dance, and communion celebrations became veritable feasts—practices fit for the voluptuaries of Baal and Satan, according to Kerssenbrück, rather than acceptable ways of celebrating fellowship.

Rothmann's arguments were familiar and to a degree persuasive even to some Catholics, who agreed that discipline was needed to restrain abuses of faith such as the worship of Mary as a divine being. But Holy Communion and the Latin Mass were integral to Catholic faith. To denounce them was bad enough; to forbid them was to declare religious war. The new Bishop would have no choice but to respond with force if Rothmann, the instigator of the trouble, was not now expelled from Münster. But not only was Rothmann allowed to remain and to preach, he was given the grandest church in town for his own, St. Lambert's, and an apartment over a neighboring shop.

By this time Charles V, far to the south in his court in Regensburg, was hearing troublesome reports of the events in Münster and decided to intervene, even before he announced his more wide-sweeping measures for the empire. Some measure of the importance of Münster to the young emperor (born in 1500, he was only thirty-two) is suggested by the magnitude of the other problems he had to deal with: war with the Turks, constant contention with the French King Francis I, and resistance and defiance by princelings in every corner of the realm had combined with the incessant religious strife unleashed by Luther to endanger his own survival. The unrest in the small city on the edge of his empire had turned Münster into a bothersome symptom of the larger problems facing Charles. Impatient with von Waldeck's inaction, and suspecting him of harboring secret sympathies with the Lutherans, the Emperor warned him that the radicals were deluding the ignorant people, leading them into error and away from the true word of God: "If they do not desist there will soon be violence and bloodshed; therefore we earnestly desire that you, the Bishop, remove the Lutherans and expel them from the city. The rebellious citizens should receive the appropriate punishment and be forced to acknowledge and obey their superiors, so that they and the remaining inhabitants should be able to live quietly and peacefully."

Von Waldeck forwarded the Emperor's message to the city council with the strong warning that his "pious wishes and friendly requests should be heeded so that you do not draw down on yourselves his anger and scorn." At the same time, correctly anticipating that the Lutherans would ignore the Emperor, the Bishop summoned all the wealthy landowners and nobles to his palace in Billerbeck to ask for their support in bringing the city to heel.

The city did indeed ignore the Bishop; the result, beginning in late October 1532, was a blockade. This was a relatively easy and inexpensive measure designed to bring the city to its senses without actual attack. Münster was situated in the middle of a wide, flat plain like the hub of a wheel; the Bishop now blocked its spokes with soldiers to hinder merchants and traders from entering or leaving the city, including the local farmers who had no other market for their products or source of hardware and other supplies. Even before the formal announcement of the blockade, soldiers arrested a dozen men driving a large herd of oxen to market in Cologne. The Bishop locked the men in a dungeon and sold the cattle for enough cash to maintain a company of soldiers for a month. As reports of this outrage spread through the city, hundreds of angry citizens gathered in the Market Square to shout insults and curses at the Bishop, who was fortunately not on the scene to hear angry voices proclaiming that he was a tyrant and an oppressor, he was unworthy of his honorable name, he was a short-sighted fat-gutted fool.

The members of the city council, having earlier allowed the Catholics to be deprived of their religious freedom, now grew fearful that their own survival was at risk, along with the freedom of the city. They agreed to appeal their case to a higher political authority, Landgraf (Count) Philip of Hesse, Westphalia's neighbor to the southeast. Philip was himself a Lutheran sympathizer, a man of great personal integrity and opposed to violence from any quarter. To present its political and legal argument to Philip, the council also agreed to hire as an adviser another respected outsider, Dr. Friedrich von Wyck, an attorney from nearby Bremen. On the ecclesiastical side, it appealed for help in the battle with von Waldeck to a higher religious authority, the Roman Catholic Archbishop in Cologne; he could offer no more help than to warn the council not to "rush into destruction." Neighborly appeals to nearby towns for help were mostly fruitless, although one small city, Warendorp, was outspoken in its support and the others were at least neutral. Seeing itself without allies and defenseless if mediation by Philip and von Wyck failed, the council reluctantly decided to hire three hundred mercenary soldiers to protect the city.

In the meantime, on the day after Christmas 1532, about nine hundred armed men conducted a midnight raid on the Bishop's stronghold in Telgte, yet another palace, this one only a dozen miles distant. They hoped to capture von Waldeck himself, but the Bishop was away for the holiday at his residence in Billerbeck, and they had to settle for taking eighteen men as prisoners. Among these were high church officials as well as humiliated military officers whose negligence had allowed the attack to succeed. There were no injuries and the prisoners were adequately housed in Münster. The audacious raid itself lifted the spirits of the rebels, and the hostages gave the city a much improved bargaining position with the Bishop, who still held their own men, the cattle merchants, captive.

Drawing back now from open warfare, the two sides during the next five weeks worked out a settlement that was signed in mid-February 1533. Knipperdolling was, after all, a merchant, and he could understand the deadly economics of a blockade. For his part, the Bishop agreed to release the men he had imprisoned for trying to sell their cattle, and to pay a fine to their leader, Herman Tilbeck, for compensation. He also agreed to the city's municipal independence, saying the Church would not interfere with its business. Finally, the six smaller churches taken over by the Lutherans would remain Lutheran; however, the larger churches, such as St. Lambert's and the Overwater Church, as well as the Cathedral and the cloister church, would remain Catholic. The city had to promise that Catholic parishioners would not be subject to harassment; all citizens would be subject only to the civil authority of the magistrates. There would be no more heretical preaching by Rothmann or his associates. There were to be no reprisals against the supporters of the Bishop who had fled and would now return, and all property and goods taken from them would be restored. High and low clergy alike would be allowed to pass through the city streets unhindered. Finally, von Waldeck would receive the traditional oath of submission from the city three months hence, in May 1533.

The city's autonomy was preserved, as was the Bishop's dignity, by the truce that Philip of Hesse had sponsored. But Knipperdolling and his allies blamed the council moderates for giving ground and immediately stirred up noisy protests against these men. The radicals were supported by hundreds of zealous newcomers; for months now, despite the blockade, Rothmann's sermons and other leaflets printed by Knipperdolling had been circulating through Holland, Frisia, and northern Germany. In them Rothmann explained, among other topics, that much human misery stemmed from the idea of "private property." The very idea of owning anything, of thinking in terms of "this is mine and this is yours" was evil. "God had made all things common, as today we can still enjoy air, fire, rain, and the sun in common, and whatever else some thieving, tyrannical man cannot grasp for himself." Rothmann temptingly portrayed Münster as a rich city that was now prepared to share its wealth with all who came to it as members of the Company of Christ. He invited and urged those who could contribute to its holy mission to join him, bringing with them only the weapons they would need to defend the new Kingdom of Zion, as he called it, against the ungodly. Throughout 1533, hundreds and finally thousands of the wretched, the dispossessed, and the desperate read Rothmann's word and made their way to Münster. As they came in, nervous Catholic citizens and others who had the means to leave the city began to do so.

By March 1533, there were enough of these newcomers in town to help the radicals force a new election; some of the foreigners, like the preacher Henry Roll, were even more intemperate in their demands than Rothmann, and none was reluctant to meddle in the politics of his host city. The consequence was a special election in March which resulted in a new council. All sixteen of the twenty-four members who had agreed to the pact with the Bishop were replaced by hard-liners. Now there were no Catholics and no moderate Lutherans on the council, only declared opponents of the Bishop. These were divided into two factions. The first, slightly larger and more conservative, consisted of Lutherans who thought negotiation was still preferable to conflict, and was led by the respected but elderly clothmaker Jaspar Jodefeld. The second, consisting of Anabaptist sympathizers who thought war was inevitable, was led by the equally respected patrician Herman Tilbeck, who had been among the imprisoned cattle dealers. These two men were the new co-mayors. Serving with them were twelve artisans, mostly guildmasters, and ten businessmen, including Bernard Knipperdolling.

The new council, strongly influenced by Knipperdolling and Rothmann, set out to right some old wrongs and to correct some problems of behavior among the citizens. The supervision of the schools was taken away from the priests and given to the Lutherans, under a schoolmaster from the town of Borkum, Henry Graes. The poor were given clothing, food, and shelter and put to work on civic projects, including strengthening the city walls. The Catholic monasteries and convents were forced to open their dining tables to the newcomers. Private behavior was closely scrutinized; reports of marital discord and even children's misbehavior were speedily investigated and resolved. A new sense of moral order and discipline infused the city.

Some citizens, however, were uneasy at the draconian punishments, such as public whippings, jail, even threats of death, imposed on those "stiffnecked and wayward" types who persisted in whoring, drunkenness, lying, and blasphemy. The driving force behind the earlier agitation of the Lutherans against Bishop von Wiede had been the desire for freedom—for democracy rather than autocracy in government and for religious independence from the Roman Catholic Church. Now those who had achieved that freedom, the moderate Lutherans working with the Catholics, had been driven from office. Their successors, who had claimed an even greater devotion to freedom, were either Anabaptist sympathizers or radical Lutherans, and they were beginning to act like tyrants themselves.

A key turning point occurred late in 1533, when large-scale public baptisms began, conducted by dozens of newly arrived preachers, including the young tailor's apprentice from Leyden called Jan Bockelson. Within one week alone, a total of fourteen hundred people became declared Anabaptists, and by no means were all of them the dispossessed or the ignorant rabble, as the Bishop asserted. Many of the new converts were women, some of them merchants' wives who immediately donated all of their jewels and fine clothes to the cause. Many more were farm girls who worked for these wealthy ladies as maids and housekeepers. And not a few were nuns from the Overwater Church Convent, where the Abbess Ida von Merveldt wrote

despairingly to the Bishop that her charges were becoming obstrep-
erous, singing German psalms in church instead of Latin chants, not
wearing their habits, ignoring her commands and her tears alike.

Older men and children above the age of twelve were also baptized
during this period. As 1533 drew to a close, it was estimated that as
many as one third of the population of Münster consisted of people
who were sure that the apocalypse and the Second Coming were at
hand. Many of the converts were men whom Jan Bockelson and other
leaders immediately organized into armed quasi-military units that
operated independent of the city's own defensive force of mercenary
soldiers.

Jaspar Jodefeld, the co-mayor and leader of the Lutheran faction of
the council, saw the city slipping into chaos. The Bishop would feel
justified in destroying all of them unless Rothmann and his noisiest
assistant, Henry Roll, were stopped. On November 4, 1533, Jodefeld
told the council that he intended to send an armed guard to evict the
two preachers from Münster, in what would be the first armed encounter between the erstwhile allies. As a council member, Knipperdolling knew of the plan and led the preachers to safety in St.
Lambert's Church, along with hundreds of their armed followers.
Jodefeld and the other mayor, Herman Tilbeck, who sided in this
instance with the less extreme faction of the council, established their
own redoubt in the City Hall, a stone's throw down the street. The
two sides exchanged fiery messages until Dr. von Wyck, the Bremen
lawyer, persuaded them both that they were guaranteeing a victory
for the Bishop by their behavior. A resulting agreement stipulated that
the Anabaptists, including Rothmann and Roll, would be allowed to
stay, on condition that they refrain from public disturbance. The principle that all were free to choose their own faith was reasserted.

As part of the settlement between the factions, a Lutheran minister
from the court of Philip of Hesse, Dietrich Fabricius, arrived to preach
in St. Lambert's Church. There, in the citadel of the Anabaptists,
Fabricius charged that Rothmann was violating the rules of the recent
agreement by continued public agitation. On January 4, 1534, a crowd
of Anabaptist women rebuked Fabricius for his foreign tongue—
Latin—and chased him out of St. Lambert's, saying the church was
properly Rothmann's, not his. When the mayors admonished the

women to go home and look after their children and husbands, Kerssenbrück reports, they withdrew, cursing. They returned to the City Hall the next day with half a dozen apostate nuns from the Overwater Church Convent, who had "shamefully" removed their habits. The women loudly demanded the return of Rothmann to St. Lambert's; the mayors refused, and were berated by the women, "the nuns the loudest and most profane." Fabricius was a villainous imposter who deserved to be hanged, the women screamed. When reprimanded by the city fathers, they picked up clods of sheep, pig, and cow dung that lay about the street and hurled them at the hapless men until they retreated behind the locked doors of the City Hall.

Rothmann himself denied inciting anyone to violence or to rebellion. But if war was to come, the cornerstone for their faith had been securely laid and the walls of the city greatly strengthened. No matter how powerful the Papists might appear, they could never destroy the new Company of Christ. Remember the words of Saint Paul, Rothmann exhorted: "Night is passing, a new dawn is coming."

Bishop Franz was by now almost beside himself with fury. On January 20, 1534, he complained in a letter to Philip about the "disgusting heresies of this damned sect of Anabaptists and their misguided leader Bernard Rothmann, who along with his helpers is trying to pull everything down." They were particularly dangerous, he complained, because they spent so much time with the poor, telling them that when they adopted their proper Christian way of living there would be "no poverty—on the contrary, all property, as in the time of the Apostles, would be commonly shared by all neighbors." He went on to complain about the rejection of infant baptism and about their denial of all authority, including the Pope's. He warned that "if the growing number of Anabaptists get the upper hand in Münster" there would be a bloody confrontation ahead. Shortly afterward, von Waldeck wrote directly to the city council, saying, "We, Franz, Bishop of Münster by the Grace of God, do hereby declare that the damned, forbidden, and treacherous teachings of the Anabaptists are being spread by heretics," whom the council must expel or suffer the consequences. He summoned Jaspar Jodefeld and Dr. von Wyck to discuss the matter with him in Telgte on February 2.

When Jodefeld announced the coming meeting to the council,

Knipperdolling insisted that two other men be included in the party. One was the shoemaker Herman Redeker, the other a formidable thug, a gigantic man called Tile Bussenmeister and nicknamed the Cyclops because he had only one eye—a signal advantage, as some joked, in sighting a rifle. Knipperdolling must have known that the presence of Redeker would have been enough by itself to sabotage any attempt at a meeting, for the shoemaker was charged by the Bishop with having looted a Catholic church in an earlier disturbance; Bussenmeister's villainous presence was an even greater affront. When the odd delegation arrived at Telgte, the Bishop was outraged at its constitution and sent a messenger to turn it from his gate. He was particularly insulted that Dr. von Wyck, an attorney, should have joined company with thieves and rogues. The attorney should know, the Bishop told him through his messenger, that he was placing his life in great danger.

Back in Münster, the Anabaptists reacted gleefully to the assurance, at last, of an attack by the Bishop that would confirm their apocalyptic expectations. Seething with religious fervor, they began to call for the expulsion of all who were not prepared to fight in their holy war. The nonbelievers, especially the Catholics, would have to leave the city or convert to Anabaptism. Some of the more extreme rebels even called for the execution of the godless ones, as they called their opponents.

It was in this context, then, that Bernard Rothmann went to the convent at Overwater Church on the evening of February 6, 1534, and terrified the nuns with his prediction of coming disaster. He was very convincing: most of the nuns fled the convent, taking their belongings with them to the houses of Rothmann's supporters, leaving only the Abbess Ida von Merveldt and a few others behind. The wayward nuns joined the huge crowd that gathered during the hour before midnight to watch the cloister's promised destruction. When the twelfth hour had been tolled by the great bell at St. Lambert's without the collapse of the cloister, Pastor Bernard Rothmann was unabashed. Surely they must all know, he shouted to the waiting faithful, that a prophet is not false simply because his prophecy fails to take place at a given time. "Jonah foretold that Nineveh would be destroyed in forty days. But the inhabitants repented, and the city remained standing. The anger of the Heavenly Father had been allayed." So it was now with the convert; it did not fall because the nuns had seen the errors of their ways, causing God to be merciful. This was an occasion of great joy, as great almost as that of the final moments that were still certain to come, sometime. They should all shout their gratitude to the heavens, Rothmann declared, proceeding to lead them all on their mad merry dance through the streets of Münster.

2

THE GODLESS EXPELLED

And the Lord your God, he shall expel them from before you, and drive them from out of your sight; and ye shall possess their land, as the Lord your God hath promised unto you.

—Joshua 23:5

THE FRANTIC REVELRIES of thanksgiving inspired by Rothmann had served to obscure a more sinister aim. As the gray winter dawn broke over Münster a few hours later, on February 9, most of the city council clustered apprehensively behind the heavy stone walls of the Overwater Church Square, next to the river Aa which ran through the heart of the city. With them were several hundred supporters who had rushed to their aid upon hearing that the Anabaptists were about to mount an attack on the City Hall and overthrow the council. One of these was Assola, the young maid of Hermann Kerssenbrück's landlord, Dr. Johann Wesseling, who had sent her to the church with a musket concealed beneath her long skirts. Discovered by the Anabaptist guards who now controlled the Market Square through which she had to pass, Assola was deprived of her weapon and roughly treated until a friendly neighbor intervened on her behalf and she was allowed to pass.

There was no shortage of arms among the more than five hundred Anabaptists who now circulated outside the City Hall, waiting for instruction from their leaders as to their next step. The initial attempt to capture the council had failed with its escape into the Overwater

Church and the partial destruction of the wooden bridge across the river. Now the two factions—Lutherans and Catholics on the one hand, Anabaptists on the other—faced each other and tried to determine what the third party to this dispute, the Bishop, was about to do.

The immediate cause of the Anabaptists' attack was the rumor, circulating now for several days, that the Bishop had gathered several hundred knights and soldiers in addition to three thousand farmers outside the city. The Bishop had made it known that he considered the Anabaptists his major enemy, not the council. As Knipperdolling and the increasingly influential young Jan Bockelson, or, as he was usually called, Jan van Leyden, saw it, the council's persistent attempts to rein in Rothmann were not prompted by the desire to ensure religious freedom for all but to placate the Bishop. They thought that Jodefeld and the other moderates had lost heart and were negotiating to save their own skins and deliver the Anabaptists up for certain execution. Also alarming was the report that Dr. von Wyck, the Bremen lawyer who had been responsible for holding the factions together, planned to flee the city; if this prudent man foresaw disaster, then only drastic action on the part of the Anabaptists, as they must have seen the matter, could now save them.

While it seems unlikely that the council did intend to surrender so easily, after years of staunch resistance, the actions of the Anabaptists indicate a sincere belief that an attack by the Bishop was imminent. Several cannons were set in the tower of St. Lambert's Church, capable of firing over the city walls or into the square below if the Bishop's men broke through. Others were dragged by teams of horses into critical intersections. Streets were blocked with iron chains, and barricades were constructed of cobblestones, wagons, and furniture lowered from apartment windows. A last-ditch defensive redoubt was established in the Cathedral Square. The day wore on, the Anabaptists waiting for the Bishop to attack them, and the council waiting for an assault from the Anabaptists.

Soon the collusion between Bishop and council that the Anabaptists feared seemed about to take place, though it was probably their own actions that prompted it: a messenger managed to reach von Waldeck with a desperate plea from the city council to send military help. The

Bishop had indeed been gathering his forces in nearby Telgte, probably more from a hope to intimidate the city into surrendering than
because he planned to attack. Word came back that the Bishop would
send his delegate Melchior von Buren, the knight charged with the
military protection of the Cathedral, with a message for the city's
representative. Herman Tilbeck, the co-mayor, was safely seen
through the gate near the Overwater Church and taken to von Buren's open campfire beyond the outer wall.

Tilbeck was the logical choice for this mission, despite the earlier incident with the cattle that had resulted in his being held hos-
tage. He was on an approximately equal social level with von
Waldeck, as the only member of the present council to come from
the local landed gentry, the "patriciate," and he had a reputation
as a reasonable man. He returned from his meeting with only an
oral message, and that a discouraging one: the Bishop would not
make any kind of a deal.

The next day, February 10, Bernard Knipperdolling approached
the Overwater Church. "You must repent!" he shouted to the defenders within. The elderly Jaspar Jodefeld rushed at the merchant
with a spear, intent on running him through, before he was restrained. Knipperdolling was thrust into a cell with half a dozen
other Anabaptists whom the council had discovered among their
ranks and warned that his life would be forfeit if his fellow believers attacked them.

As the day wore on, farmers by the hundreds began filtering into
the city, admitted by the council through the gate which it still denied
to the Bishop's soldiers. The farmers were armed with scythes, pitch-
forks, heavy hammers, clubs, and wooden staves. They must have
looked to the Anabaptists, whom they now threatened, like the peasants in Brueghel's paintings: sturdy, superstitious, and ignorant, their
brutality and potential for violence obvious in their heavy shoulders
and thick-featured, low-browed faces. To the Catholic citizens of
Münster, however, who had placed straw crosses on their doors to
signify their fidelity to the Bishop, the farmers were devout companions in the only true faith and their potential saviors.

The pressures for some kind of rapprochement between the two
city factions grew more intense. Mayor Tilbeck argued that the coun-

cil should make a pact of mutual defense with the Anabaptists. Supported by an apparently shaken and repentant Knipperdolling, and despite the reservations of Jodefeld, the council agreed to meet with Jan van Leyden and Rothmann. A truce was struck by mid-afternoon. Prisoners and hostages were to be immediately released; each side agreed to refrain from interfering with the other's right to worship as it chose; and each swore to support the other in their common quarrel with the Bishop.

When word of the truce between the supposedly responsible Lutherans and the heretic Anabaptists was passed to the Bishop's officers waiting outside the gate, they received it, according to Kerssenbrück, "with tears and sighs." The Bishop said that the truce was the work of the devil. He felt that he had made the city a legitimate offer that had been spurned and he was angry—justifiably so, for as was later revealed, his offer had never reached the council: Herman Tilbeck, the reasonable man, the patrician, had secretly joined the Anabaptist cause sometime earlier and was functioning as Knipperdolling's agent when he received the Bishop's message. That message was not the dismissive oral communication that Tilbeck conveyed to the council, but a written document in which the Bishop swore that he wished only to defend and guarantee the freedom of the city. The Anabaptists were his enemy, and he would destroy them if the council would see to it that the gate by the Overwater Church was opened for his soldiers. The others who had resisted him, including the council, would not be harmed. Tilbeck burned the Bishop's offer and misled the council into thinking it had no other course than a truce with the Anabaptists.

The last chance to avoid disaster had just been lost to treachery and deceit, but few could see that at the time. The farmers, who had earlier looked so menacing, stacked their scythes and crowded into the taverns for beer and sausage before they "made their way home to their wives." At sunset, as the last one disappeared, the main gate was pulled shut and locked, and the Anabaptists burst into songs of thanksgiving. They could not doubt now, Rothmann and the other preachers assured them, that God was on their side—they all knew from their memories of the Peasants' War that you did not often buy off a mob of fanatical farmers with a few beers!

But it was well for the peasants that they had left, for now, as Rothmann wrote shortly afterward to a friend, a wonderful event occurred: the setting sun was not just one sun but three, a true miracle sent from God. The clouds appeared to be on fire, and the faces of all of the faithful were golden, as were the stones on the street. The divine flames that illuminated the faithful, they all knew, would also destroy their enemies: "If the farmers had remained a half hour longer," Rothmann said, "they would have been consumed by these flames and sent to Hell." He sent off messengers immediately to Holland and Frisia with descriptions of this miraculous salvation and manifestation of God's saving grace. At the same time, Jan van Leyden sent a message to the man who had replaced the pacific Melchior Hoffman as the leader of the northern Anabaptists, Jan Matthias. The time has come at last, the younger Jan informed Matthias: he must come immediately to Münster.

In the meantime the Anabaptists celebrated their victory in the streets with what Kerssenbrück described as shameless abandon. They leaped into the air "as if they wanted to fly," especially the women, who let their hair down and opened their garments or threw them away entirely, and flung themselves in the street in the shape of a cross, rolling in pig- and cow-dung. Their shrieking reminded the boy of a thousand squealing pigs. Men and women raced about in circles, foam spilling from their lips: "Nothing could have been more frightful, more insane, or more comic." A single incident combined all three of these elements for the young Catholic; the clouds referred to by Rothmann were not simply on fire, one man declared. They were fiery horses on whose backs rode angels with waving swords. Looking up, the boy saw only a beautiful sunset whose rays reflected blindingly from a weather vane in the shape of a gilded cock. As he watched, another believer, presumably suspecting witchcraft, shot it from the roof with an arrow.

The celebrations shortly took on a more organized character: it was carnival time, the pre-Lenten festival that had traditionally served as a release for Catholics before the stringent observances of the Easter season. The Anabaptists seized upon the occasion to parody the Catholics and Bishop Franz himself in a public procession. A company of maskers dressed as priests, monks, and nuns led a parade of revelers, singing hymns with obscene lyrics. They were followed by a chariot pulled by six men wearing the habits of different religious orders; on the box sat a mock Bishop with a miter looted from a city church, urging his steeds forward. Behind him a priest wearing hugely exaggerated spectacles intoned a parody of the last rites over a "dying" man. A sturdy blacksmith named Rusher had harnessed himself to a farm cart in which two young men rode and pretended to scourge him with whips.

Within a few days the persuasive accounts of their deliverance from evil sent abroad by Rothmann drew scores of ardent supporters to Münster, who passed with contemptuous ease through the Bishop's all-but-abandoned blockade. Among them were the two Krechting brothers: Henry, the surveyor with whom Jan van Leyden had lived for several months in Schöppingen, had brought with him not only his younger brother Bernard but his own wife and their two sons, both under ten years of age. These men, like hundreds of others, were so certain of the righteous cause of the New Zion that they did not hesitate to risk the lives of their families as well as their own.

They took the place of other men who saw nothing but trouble ahead and chose to flee, like Jaspar Jodefeld, who soon found safety in the small city of Hamm, and like the Bremen attorney, Dr. Friedrich von Wyck. Jodefeld was too old to be effective and was no great loss. Von Wyck, however, was a much more impressive man, a true statesman who would have been capable of great work in the right setting. He had left his lucrative practice in Bremen at considerable personal sacrifice to help his birth city regain its balance, but he was compromised by being caught in the middle. His frustration had peaked earlier when he had been saddled with Redeker as part of the truce team during their failed negotiations with the Bishop: the Anabaptists hated him for calling Redeker a thief, and the Bishop had threatened him for allowing that same thief to accompany him, and for choosing to help the city separate itself from his power.

The Bishop's soldiers overtook von Wyck shortly after he left Münster, quietly and in the dead of the night. He was taken first to

Bevergen, then to Iburg, and finally to Fürstenau. There he would remain in the charge of one of the Bishop's most trusted men, Count Eberhard von Morrien, until von Waldeck decided his fate.

Until now the unrest in Münster had resulted only in physical intimidation and harassment; neither the Anabaptists there nor their opponents had been charged with any deaths. Von Wyck must have assumed that he would be punished by having to ransom his freedom. Von Morrien and he were well acquainted, and he was made as comfortable as if he were an honored guest and not a prisoner. But one morning soon after his arrival, as the knight and his illustrious guest were playing their customary leisurely game of chess, a messenger arrived with a note from the Bishop. It was the Bishop's order, he said, that the message be read immediately. Von Morrien broke the seal and read the letter. His face grew pale. Von Wyck asked him what was the matter. "Herr Doktor," von Morrien replied heavily, "it has to do with your life. The Prince orders that you be beheaded immediately."

He handed the letter to the attorney. Von Wyck read it and responded angrily. Even if he had offended the Bishop, it was not possible that he should be secretly charged, tried, and executed. He demanded a proper trial. Von Morrien interrupted the lawyer and begged him not to blame him for ordering his death. He reminded him that he, von Morrien, was bound by a holy oath to follow his orders, and that his own life was forfeit if he failed to do so. Von Wyck reproached him, saying that a man had a higher duty to God when he was given such an order, and that God alone had the right to determine his guilt or innocence, not the Prince-Bishop. All his protests were in vain: the messenger had arrived with both a priest and an executioner, who waited below in the courtyard. Von Wyck rejected the ministrations of the priest with contempt, commended his soul to Heaven, and bared his neck to the executioner.

When news of the execution reached the city council in Münster, they sent a message to the Bishop asking the cause. He responded promptly that von Wyck had not been condemned as a supporter of the Anabaptists but because he had been a "rebel" who used his office in Münster to challenge the old ways and to stir up agitation. Any further hope on the part of the council for mercy from the Bishop was buried with the Bremen attorney.

As the model of tempered good sense and goodwill in the person of Dr. von Wyck passed from the stage, another, very different, kind of man entered onto it. When Jan van Leyden sent his message to Jan Matthias, saying that the time for his presence had come, it was as a pupil to a teacher, or as a servant to a master, for Matthias had himself baptized the younger man two years earlier. But Matthias was much more than one man's exemplar: he was now the titular head of the Anabaptists, in place of the jailed Melchior Hoffman. For him to come to Münster was analogous to a visit from the Pope or the Emperor, but it was even more significant to his followers because he was seen as the revivified presence of the Prophet Enoch, sent hither to announce the Second Coming.

Jan Matthias had been a humble baker in Amsterdam until he was converted and baptized by Melchior Hoffman in the 1520s. After that, he dedicated his life to following Hoffman, baptizing thousands of men and women and gradually assuming dominance over the now-imprisoned leader. At some point in recent years, he had determined that Hoffman's pacifism was completely wrong; the only proper response to oppression was violent resistance. It was not Christ that the Anabaptists should choose as their model but Jehovah, the God of wrath and vengeance. As official repression grew during the 1520s, so did Matthias's propensity for violence, though as yet it had borne little fruit.

Now in his mid-fifties, Matthias's tall figure was gaunt and stooped, his muscular baker's forearms wasted. His skull, almost bald, was enormous, his black eyes huge and piercing, and his flowing beard reached almost to the rope belt of his black robe. He stalked the streets of Münster, always accompanied by his beautiful dark-haired wife Divara, a former Carmelite nun some twenty years his junior. The vivid contrasts in their physical appearance were heightened by their dress: Matthias always attired in black robes, Divara in white. They were both attended constantly by worshipful crowds. It was not difficult to see him as an Old Testament prophet, in spirit if not in fact, as he inveighed against the evils of the godless ones who still infested the

New Zion—that is, the Catholics and Lutherans who had refused to undergo a second baptism. There were no figures among his allies to challenge Matthias, even if they had been so inclined. Bernard Rothmann, for all his eloquence, paled in comparison to the Prophet, as did Bernard Knipperdolling, for all of his fervor and passion. Only Jan van Leyden seemed able to maintain his composure in the presence of Jan Matthias.

The Prophet had not been in Münster more than a few days when he asserted that the city council had to be changed; the people should be represented by those who "did not follow the instinct of the flesh but of the spirit"—the council should be composed entirely of Anabaptists or those who were about to convert. Only a few months earlier the truly representative city council had been replaced by one more amenable to the demands of the radical Lutherans and their Anabaptist allies. Now these men were in turn dislodged from power as insufficiently devout. A second special election returned only six of the twenty-four men to office. The new members were all declared Anabaptists or soon to become so. Losing their positions were Jodefeld, who had already fled, Henry Mollenheck, the prominent leader of the blacksmiths' guild, and Herman Tilbeck—who, despite his valuable service in betraying the city and the recent public baptism of himself and his family, was not fully trusted, perhaps for reasons of class.

The new co-mayors were Bernard Knipperdolling and the wealthy clothier Gerd Kibbenbrock, a tiny man famous for his hot temper. These two were the only men of property on the council; the rest, in a radical departure from the principle that only men with a large personal stake in the fortunes of the city should serve, were workmen—carpenters, tailors, masons, blacksmiths, and furriers. Communist dialecticians a few centuries later would praise the results of this election as the first dictatorship of the proletariat. For Jan Matthias, it was the realization of the theocratic state that he vowed would destroy the larger state that contained it.

The destruction began as the Anabaptists celebrated the election with drunken parties in the streets, which soon became violent. The Bishop was hanged in effigy. Houses that had been decorated with straw crosses were looted and their owners beaten. Abbess Ida von

Merveldt and the Bailiff of the Cathedral, Dirk von Merveldt (the two were not related) had already fled the city with the lesser clergy, along with Melchior von Buren and his men. The great domed Cathedral, now undefended, was invaded by men carrying axes, sledgehammers, and long knives. Latin Bibles and a painting of the Virgin Mary were smeared with human feces. The tombs of long-dead Church leaders were broken open and the bones and ashes strewn on the floor. The altars were hammered to kindling and the stained-glass windows shattered with arrows and axes. Other paintings were destroyed and their frames turned into toilet seats for the guardhouses. Wooden statues were burned, those of marble shattered. A collection of medieval manuscripts assembled by the poet Rudolf Lange and other books not hidden by the staff were burned. The great organ was torn down and its brass pipes hauled away to be melted into shell casings. Bronze plates were pried loose from coffins for a similar fate. The glass and gears and finely inlaid wood of the recently completed great ornamental clock had no utility when the clock was destroyed and were merely left on the cold stone floor.

Such barbarous vandalism was neither aimless nor irrational in the eyes of the Anabaptists: the contemptible and disgusting symbols of Catholic religious authority had to be desecrated and destroyed—and, most of all, made vulnerable to attack, in order for the institutions of Church and state themselves to be overthrown. Much of Jan Matthias's power came from the simplicity of his message to people who had long suffered from oppression and were not open to subtleties of argument and debate: his message was as direct and forceful as a boot in the face, to paraphrase George Orwell's later observations about fascism. Insofar as Matthias had a coherent ideology, it consisted of destruction in order to achieve salvation: "We preach the separation of the world. The state is to be used to destroy the state." He demanded a theocracy devoted to the worship of God the Father, the jealous and demanding and wrathful Father, not his meek and mild and loving Son. He railed against Satan, who spread himself outward like the limbs of a great oak tree, against the wicked idols of Moloch, against unbelievers in the saddle, against false Christs and false prophets. And he spoke fervently of the New Zion in Münster, where only the newly baptized could expect forgiveness from the Lord. All others would be executed or expelled into the outer darkness.

The Catholics, many of whom had roots in Münster going back for centuries, began to leave their home in mid-February 1534, in the first of two major departures during that month. The first time, the departing citizens were allowed to take what they could with them, except for food; it was clear to the Anabaptists that the Bishop would be forced to besiege the city, and they were already filling the warehouses with provisions. Some ingenious women, looking at a long few days on the road, tried to smuggle sausages under their skirts. One of them, Kerssenbrück says, was intercepted by the furrier Sundermann, on guard at the gate, who thought she looked uncommonly fat, and upon feeling her body in a very familiar manner discovered the sausages. Guards then began to force the evacuees to hand over their heavy coats and to open their bags for inspection, and men were assigned to poke through mattresses and bedding with long knives. Any protests were met by mockery and curses such as "On your way to the hangman, you gallows birds—you'll never come back here!"

But many Catholics remained in the city, unwilling to give up their homes and their belongings and hoping that the Bishop would somehow intervene to save them. Matthias now demanded again in a public sermon that not only the Catholics but the Lutherans be killed, so that "true Christians can serve God the father without hindrance." The translation by the Victorian scholar Baring-Gould endows Matthias with a degree of rhetorical elegance: "The Father demands the purification and the cleansing of His New Jerusalem. Our republic cannot tolerate the confusion sown by impious sects. I advise that we slaughter without delay the Lutherans, the Papists, and all those who are not of the right faith. None may remain alive in Zion but those who can offer to the Father a pure and pleasing worship. The only way to preserve the righteous from the contagion of the impure is to sweep them from the face of the earth. We are supremely strong and can do this immediately without fear of interference from within the city or without." A more accurate sense of what Matthias actually sounded like can only come from seeing his words in the original breathless German: *"Draussen aber sind die Hunde und die Zauberer und die Huren and the Totschläger und the Abgöttischen und alle die die Lügen lieben and tun!"* ("Everywhere we are surrounded by dogs and sorcerers and whores and killers and the godless and all who love lies and commit them!")

Such mad passion was beyond the Prophet's chief disciples, who thought the city was not yet strong enough for a full-scale war with the Bishop. Only Knipperdolling had the courage to challenge Matthias and his plan to exterminate the godless ones. They would ruin themselves by so doing, Knipperdolling argued. It was not that he valued the lives of the Catholics or indeed of the Lutherans—his townsmen and business partners for many years though they had been. And it was true that the Bishop by himself could do them little harm at this stage of the conflict. But if the Schmalkaldic League, the association of northern cities of which Münster was a part, grew fearful that any city could find a third of its population murdered, then it would give the Bishop enough arms and men to overwhelm them. Until we are stronger, Knipperdolling advised, let us settle for simply expelling the godless ones from the city. This time, however, those who were driven away would have to leave everything they owned for the benefit of the Company of Christ. Thus would the city be purged of those miserable wretches who refuse the New Covenant and at the same time be enriched by their wealth. Matthias reluctantly agreed to settle for the expulsion of the unbelievers.

The next morning, February 27, was bitterly cold. A hard frost had glazed the cobblestones. A sleeting rain, driven almost sideways by a fierce north wind, would normally have kept most people indoors, but the squares were thronged with armed Anabaptists who had been told of the coming expulsion and some worried citizens who did not know what was going on. Hooded preachers carrying long staffs moved among them, kissing the true believers, both men and women, on the lips, as Jesus was said to have done. Those few who resisted were clearly not of the faith, and were driven toward the main gate, where a double guard thrust them out of the city. Matthias appeared now, taller than any of the others and looking like the very Angel of Death in his hooded black robe. Facing the shuttered windows of the houses that lined the square, behind which,

he knew, cowered the unbelievers, he screamed threats and warnings: "Turn, turn, O sinners. See the storm of sleet and snow that
the Father has sent against you? The very elements themselves de-
spise your presence if you do not join us now!" He threw himself
face down into the freezing slush and, his arms extended, fell into a
trance. Rothmann, Knipperdolling, and Jan van Leyden rushed to
his side and announced that the Lord was about to reveal Himself
through His Prophet. Matthias opened his eyes like one awakening
from a dream, rose to his full height, and said, "Hear now the word
of your God! Cleanse this holy city of its impurities! Drive away the
sons of Esau! This place, this New Jerusalem, belongs to the sons of
Jacob!"

Released now to action, the Anabaptists roamed the city, invad-
ing every house, scouring every garret, every cellar, driving from
their hiding places old men and women, entire families, invalids,
kitchen maids and laborers as well as their masters, whose fine
clothes and jewelry were stripped away and tossed into baskets.
The men were pushed and shoved if they moved too slowly, or if,
like the hapless Fabricius, they had made themselves known as opponents. Matthias himself stopped a wagon driven by the old clergyman Dr. Johann Dungel, of St. Mauritz, and put a spear to his
chest: "You won't escape unpunished, you old traitor! You can
keep either your money or your life." Dungel protested that
Knipperdolling had assured him he would be allowed to leave un-
molested, to which Matthias responded, "I never made such a
promise!" He pulled the rings from the old man's fingers and finally let him go, minus the wagon, on foot.

Herman Kerssenbrück and his landlord Dr. Wesseling were among
the expelled though both remained in the vicinity of the outer wall
for the day, hoping they would be allowed to return. Until recently
the boy had regarded what he had seen as a comedy. Now he saw
terrible things that imprinted themselves on his memory, to be recalled
years later as the last of his personal experiences with the Anabaptists.
"The women carried their naked nursing babies and begged in vain
for rags to clothe them in. Other women, driven from their maternity
beds, gave birth in the streets. Miserable children, barefoot in the
snow, whimpered beside their fathers. Old people, bent by age,

tottered along calling God's vengeance down upon their persecutors." Unmoved by pity, the preachers watched the old and the sick, women and children, leave through the gates for an uncertain fate. It was unfortunate, said Pastor Bernard Rothmann; but they had to be sacrificed for the sake of the chosen who remained as the Company of Christ.

Those who could not bring themselves to leave town and who consented to conversion were subjected to a chilly baptism in the Market Square, where the preachers poured water over their heads from large copper vats. Others who were physically unable to leave were carried to the square and baptized. One doughty old woman resisted Rothmann's efforts to convert her, saying that she had been baptized already, as had her ancestors; she did not require another ceremony. Rothmann grew impatient. "Then you must be separated from those who do believe by death, so that the wrath of the Father does not descend upon us." "Well, then, let it be so," she replied. "You may baptize me in the name of the devil, for I have already been baptized in the name of God."

The revolution was now complete, but its leaders were shaken immediately by two events. The first was the arrival of bad news from Amsterdam. A week before the expulsion of the unbelievers, the most militant of the Anabaptists, Henry Roll, had left Münster for the Dutch city of Maastricht. His mission was to raise support for Münster among the Anabaptists in Holland—their money, their weapons, their physical presence, if they were fighting men. However, the Spanish rulers of Holland, alarmed at the increasing unrest in neighboring Westphalia, were keeping a close watch on their own religious rebels. Now word was received that Roll had died, burned at the stake in Utrecht, his ashes scattered in the neighboring fields. More disturbing even than the news of his death was that he had prophesied it and done nothing to avoid easy capture. The Anabaptists professed to envy him his selection for the special blessing by the Lord, but they must have seen that suicide was not the message they wanted their converts to receive.

The second event was less surprising, as it had been both anticipated and provoked. The morning after the expulsion, on February

28, the fog lifted from the moat to reveal the figures of hundreds of laborers erecting earthen barriers around the three-mile circumference of the city, several hundred yards beyond the range of the defenders' cannons. Behind the barriers, barely visible, were the first few of what would be dozens of white-walled tents with the Bishop's crest dangling limply from their peaks. The siege of Münster had finally begun.

3

A MIGHTY FORTRESS

A mighty fortress is our God
A bulwark never failing;
Our helper He amid the flood
Of mortal ills prevailing.

—Martin Luther

MÜNSTER WAS OFTEN compared to a wasps' nest during this period of frantic, aggressive consolidation of power by the Anabaptists. Franz von Waldeck, for his part, was like a lethargic, lumbering bear as he approached the nest, uncertain how to grasp it. On February 3, immediately following his disgusted dismissal of von Wyck and Redeker, he had ordered his knights to prepare for an attack, only to find them resistant and anxious to pursue further negotiations. Lashing out at easier targets, von Waldeck executed several Anabaptists in nearby towns: five women and one man were drowned in Wolbeck, and in Bevergen four women were drowned and two men burned at the stake. Everywhere in his bishopric the belongings of those who, like the Krechting brothers, had joined the rebels in Münster were confiscated. When the Anabaptists, undeterred, welcomed Jan Matthias and took over the city council on February 23, the Bishop met with his command staff yet again to discuss the growing probability of a siege. His chief lieutenants were Johann von Buren, Hermann von Mengerssen, Eberhard von Morrien, and Johann von Raesfeld as his commander-in-chief. He assured them that their services would only be needed for one or two months, at most.

Two days later, on February 25, the rebels sent a force of men outside the city gates to the St. Mauritz Church, a few hundred feet from the city's outer wall. The high and sturdy stone walls of the old church would have provided the attackers with an excellent platform for their cannons. The Anabaptists set explosive charges and blew it up, leaving the Bishop a heap of rubble for his cannon mounts.

The expulsion of the unbelievers two days after that had been the final insult. The Bishop was now forced to respond in earnest; the rusty, creaking machinery of late-medieval warfare was about to grind into action.

To begin with, von Waldeck had no artillery of his own and had to borrow cannons, wagons, and horses from various sources. Philip of Hesse sent two gigantic siege cannons, nicknamed the Devil and the Devil's Mother. Lighter cannon and field artillery pieces arrived from other sources, including the Prince of Cleves, the Archbishop of Cologne, and the Prince of Bentheim. A total of forty-two heavy weapons would ultimately be positioned in front of the Judefelder Gate, the Hörst Gate, and the St. Mauritz Gate; in the latter location they were protected from attack by the defenders of the city by the fallen stone walls of the destroyed church, but elsewhere they were screened by more than three thousand "good, strong, portable" lattices of braided reeds and rushes and tree branches, each eight by twelve feet in size.

Huge quantities of munitions and other supplies arrived in wagon convoys from near and distant cities: nearly three hundred barrels of powder from Brabant and Amsterdam, an equivalent amount of saltpeter and sulfur from Mengen, iron musket balls from Deventer, three hundred and thirty wheelbarrows and twenty-two hundred shovels from a variety of sources. Secure armories were built to contain these materials as well as the weapons the soldiers needed—muskets, halberds, lances, spears, small portable bombs for blowing up wooden gates. Powder mills and smelters in Osnabrück and Iburg were commissioned to replace supplies as they were depleted.

The soldiers who were to enforce the Bishop's will began to assemble during the middle of February, as the Anabaptists had already observed. While many were from nearby, not a few had come great distances—from the Rhine Valley, from Saxony, from the Netherlands, from Denmark. By May there would be nearly eight thousand of them, almost all mercenaries who fought only for money. At their best, these *Landsknechte* lived up to the model set in the Middle Ages by the Swiss guards, whose discipline, courage, and long lances had become legendary. With their fantastically colorful costumes and their freedom from the ordinary constraints of life, they may now appear to us as romantic figures. More often, though, they were neither heroic nor romantic, living lives that, in Thomas Hobbes's memorable phrase, were nasty, brutish, and short. Victims of their century—peasants, laborers, and artisans whom plague, religious wars, and economic dislocations had turned into wandering adventurers—they roamed the continent with their wives or their camp followers, with their horses, their dogs, and their weapons ready for hire.

Such men were often notoriously unreliable and undisciplined. Many who wound up fighting for the Bishop had come to Münster after hearing rumors that the Anabaptists were willing to pay well for professional protection. The Bishop's men told the mercenaries that they had two choices, neither of which included being allowed to fight for the Anabaptists: they could either sit out the siege in chains or they could join the Bishop. Once they were hired, all soldiers were subject to clear and harsh rules of discipline, violation of which meant torture or death. The rules of engagement included division of the booty after victory, which provides insight into what the Bishop hoped to accomplish in Münster. In addition to pledging that they would "fight bravely" for their commanders, the soldiers had to acknowledge that they were aware of the following: (1) powder and bullets taken from the enemy have been promised to the Bishop; (2) the Bishop is not obligated to pay any soldier who engages in plundering; (3) the City Hall is not to be plundered or damaged, whatever booty is found there belongs to the Bishop; (4) anything found belonging to the Church officials who had been expelled from the city must be returned to them; (5) everything must remain in the private houses after the conquest, including carpets and wall hangings; (6) the soldiers must formally acknowledge the authority of the Bishop once they are in control of the city; (7) the soldiers must leave the city within eight days after the trumpet sounds victory—during this period they will receive their assigned shares of the booty and the salary still owed to them; (8) the soldiers must not kill the leaders of the rebellion but try to capture them alive, in which case they will be amply rewarded.

The soldiers were divided among seven tented compounds situated in a line that stretched for nearly four miles around the city, just outside of cannon range. Each compound was about a half mile from its neighbors. All were easily visible from the city gate towers. It was a constantly busy scene. Neighboring village merchants, at first distressed because Münster had been their best customer, set up shop in and between the tent compounds, selling the soldiers whatever they needed in the way of food and drink and supplies. The soldiers' wives and mistresses hung out their laundry, and their children played in the fields. The scene from the city walls must have looked almost festive with the white pinnacled tents, the vividly colored princely crests fluttering under von Waldeck's coat of arms, the smoke from cooking fires drifting into the damp spring skies, and the sounds of trumpets and drums as the men practiced their formations . . .

But it was dangerously expensive as well, not only for von Waldeck but for his numerous creditors—the monthly payroll for the lounging soldiers alone was 34,000 guilders, plus expenses for supplies, transportation, and administration. The Bishop did not lack for allies. Since the Peasants' War had ended, the Emperor had impressed on all his princes the necessity of mutual defense in time of trouble; anarchy would be loosed in the land if one member of the confederation was allowed to fall. In addition to weapons, supplies, and money provided by Hesse, Cleves, and Queen Marie of Burgundy, von Waldeck received loans from church authorities in Paderborn (2,100 gold guilders), Osnabrück (one thousand gold guilders), and Capenberg (two thousand gold guilders). But far more came in the form of loans from nobles and businessmen—a total of nearly 25,000 gold guilders borrowed at rates of five to ten percent yearly interest. (A gold guilder would be worth about $50 in today's dollars.)

The economic pressures on the Bishop trickled down to his subjects. He had ordered the Catholic churches in his domain to turn over to him their jewelry and gold and silver; in addition they now had to pay a ten percent yearly tax. The farmers were also assessed a war tax on each "plow and cow," even as they were compelled to leave their fields during spring planting and dig trenches and earthen assault barriers for the Bishop's soldiers.

By early May the Bishop's subjects, his creditors, and his superiors— the Archbishop of Cologne and Emperor Charles V—were reaching the end of their patience with the delay in prosecuting the war. After two months the heretics still owned Münster and seemed to be growing stronger, not weaker, even though it was known that some recent events in the city seemed to signal some fatal flaws in its leadership. But not only had the Bishop not attacked, he also had begun to fall behind on his payments to the soldiers; while many stayed in their camps, hoping eventually to be paid, others were beginning to drift away. Some, including a company-grade officer, Gert von Münster, had even deserted to the Anabaptists, taking with him several of his men.

The Bishop's hesitation derived, it would appear, from the hope that his huge force would intimidate the defenders into surrendering without a fight. There were those within the city who could have told him he was wasting his time: not only was the city virtually invulnerable to direct assault, it was defended by people who, whatever their theological peculiarities, were well-led, fearless, and fighting for their lives.

Long before the Anabaptists or the Lutherans came on the scene, in the middle of the thirteenth century, Münster had become a virtual state within a state, with the right to levy taxes, issue its own coinage, and elect its own government. It had been, from its earliest days, one of the most securely fortified cities in northern Germany. Lacking the natural advantages of such mountain fastnesses as Rothenburg on the Tauber and Coburg, as well as ready access to large quantities of stone, the engineers who designed Münster's defenses over the centuries had used the river Aa that bisected the city as the key to its protection. Since the first castle on the site had been built in the eighth century, walls and moats had been added as well as a gun tower, or Zwinger, near the New Bridge Gate, where the Aa leaves the city. There were ten gate towers, connected by a twelve-foot high broad inner palisade with a stone foundation. Each gate led to a drawbridge across the inner moat, nearly one hundred feet across. Beyond the moat was a second, lower, earthen wall, anchored by eight squat round stone towers and the more substantial *Zwinger*, all of which housed cannons and sharpshooters. And beyond that wall there was yet another barrier, a second moat—all together, the combined defenses of walls and moats kept attackers more than three hundred yards away from the city's interior.

Behind the inner wall the cobbled streets and wooden houses of the city lay secure against all but lucky cannon shots or flaming arrows designed to set thatched roofs on fire—all of which were destroyed by the defenders before they could become a hazard. There was in any event abundant water from the river Aa for fighting fires. The river also provided water for drinking and for irrigating crops, in addition to carp, bass, and eels for food. Münster was a market town as well as a commercial trading center, and all of the cottages on the outskirts and many within the city proper had their own vegetable gardens. Smokehouses and granaries, breweries and barns in abundance made it unlikely that Münster would be starved into submission for at least a year, and few medieval sieges lasted that long.

But armed defenders, not walls and garden plots, are needed to protect a city against a professional army nearly as large in numbers as its nine thousand inhabitants. On its face, Münster may have looked woefully undermanned: most of the approximately sixteen hundred men between the ages of eighteen and fifty were not trained soldiers but artisans and merchants; about four hundred adolescent boys and old men might also serve in an emergency. More than half—five thousand—of the total population were women, and two thousand more were young children. In an ordinary army, assuming three guard shifts per day, only about five hundred men would be ready to fight at any given moment. Many of these would presumably be handicapped by fear of what would happen to their families if they failed to defend them adequately.

In Münster, though, virtually everyone became a vital part of the city's defense; few of the nine thousand were allowed to be dead weight. Moreover, many of the new arrivals were true believers like Henry Krechting, who had not only brought his family but heeded Rothmann's command to bring weapons: "He who has a knife, or a sword, or a gun should take them along, and if he does not have them, buy them, because the Lord is going to save us through His mighty arm but He requires evidence that we are willing to fight for ourselves and for His Kingdom." Thus most of the men, though they might not be soldiers by profession, were not only ready to fight but were armed as well; in all, four hundred and fifty muskets as well as shorter firearms, swords, pikestaffs, and bows were available for the defenders, plus eighty-six cannons—twice as many as the Bishop had, and all nicely protected in stone battlements, not hiding behind straw lattices.

From the start the Anabaptists aggressively challenged the Bishop and his soldiers, burning his mills, destroying a brickworks, and killing a number of the enemy. As a warning that the soldiers could expect nothing from them but trouble, they cut off the head of a captured drummer and stuck it on the peak of the Bisping Gate. Night forays into the very tents of the soldiers left some of them with their throats slit and messages inviting the others to desert their godless and losing cause and to join the Company of Christ instead.

But for the most part, more attention was paid in these early days to preparations for defense. The fighting force was divided into ten companies, one for each gate, and it maintained the active watch. Elderly men were assigned to night patrol duties and fire brigades. The older boys, laughing and excited, were given archery lessons by Tile Bussenmeister, the one-eyed giant, and taught how to charge and how to retreat in good order. Older women and young girls prepared meals in the new kitchens and dining halls near each gate where all now took their meals together, presided over by the Anabaptist preachers.

The defenders knew that in an attack the enemy's cannons would be brought to bear on selected sections of the wall. Repeated pounding with thirty-pound iron and stone balls would destroy any wall, which meant that it had to be reinforced from within, a major project. Trees outside the walls were cut down at night to deprive the Bishop's troops of cover and dragged back to be used, along with the decorative linden trees that had shaded the city's streets and squares, to shore up the walls. When these ran out, unoccupied wooden houses were torn down for their heavy beams and structural members. Paving stones, grave markers, and marble slabs wrenched from the Catholic tombs in the churches were used to finish off the reinforced inner wall.

The defenders built their own powder mill next to the Cathedral and a charcoal kiln in the nearby Rosenthal Church. Crews of women brought the charcoal to the men operating the mill. Others scraped the accumulated deposits of saltpeter from the caked walls of animal stalls and dumped them into vats of boiling water; what remained after the water had boiled away was saltpeter ready for use in making gunpowder. Pitch and quicklime were readied for cauldrons on the ramparts; the older women fashioned wreaths made of flax and hemp and dipped them into the seething cauldrons. The younger women would, when the time came, light them with torches and hurl them as flaming necklaces upon the enemy soldiers as they tried to scale the walls.

A foundry was placed in front of Melchior von Buren's house near the Cathedral Square, and lead from the destroyed church tower of St. Maurtiz was melted down for bullets. Blacksmiths hammered out spearheads and sword blades and reinforced rims for the wheelwrights to use in making heavy carts for moving the cannons. The stablehands groomed the horses and fed them well to be sure they were strong and ready for battle. Private gardens were taken over as city plots and readied for an early planting during what was proving to be an unseasonably warm spring.

The city's only serious and irremediable deficiency was sulfur, necessary for gunpowder, and throughout the siege it would be essential to use their firearms sparingly.

It was Jan van Leyden, aided by Knipperdolling and Henry Krechting (who had been a soldier with the German troops when they sacked Rome in 1527), who devised the plan of defense and organized the different units effectively. This was no small achievement, and for a time the new Company of Christ achieved a kind of perfect balance; outside the walls was the enemy, the Bishop and the Church and state that he represented—brutal but incompetent and incoherent. Inside were they, the Chosen Ones, a family of brothers and sisters whose Father was the Lord and whose essence was unity and clarity of divine purpose.

Morale was high and kept so by mass meetings and religious assemblies. Aflame with religious passion, the Company of Christ was assembled to the sound of trumpets at all times of the day and night to hear public announcements by one or another of their leaders. After these gatherings the people lifted their voices in song, led by Jan van Leyden's clear high tenor. The sight and sound of thousands of devout believers joined in song must have deeply stirred the members of the besieged community, whose musical preferences were less radical than some of their other tastes, tending toward familiar Lutheran hymns that they adapted. Among the most popular was one drawn from Psalms 124:7, celebrating an escape from evil pursuers: "Our soul is escaped as a bird out of the snare of the fowlers: the snare is broken, and we are escaped." Bernard Rothmann adapted another from Psalms 6:9, concerning the return of David to the world and the joy of his followers at the destruction of the godless. The most stirring song of all was *"Ein' Feste Burg Ist Unser Gott"* ("A Mighty Fortress Is Our God"), too famously Luther's own words to be denied by the Anabaptists, much as their author was by now despised. The Bishop's soldiers, within easy earshot, surely heard the singing as it lifted over the walls:

> A mighty fortress is our God
> A bulwark never failing;
> Our helper He amid the flood
> Of mortal ills prevailing.

Even now, Luther's source, Psalm 46, conveys the emotional force that the Anabaptists must have responded to: "God is our refuge and strength, a very present help in trouble" (46:1), and "The heathen raged, the kingdoms were moved: he uttered his voice, the earth melted" (46:6).

But the defenders' delicate sense of community and common purpose was soon challenged by two acts of Jan Matthias, who had a genius for discord. The first involved, among others, Henry Graes, the schoolmaster from Borkum, who continued to meet daily with his charges, assisted by several other preachers; in mid-March, his task was complicated by the decision of Jan Matthias to burn every book in the city, including schoolbooks, finishing the job he had begun earlier. Every house was scoured for hidden books, as well as the churches, cloisters, and convents, and a second great bonfire was built for them in the Cathedral Square. Even religious works that were unconnected to the present controversy were destroyed. Only the Bible was spared. The justification for this action was that there was no past, no history, other than what the Bible recorded. Fruitless theological speculations such as those of Aquinas and Augustine vanished in the flames, as did Luther's quarrelsome and nitpicking disputations. Guidance in the meaning of the Scriptures would now be provided only by the Bible and by the preachers who helped their flocks to comprehend its message.

Such at least appears to have been Matthias's argument. The adults whose books he burned could at least retain their memories of books read and lessons learned. But the sight of those fresh-faced young children, marching hand in hand in double rows to the Overwater Church for their education from men who burned books, must have saddened more than one parent, for most of these people were not so zealous as the Prophet. Later events suggest that it also profoundly disturbed the schoolmaster, Henry Graes.

Jan Matthias's other major action during this period was better received, at least by the poor who had made their way to Münster in response to Rothmann's widely circulated assertions that private property was a curse, as was all commerce: "Everything which has served the purposes of self-seeking and private property, such as buying and selling, working for money, taking interest and practicing usury, or eating and drinking the sweat of the poor—that is, making one's own people and fellow creatures work so that one can grow fat—and indeed everything which offends against love—all such things are abolished amongst us by the power of love and community. And knowing that God now desires to abolish such abominations, we would die rather than turn to them. We know that such sacrifices are pleasing to the Lord. And indeed no Christian or Saint can satisfy God if he does not live in such a community or at least desire with all his heart to live in it." Or, as the ever-succinct Bernard Knipperdolling summed up Rothmann's idealistic community: "One God, one pot, one egg, and one kitchen."

Now Matthias confiscated the houses of the departed unbelievers and installed the newcomers in them. He took all the bedding, furniture, food, and clothing that he could find and placed them in central depots under the charge of seven "deacons," whose names were revealed to him after three days of prayer. He assigned one deacon for meat, one for grain, one for beer, one for clothing and shoes, one for furniture, one for weapons, and one for valuables, including jewelry. As all property and goods were now held in common, Matthias decreed that all debts and obligations were abolished. He gathered up the account ledgers and IOUs left in shops and businesses, churches and private homes, and burned them all. As might have been anticipated, he abolished currency itself, along with the idea of working for pay; all would contribute their labor for the greater good, and would receive what they needed in return free of charge.

But opposition to the dark prophet, as some were calling Jan Matthias, was growing within Münster even as the Bishop's preparations for attack floundered. The religious fervor of its citizens was matched by—on the part of some—their stubborn resistance to arbitrary rule, no matter what its source was. The powerful merchants like Knipperdolling, educated and articulate, had provided the spear point of the original resistance to Catholic dominance of the city, but they would have been helpless without the cooperation of the guilds and their leaders. Builders, blacksmiths, weavers, carpenters, tanners, millers, brewers—these were men who worked with their hands and trained and directed others to do so. Often hostile to the merchants by reason of temperament and class, the tradesmen were hardworking and thrifty, early models of what would later be called the Protestant ethic of self-discipline and self-denial. Many had actively supported the farmers in the Peasants' War, and some of them had died for their allegiance to the rebellion. There were many of these men in Münster, devoutly religious but not fanatical. Two were friends and colleagues: Herbert Rusher and Henry Mollenheck. Both would offer courageous challenges to Jan Matthias, at great personal cost.

Initially, Rusher's enthusiasm for the new order had seemed boundless, as was evident when he let himself be lashed through the streets during the carnival a few weeks earlier. His disillusionment must have set in almost immediately, for now, in mid-March, he was arrested and charged with treason. As plausibly reconstructed by the German novelist Helmut Paulus, using contemporary sources, Rusher was standing guard one freezing midnight with a recent arrival, a young carpenter called Henry Gresbeck, and Mollenheck, among others. As the men listened to the Bishop's soldiers singing and carousing, warm and comfortable around their blazing campfires, Rusher grew indiscreet in voicing his complaints. Why was it that the Hollanders and the scum they had brought with them never stood guard duty? Why did they have to stand in the open, exposed to the northern night wind with no shelter, no fire? Why should he have to stand guard after working all day at his forge? Who gave the stranger Henry Krechting the authority to throw their women and others who complained into the Rosenthal Church dungeon? How could they concede to Jan Matthias the right to take all of their hard-earned property and cash? Rusher grew more vehement in his denunciations of Jan Matthias. He no doubt believed he was among friends who would not betray him; but Matthias had already instructed his preachers to tell his followers that children must report their parents for slanders against the Prophet. Families, neighbors, friends—all had to recognize a greater loyalty to God's anointed messenger than to anyone else.

Accounts vary as to how Rusher was taken into custody: he was in a tavern, he was home in bed with his wife; he was, as Paulus has it, on guard duty. There is some variance as well in what he actually said about Matthias. The polite Victorian version is that he called the Hollander a "lying villain who was misleading others, nothing more than a lying traitor." Henry Gresbeck, who left a record of his days in Münster, reports that Rusher called Matthias "a crazy lying *Scheissprophet* [a shit-prophet] who was not worth a baker's fart"—a livelier and more credible rendition. But the sources agree that Rusher was brought before the Prophet in the Cathedral Square for public exposure and questioning. Rusher was a tall man and, like blacksmiths generally, heavily muscled. He was tightly bound with rope, his hands secured behind him. Hundreds of Rusher's fellow citizens, all of whom had known him for years, crowded closer, as did the foreigners he had railed against, standing on tiptoe to see him and straining to hear the Prophet's words.

Matthias glowered at the frightened blacksmith. "Perhaps this man has gone mad," he shouted to the crowd, "or perhaps an evil spirit has misled him"—he could not say with certainty. But it was clear that Rusher was "one of the godless ones of whom God had said, 'You who allow such to remain in your company will become godless yourselves.' " It is not difficult to imagine the mad Prophet growing more excited, his dark forked beard stabbing downward as he worked himself into a judgmental fury. As Kerssenbrück recounts the episode, Matthias proclaimed that the whole Company of Christ was threatened with God's scornful wrath unless it purified itself through punishment of the evildoer. "He must be cast out of the ranks of the living into death," Matthias shouted. "It is written!"

At this point two of the most prominent and influential Anabaptist leaders stepped forward to protest. They were Herman Tilbeck, whose earlier duplicity as co-mayor with Knipperdolling had delivered the city into the hands of the Anabaptists, and Herman Redeker, the shoemaker accused earlier by the Bishop of looting a church. Both now said that although it appeared that Rusher was deserving of punishment, there should first be an official inquiry. He should be locked up until the inquiry had found him innocent or guilty, and then punished if necessary. These were both men who believed entirely in the divinity of Matthias's mission, and had been ready to plunder churches and to betray their comrades for that mission. For them now to question the Prophet's authority in public indicates how profoundly troubled they were by this attack on one of their own, even though he was a doubter. Matthias flew into a rage and ordered Tilbeck and Redeker thrown into the Rosenthal dungeon to await his later judgment.

Turning back to the condemned man, who must have watched with hope and then anguish as Tilbeck tried and failed to help him, Matthias prepared to lift his sword. Gresbeck's account suggests that he now hesitated to deliver the fatal blow; perhaps some residue of compassion still existed in a man who was, after all, a baker by profession, not a soldier and not a criminal, and there is no record of his having ever killed anyone before. It was Jan van Leyden who concluded the matter; he must have seen that any weakness or hesitation would have doomed them all. Although the young tailor's apprentice, tavern owner, and actor presumably had no more personal experience of bloodletting than the elderly baker, he now stepped in front of Matthias and, seizing a halberd from one of Rusher's guards, drove it deep into the kneeling man's back. Rusher toppled to his side in the street. Though the wound was enough to kill a weaker man, he remained conscious, groaning loudly but nowhere near death. Van Leyden seized a short firearm, a primitive pistol, from another guard, and fired point-blank into Rusher's back. Still the blacksmith clung to life. Two men stepped out of the crowd and carried Rusher to his home. "He will recover!" Jan said. Rusher lingered in great pain for eight days until he died.

Tilbeck and Redeker were released unharmed from the Rosenthal dungeon after a few days, chastened, obedient, and destined to be with the cause until the end. Matthias's shrewder disciples, such as Jan van Leyden and Henry Krechting, saw that they had nearly lost control of the situation with Rusher. Now they acted to tighten that control. First, they reiterated the demand for all citizens of Münster to bring all of their gold, silver, and jewelry to the City Hall, on the ground that true Christians had no need of such things but the New Zion could use them to pay for its defense. Most obeyed, but many buried or hid their treasures. To guard the new city treasures, Matthias appointed Cord Cruse, a jeweler who had just returned after a seven-year banishment by the prior Prince-Bishop, and Anna Kolthave, formerly the concubine of a Catholic priest, since departed. These two were charged with the task of relieving their Christian brothers of their guilty and heathenish dependence on material possessions.

But more than reluctant cooperation was needed from the people of Münster. The two Jans knew that many of the new converts, like the elderly woman threatened with death by Rothmann, had only converted to avoid execution or exile. They had to be reminded of their falseness and hypocrisy. Hundreds of the suspect converts were herded into the Cathedral and forced to lie on their faces on the cold stone floor for three hours while Matthias harangued them for their uncertain devotion to his holy cause. Several dozen of the most recalcitrant among them were locked in St. Lambert's Church to await their fate; given what had just happened to Herbert Rusher, they were reduced after several hours of waiting to a state of nervous terror. When the doors were finally unlocked and Matthias strode among them, they groveled before him and begged him to forgive them their sins. Matthias let himself be softened toward the sinners, as Henry

Gresbeck sarcastically wrote in his journal; he knelt beside them and gave thanks to God for having heard his prayers to be merciful to the sheep who had been lost and now were found, who now wept with him and gave thanks.

4

DEATH OF A PROPHET

There is a way which seemeth right unto a man, but the end thereof are the ways of death.

—Proverbs 14:12

For when he dieth he shall carry nothing away; his glory shall not descend after him.

—Psalm 49:17

THAT TWO DUTCHMEN were able to murder a respected citizen of a German city in full public view shows two things: first, a sudden escalation in the level of violence, far beyond anything that had yet occurred in the city; and second, a loss of control to foreigners whose actions and motives seemed beyond reasonable comprehension. Both the violence and the tyranny become more understandable when seen in the broader context of which Münster was only a part.

That context includes the cultural and geographical homogeneity of Holland and northern Germany; the languages of Dutch and "low," or north German, were close enough to be mutually understandable, and many, like Henry Gresbeck, who would leave a written account of his days in Münster, spoke a mixed German and Frisian dialect that modern German speakers need help in translating. There were no geographical features such as rivers, seas, or mountain ranges to separate sections of Germany and adjoining nations such as Denmark and Holland, both of which at various times claimed sovereignty over

German-speaking regions; indeed, "Germany" as a nation did not exist, only a collection of rival duchies and principates. Merchants like Bernard Knipperdolling worked as comfortably in Antwerp and Amsterdam as in Bremen and Lübeck, and religious missionaries like Melchior Hoffman and Jan Matthias were indifferent to so-called national boundaries. The "foreignness" that Herbert Rusher had so vehemently opposed, then, was not so much a matter of nationality as of outsiders moving in and taking over, like cuckoos displacing other birds from their nests.

The violence of official repression was another element of context. The flagrant injustice on the part of secular as well as religious authorities in executing so many Anabaptists for heresy erased any sense of moral obligation to authority that the survivors might have felt. It also provided a compelling model for emulation: Jan Matthias, when he murdered Rusher, was following the logic of the times—how else could one deal with insurrection? He simply dispensed with the state's charade of a judicial hearing.

It was, ironically, the state itself that Matthias looked to for the salvation of Münster—the officially sanctioned repression of the Anabaptists in the Netherlands would drive them by the thousand to Münster as their sanctuary. From there the invincible Company of Christ would issue forth, sweeping the puny forces of the Prince-Bishop aside and establishing with the cross and the sword a thousand-year kingdom of God throughout Europe. Or so Matthias hoped.

In practical terms, this meant that the Dutch Anabaptists, over whom Matthias had such influence, had to be incited to revolution and to the support of Münster. In the middle of February, shortly before the expulsion of "the godless," Matthias sent a group of nearly thirty men to spread the word throughout the Netherlands. They were armed with *Flugschriften,* or leaflets, written by Rothmann and printed in Knipperdolling's basement. Rothmann was a master propagandist and understood that even the faithful would respond best to appeals based on self-interest as well as on duty. Münster had become the promised land of milk and honey, he wrote, because now all shared equally in the wealth: "The poorest among us, who used to be despised as beggars, now go about dressed as finely as the highest and most distinguished . . . By God's grace they have become as rich as the mayors and the richest in the town."

Rothmann also appealed to his listeners' sense of duty and of self-preservation: "God has made known to us that all should get ready to go to the new Jerusalem, the City of the Saints, because he is going to punish the world . . . No one should neglect to go along and thus tempt God to punish him, because there is an insurrection all over the world. As it is written in Jeremiah 51:6, the Lord decrees that every man must flee out of Babylon and deliver his soul, for this is the time of the Lord's vengeance. I do not simply tell you this," Rothmann continued, "but *command* you in the name of the Lord to obey." He reassured those who were concerned about leaving their property and families behind that there was enough food and clothing for all in Münster, in addition to housing. As for unbelieving wives and families, they were best left behind in any event.

Rothmann's command invitation found a ready audience in the Netherlands, already stirred by considerable agitation. On February 10, seven men and women had stripped off their clothing and run through the streets of Amsterdam, proclaiming the "naked truth" to the godless. This kind of behavior, common in Münster and elsewhere, tended to alarm those who wanted to see the human species as either rational or spiritual: surely only lunatics or the demon-driven could act in such a fashion. As the Anabaptists saw it, they were simply following the implied directive of Melchior Hoffman, who had said that all true believers would ultimately come to the Kingdom of God "completely naked, having put the old Adam aside completely." Hoffman was clearly referring to the curse of Original Sin that caused Adam and Eve to cover their nakedness with leaves from the Garden of Eden. His followers read the biblical symbolism as literal truth. If clothes were invented to cover sin, then those who were innocent of sin should shed their clothing and go naked.

Such extreme insistence on the literal truth of symbolic statements may or may not have been madness, but the frenzied naked dashes through the streets that resulted from it must certainly have estranged the believers from ordinary citizens, let alone the authorities who had to keep order. The naked seven in Amsterdam, who had burned their clothing before they took to the streets, were hardly chastened by their arrest; thrown into cells with their clothed brethren, they made them strip as well. Unfrightened and unrepentant, they called their trial judges "bloodsuckers" and went proudly to their deaths, along with a Catholic woman who had been swept up by the prevalent hysteria and had joined them in the streets.

At about the same time as the incident in Amsterdam, "flying columns" of soldiers sent out by The Hague were roaming throughout the Netherlands, rounding up hundreds of Anabaptists and imprisoning them. Tortured into recanting their re-baptism, flogged when they hesitated, beheaded and drowned when they refused, the Anabaptists were harried mercilessly. Still they persisted. On March 22, another outburst occurred in Amsterdam when five prominent Anabaptists were arrested after they had wandered through the city streets waving swords and crying out "Repent!" and "Woe, woe to all the godless!" Three were tortured and executed. A Dutch Anabaptist who had not been involved in this current disturbance, Obbe Phillips, went in disguise to watch the execution because he knew that among these men he would find the one who had baptized him and given him his calling. But the bodies of the men were so "frightfully" distorted by the effects of fire, smoke, and the rack and the wheel that he could not recognize any of them.

As these men were being executed, thousands more were marching from all over Holland toward a harbor village on the Zuider Zee (IJsselmeer). They were responding to copies of a secret letter from Matthias signed "Emmanuel," carried by trusted preachers and circulated by word of mouth far beyond the preachers' range. Entire families had left their farms, their houses, and most of their belongings behind to travel by horse and on foot through the late-winter rains to the harbor. There they were to board boats and be taken across the harbor to the designated meeting place in Hasselt. Guides from Münster would then lead them to the New Zion, where they would force the Bishop to raise his siege.

Something of Matthias's appeal to his followers as well as his judgment of their needs is revealed in the great numbers of people in the Netherlands willing to give up everything in response to his call. Even the preachers he had sent with his message had anticipated far fewer recruits; according to confessions later extracted by the authorities, the preachers had believed that only those who were most visibly persecuted would respond, at most a few hundred. Instead, as many as fifteen thousand uprooted and troubled souls converged on Hasselt. But the Prophet's political naïveté was evident in his assumption that his incendiary letter could be kept secret, or that so many thousands of people could openly travel hundreds of miles in a country infested with both Dutch and Spanish governmental agents.

On March 27 the great trek to Münster was rudely aborted. It had progressed far enough so that some three thousand Anabaptists were ferried across the Zuider Zee to the meeting place at Hasselt, carrying with them a quantity of weapons: fifteen hundred spears, many guns, halberds, and swords, and four flag standards and drums, clear indications of martial purpose. The weapons were not used, however, and no resistance was offered when a handful of Dutch officials arrested the lot and took them into custody. Eventually the Court of Holland ruled that most of the sojourners were simply "poor and innocent people" and sent them home, minus whatever weapons and money and valuables they had brought with them. But about a hundred men were executed, this constituting what was considered a mild response to a dangerous provocation.

There is no record of precisely when the terrible news of the rout at Hasselt became known in Münster. Spirits there seemed to have been high enough on the morning of Good Friday, April 3, nearly a week later. In a typically theatrical episode, the Anabaptists had found a new way to assault the sensibilities of the Prince-Bishop. They brought out the treaty that Philip of Hesse had arranged the previous fall, guaranteeing peace to all sides, and conducted a new mock treaty ceremony, accompanied by bellicose sermons and street festivals. The highlight of the morning came when the treaty was tied to the tail of an old nag. To the sound of pealing bells, blaring bugles, and raucous laughter, the massive Ludger Gate was opened and the horse was driven toward the Bishop's soldiers, dragging Philip's treaty in the mud.

The rulers of the New Zion, the two Jans and the two Bernards and their confederates, had cause to feel confident in their power. The more vocal dissenters such as Rusher had been killed or frightened into silence, and the continuing excitement of incoming supporters and their stories of rebellion brewing throughout the region raised the morale of the rest. Wisely, though, the ordinary rituals of calmer times, such as weddings and funerals, were permitted to continue as before. One of these events, the wedding of two recent immigrants from Holland, occurred on the evening of Good Friday, and was attended by the young carpenter Henry Gresbeck, who by now had come to occupy a position on the Anabaptists' periphery of power, and whose journal of his adventures perfectly complements that of Kerssenbrück.

The host for the celebration was a Münster native, Evart Riemensneider, who kept a tavern near the Ludger Gate that could seat the several dozen members of the wedding party and guests. Radical though the Anabaptists were in matters of faith (and matrimony, as would soon be revealed), this seems to have been a typical German wedding, which would have meant a long table covered with white cloth and fir branches, groaning under the weight of roasted ox, broiled chicken, fried pork chops, heavy dumplings, sauerkraut, and strudel, and maids pouring dark beer into steins from Riemensneider's shelves and into the chalices looted from the Catholic churches. We can be sure that lusty drinking songs and coarse jokes about food and sex drifted through the smoke-filled air—Anabaptist doctrine, as they consistently asserted, held that that the Lord intended His people to enjoy the pleasures of the flesh when they could. Only the always sober and reserved Knipperdolling and the constitutionally dour Jan Matthias abstained.

When the festivities were at their peak, Jan Matthias, who had been sitting with his great gray head drooping to his chest, groaned audibly and raised his stricken face upward. Pale as death, he shuddered violently and fell face down on the table before him, completely unconscious. The room grew instantly silent. None dared touch the Prophet for fear that he was again receiving a divine message. At length Matthias lifted his head and stared with unseeing eyes. "Oh, dear Father, my Lord and my God, I hear and obey," he cried. "Not what I want, but what You demand!" With that he rose unsteadily to his great height and solemnly kissed the lips of every man and woman in the room. To each he said, his hand clasping theirs, "God's peace be with you and with this city." And with these words he left the wedding party.

It was left to Rothmann and the other preachers to figure out what the Prophet's strange behavior meant and to explain it to the people. Matthias, they said, had received word late in the day of the failure of the Dutch mission. The New Zion, unable now to count on help from abroad, was therefore in great peril. The Lord had revealed to the Prophet at the wedding feast that he should don the armor of battle and go forth alone, as David had done against Goliath, as St. George had done against the dragon, to slay the giant beast that was the Bishop and his army. At high noon on Easter Sunday, Jan Matthias would valiantly seek out single combat with the Bishop's army, taking with him only a few selected members of his honor guard.

Jan van Leyden and the other Anabaptist leaders were practical men as well as religious revolutionaries; he and Knipperdolling and Rothmann must have known that such a suicidal mission could only undermine the faith of those the Prophet would leave behind. And yet these men also believed in both the literal truth of the Bible stories and in divine ordination, which would have made it hard for them to dissuade the Prophet from his folly. As for Matthias, his stricken reaction to God's command to do battle with the Bishop's army suggests that he knew he was doomed. If so, how much more terrified must have been the dozen men Gresbeck says went with him?

Everyone in Münster knew of the heroic forthcoming challenge by the Prophet to the Prince-Bishop, and all who could be there thronged the city walls on April 5 to watch. What they saw on that warm April morning was an old man in full armor, carrying a lance and a sword, slowly guiding his horse toward Miller's Hill, a low promontory east of the Ludger Gate. A dozen or so riders accompanied him. Then a regiment of black riders, the Bishop's shock troop of cavalry whose horses and armor were of the deepest shining sable hue, rose from behind Miller's Hill. At a signal, five hundred knights charged the Prophet and his men. Cries of pain, shouts of glee, the creak of horses' harnesses and the clang and bang of metal against metal, clouds of shimmering dust in the spring sunlight—the pathetic challenge was over in a matter of minutes. Kerssenbrück relates with smug satisfaction that "every limb and part of 'the new Samson' was run through with countless swordthrusts until he was entirely in pieces." The Prophet's severed head was paraded in front of the watching Anabaptists by a galloping black knight, then stuck on a pole and planted before the city. His private parts, according to one story, were nailed that night to the city gate through which he had departed.

Miguel de Cervantes was born thirteen years after the death of Jan Matthias, and we know that he had models other than religious zealots in mind when he created Don Quixote, our touchstone and archetype of misguided idealism. The fictional knight was a fondly satirized exponent of a collapsed feudal system, good-hearted in the comically confused quest that led him to mistake whores for nuns and windmills for dragons. The semiliterate baker Jan Matthias was all too real to be regarded so sentimentally; and yet there is pathos as well as courage, even a certain nobility, in the picture of the doomed old man in his dented armor venturing forth with only a spear and a sword to slay his dragon.

This putative man of God nevertheless did lasting evil, for it was with the arrival of Jan Matthias that murder became a political tool of the Anabaptists. With him gone, Bishop Franz would have been justified in seeing the threat to Münster as virtually ended. The Bishop was well versed in contemporary realpolitik. In ancient times Spartacus led the slaves to revolt against the Romans, and only four decades before the siege of Münster Savonarola threatened the power of the Catholic Church in Florence; both men were martyred and both movements collapsed upon their deaths, just as countless others had when their inspirational leaders were gone. The Bishop had only to wait for the motley crew of preachers, merchants, and artisans who had inherited the Apostle's New Zion to beg for a merciful justice.

Modern scholars, in particular Max Weber, have confirmed the Bishop's grounds for optimism. Weber, a German sociologist and economic historian who died in 1920, described three types of rule. In modern democracies, and as it was in ancient Greece and Rome, there is rule by law, under which the law rather than the person implementing it is what is obeyed. But throughout history most people have lived under "rule by tradition," either patriarchal tradition, as described in the Bible, or the feudal pattern of the Middle Ages. Both versions of traditional rule required inherited authority, customs, and patterns of organization. They differed in that the older patriarchal systems, most prominent in the biblical chronologies, were based on families; the more recent medieval feudal systems, like the one in which Franz von Waldeck lived, relied more on networks of prominent allies who gave an oath of allegiance but remained in control of their own domains. Both systems depended on obedience to arbitrary commands, such as the one that forced Eberhard von Morrien to allow Dr. von Wyck to be executed in his own house.

The third type of rule, which Jan Matthias represented, is what Weber was the first to call "charismatic." It is one that our own age of political turmoil sees frequently, and that Weber himself sought to understand through his discovery of earlier exemplars of charismatic leadership. The essential nature of charismatic rule is that it is short and turbulent. The charismatic leader claims special powers, commonly revealed through magic, through visions, dreams, and revelations, through heroic deeds, and through his extraordinary powers of persuasion. He—with rare exceptions, such as Joan of Arc, such leaders are always men—derives his authority not from rules or traditions but from devout followers, disciples who believe in his personal qualities. The charismatic leader is not elected or appointed, he simply assumes command; his followers similarly have no set titles or time of office, and no specific duties or spheres of influence that cannot easily be altered.

Weber says that elements of the patriarchal, feudal, and charismatic types of rule have frequently been mixed, as in the case of England's Henry VIII. But there are inherent paradoxes in such a mix. The charismatic ruler is hostile to rules or traditions, but he wants his followers to revere his memory and continue what he has begun—and there is always much to be done, for charismatic leaders are prominent in troubled times. During wars, revolutions, plagues, and natural disasters there is a "collective excitement through which masses of people respond to some extraordinary experience and by virtue of which they surrender themselves to a heroic leader." This leader is commonly seen as "pure" when he first appears; he is indifferent to money, to material goods, to personal comfort; he has no regular occupation, and if he has a family, it is often left behind or rejected. He is "a radical who challenges established practice by going to 'the root of the matter.' . . . [he] dominates men by virtue of qualities inaccessible to others and incompatible with the rules of thought and action" of normal life. "People surrender themselves to such a leader because they are carried away by a belief in the manifestations that authenticate him."

This "surrender" means that the comforting "external" structures of religion, society, and even family are lost to his followers: he is all that they have left. Followers of conventional beliefs can pretend an external commitment by observing public rituals of church attendance and the like. But no one can fake an internal commitment to a charismatic leader, and it cannot be modified or partial, it must be total. (A favorite passage of charismatic leaders, including those in Münster, is in Luke 14:26, where Jesus says, "If any man come to me and hates not his father and mother and wife and children, and brethren, and sisters, yea, and his own life also, he cannot be my disciple.") Thus the degree of commitment to a charismatic leader will often be far greater and more intense than that to one who rules by law or tradition. His adherents do not "choose" to follow his dictates; it is simply impossible for them not to obey. If they do balk, it means the leader has lost his charisma. Both charismatic leaders and their followers need constant reassurance that they are pursuing the right course of action because the world around them insists that they are wrong. Thus they manufacture emergencies and challenges even when none exist and live in a state of unending tension and instability.

The great problem for the followers of the charismatic leader is that his is always a "uniquely personal response to a crisis in human experience," often the result of a vision that only he sees. Thus the alchemy that produces him is impossible to pass along to a successor. When a charismatic leader dies or is proved unworthy, the followers are not only distraught but powerless; they have neither the external structures that sustained them before he appeared—church, family, government—nor the internal conviction that he inspired. On those rare occasions when the leader does designate a follower to succeed him, or his disciples pick one, the result is always less intense than the original. Sometimes, as with Christ, when the leader's influence is benign, the followers are able to create a traditional structure to replace the original charismatic rule. More often, though, charismatic leaders see themselves as the end rather than a means, and the movements they establish simply disintegrate when they die.

That is what by all rights should have happened in Münster. Bernard Rothmann and Bernard Knipperdolling were persuasive and clever but not charismatic figures; it took the intervention of Jan Matthias to turn them into his disciples and into willing accessories to the murder of Herbert Rusher. With the death of Matthias, the catalyst that had turned rebellion into religious war was gone. The feudal structure that supported Franz von Waldeck could easily survive his death because it relied on institutional authority. Until Luther, no rebel had yet been able to create a counterbalancing authority, and Jan Matthias was certainly no Luther. Nevertheless, the rebellion in Münster did not fail after the death of Jan Matthias; it grew more intense under the direction of a second, even more charismatic leader, an event with few if any precedents or sequels.

To appreciate what young Jan Bockelson, or Jan van Leyden, was able to accomplish, we must consider the situation he faced. It is now April 5. For six weeks the passionate Matthias has dominated most of the nine thousand inhabitants of this walled and isolated city. Those who were born there have more or less willingly allowed him to take over their city government; to appropriate their houses and their money; to chase away the godless and replace them with foreign zealots; to incite the Prince-Bishop to armed warfare against them; and to enlist them as soldiers of Christ in the final battle of good against evil. Now the great leader to whom they entrusted not their lives but their souls has delivered himself up for slaughter. What could anyone say to so many people torn with anxiety and fear for their own future? What explanation could account for such a sudden and overwhelming catastrophe? Who could save them now from the Bishop's so-called Party of Order?

The answer would come that very evening, after a day of despair and confusion in the streets: they should surrender . . . they should kill themselves . . . no, they must wait—Jan Matthias would return from the dead in three days. . . . Then, at dusk, trumpets sounded, summoning the frightened people to a small church near the Cathedral. There they saw a figure standing high above them, his white-robed form illuminated by candlelight in the tall, narrow bay window of the third level of the church. It was Jan van Leyden, the young Hollander who had sent for the Prophet and who had been his constant companion and closest adviser.

As he waited for the milling crowd to grow silent, it must have been an extraordinary moment for this young man, barely twenty-four years old. How far he had come from the nearby village where the mayor had made him a bastard, then let his mother take him away to be raised in poverty in Holland! He knew he had been destined for greatness even as a youth when, despite his humble origins, his keen mind, quick tongue, and blond beauty led him to a prominent place in a local public-speaking club. Creative and imaginative, and fascinated with the still-popular medieval mystery and miracle plays, he began to write his own sketches, in which he always played the lead role, wearing colorful scarlet and green colors that showed off his handsome figure to its best advantage. Women sought him out and gave him whatever he asked of them.

But despite his gifts he was condemned by poverty and class to be no more than a tailor's apprentice in Holland. He set out, accordingly, to make his fortune in business, traveling as far south as Portugal and later residing for more than a year in England before returning in 1530, no richer than the day he left, to marry a sailor's widow in Leyden. They had two children and ran a seedy harbor tavern, the Inn of the Two Herrings. The handsome young orator, playwright, and actor had come to a dead end, barely into his twenties.

It was then that Jan Matthias came into his life with his message of resentment, revenge, and salvation. The younger Jan became his agent, discovering a talent for infiltrating and organizing groups of people as restless and dissatisfied as himself. He visited Münster briefly in 1533, having heard that "the word of God was better preached there than anywhere," and lived in the house of a Rothmann disciple, Herman Ramert. From there he went to Osnabrück, twenty-five miles northeast, which expelled him immediately. In Schöppingen he stayed with the surveyor Henry Krechting and healed a sick girl, it was said, by baptizing her. He was good at his work, and by the time he returned to Münster in January 1534, he was a wanted man: Queen Marie of Burgundy had put a price of twelve guilders on his head. He was known to Bishop Franz as a troublemaker whose mere presence in Münster was an insult. By the same token, he was drawing to him men such as Henry Krechting and others, who would later leave their homes and businesses to join him in Münster.

Unlike Matthias, Jan van Leyden took care to insinuate himself discreetly into the life stream of the city. He lived in Knipperdolling's house and married his older daughter, who was unaware that he was already married. He attended all meetings but seldom spoke publicly. His apparently impulsive attack on Herbert Rusher surprised observers who had assumed that Jan never did anything without first calculating its costs and benefits. Now some of those who watched the young man in the church window wondered how it was that he had so readily allowed old Matthias to kill himself.

We have no way of telling what went through Jan's mind as he looked out on the people awaiting his message. But we do have a full record of what he said, and it is clear that he understood intuitively how to appeal to the fears and emotions of his audience, that he was ingenious and daring, and that he was shamelessly manipulative. This would be Jan's first major performance during the long drama of Münster. For him to survive, he knew that it had to be a masterpiece.

"Dear brothers and sisters," he said, stretching out his arms, "you should not allow yourselves to be distressed. It is God's will that Jan Matthias died. His time had come." This much the crowd no doubt expected to hear, as it was the traditional consolation. What Jan said next, however, must have shocked them deeply. It was not only that Matthias's time had come, Jan said, but that he deserved to die: the Prophet had been so vain, so proud, so aspiring to fame, that he had failed to pray and to fast properly before going out to do battle with the Bishop. He had as well disobeyed God's command to go alone, taking other men with him to their deaths. Matthias had sinned in his pride and his willful disobedience and had been found guilty in the eyes of the Almighty—for could anyone believe that what had transpired had done so without God's direction?

He knew for himself, Jan continued, that Matthias had been chosen for death because of an extraordinary event well before the Prophet had received his vision. On Jan's right side, slightly behind him, stood Bernard Knipperdolling; on his left was the dead prophet's widow, Divara. He gestured now toward Knipperdolling to stand beside him and continued to speak. "The terrible end of Jan Matthias was revealed to me eight days ago by the Holy Ghost. I lay sleeping after meditating on the Divine Law in the house of this man, Bernard Knipperdolling. In my dream Jan Matthias appeared before me, pierced by the spear of an armed knight. His guts spilled out around the haft of the spear. I was frightened at this terrible sight, but the man with the spear said to me, 'Do not fear me, for you are the well-beloved son of the Father. Stay true to your calling. The judgment of God must fall upon Jan Matthias. When he is dead, you must marry his widow.'"

We may assume an astonished murmur among the crowd, as well as a strategic pause for effect as the young man anticipated its questions. "I was profoundly amazed by these words," Jan said. Knowing that he might be doubted, he had "immediately sought out a witness for this great revelation. That witness is Bernard Knipperdolling. He is here and he will confirm what I have told you."

Knipperdolling obediently shouted to the crowd that everything Jan had said was true, and the performance was over. As the people milled about in the spring twilight, they must have been mightily confused. Their revered and martyred Prophet was now vilified by his chief lieutenant as a vain, befuddled dotard. The old man's beautiful wife was now to become his lieutenant's by virtue of a dream vision conveniently confirmed by a prominent citizen. Unstated but clearly implied was that the old man's leadership would also pass to the younger Jan. Some of Jan's audience must have exited shaking their heads in confusion or dismay. But more were entranced with Jan's vision, first murmuring, then crying aloud, "Father, Father, give us your love!" A few, then many, tore off their clothing and began to dance.

It says much about this strange young man's personality and character that he could so effectively turn his mentor's disaster into his own triumph. Of all the qualities that the preceding episode reveals about Jan van Leyden—ingenuity, imagination, timing—the one that stands out most is his intuitive mastery of what would later, in our own century, be called the technique of the big lie. Told with sincerity to a people anxious for reassurance, deriving from some source beyond and greater than its speaker, the big lie is so outrageously improbable that nobody could possibly make it up. Therefore, it must be true. As a tool for demagogues and charlatans to mislead the gullible, it has never been more effectively used than by young Jan van Leyden.

It has been suggested that in Jan Matthias readers of this story might see something of Don Quixote. A contemporary of Cervantes, William Shakespeare, also drew on what he knew of the politics of his time and about human nature for his drama *Othello*. Othello, a brave general prone to delusion, has a beautiful wife and an apparently loyal servant, Iago, whose treacherous lust after his master's wife and his power eventually destroys them all. In Münster, the Prince-Bishop had rid himself of a simpleminded, rabid Quixote, only to face in his stead a cunning, ruthless, yet plausible Iago, who would prove immeasurably more difficult to overcome.

5

The Bishop and the Maiden

Who am I that I should refuse my lord? I will do whatever he desires right away, and it will be something to boast of until my dying day.

—"Judith and Holofernes," XIII: 13–14

THE PRINCE-BISHOP NEGLECTED to follow up on the opportunity that Jan Matthias's death gave him, having no plans yet to attack and unable, unlike Jan van Leyden, to improvise a response so quickly to the donation by Jan Matthias of his head. His soldiers had little to do other than to insult the besieged shopkeepers, as they considered them. Not only had they nailed the testicles of the previous prophet to the city gate but on another night they tacked up a pair of worn boots with a note requesting their mending, a dig at the humble occupations of the so-called Company of Christ, including its new tailor-prophet. And one young soldier amused his comrades by appearing every morning in the same spot to bend over and expose his bare bottom for the edification of the besieged.

The defenders responded in kind, though more imaginatively. They captured a soldier and brought him within the city walls. The next day he was released and sent back to the Bishop by way of the St. Mauritz Church ruins, jouncing along on an old mare with his hands tied behind his back, wearing a motley costume of Bishop's regalia and with obscene slogans dangling from his neck. Trumpets from the city walls announced his chagrined progress, along with the jeers and catcalls of hundreds of watchers, to the Pope's "slaves and idol-worshippers." When the Bishop's soldiers ran to help their hapless comrade, the defenders let loose a flight of arrows and shot that sent them scurrying for cover. On another occasion they allowed a horse pulling a cart with a wine cask on it to be intercepted by the enemy. The thirsty, boasting soldiers crowded around the cask with their outstretched cups and opened the spigot. What poured forth in an unstoppable torrent—the spigot had been fixed to remain locked in the open position—was not good red wine but liquid manure. And what about the impetuous and disrespectful soldier who had bared his bottom? He did it one time too many in the same location and was blown to pieces by a coordinated burst of cannon fire.

Further keeping the soldiers off balance, the Anabaptists sent them frequent assurances, tied to arrows and spears, that they bore them no ill will; we want, they said, no more than "brotherly love in Christ with all people," including you soldiers who now attack us. We know that if you allow yourselves to repent and to join us, you will be happy, for "God knows that we wish nothing more for ourselves and for all others than the Kingdom of God!"

Inside the walls, Jan set about within days after the death of Jan Matthias to establish his own control. On April 9, Jan's father-in-law and chief aide, Bernard Knipperdolling, appeared in the Market Square to declare that he had received a vision in which the Lord had commanded him to act on this essential truth: "All that is high shall be made low, and all that is low shall be high." What this meant, among other things, was that the church towers that filled the sky over Münster were to be demolished, for they were the most visible and obnoxious symbols of the Pope's tyranny, and of the Bishop's as well. The merchant who had spent his entire life in a city so beautiful that it was called the Jewel of Westphalia commanded three architects to lead squads of masons and carpenters on a horrendous mission of destruction. Even the magnificent Overwater Church tower was reduced to a stump. A few towers, including St. Lambert's, were retained as cannon mounts.

So much dust was raised by the steeples crashing onto the roofs below that the besiegers thought the city had been split in two. One tower on the Church of St. Martin resisted destruction, leaning eastward but not falling. After days of hard but fruitless efforts to pull it down, the engineers of deconstruction sent up a carpenter named Trutelink. He fashioned a set of spurs to let him climb the thin and slippery copper roof toward the cross at the pinnacle, where he intended to tie the coil of rope he carried around his neck. He was not quite halfway to his goal when the tower collapsed beneath him; those who watched Trutelink's fall were of two opinions as to why he died—either he was fulfilling the will of God or he was violating it.

The Bishop held at bay, and the city physically altered as he had ordered, Jan now turned to the destruction of what remained of its civil government. First, though, another performance was required. As the sun rose one morning about a week after the last church spire had been hauled away to the foundry, to be melted into spearheads and bullets, Jan appeared in the Market Square, his slender body entirely naked. "Listen to me, you Israelites," he cried to the curious gathering crowd. "You who inhabit the holy city of Jerusalem should fear your heavenly Father and repent of your earlier lives! The trumpet of the Lord will soon issue its frightful sound and send thousands of angels down to us!" The handsome young man raced naked through the streets until he collapsed, mute and gasping, before Knipperdolling's house. Gripped under the shoulders to be carried inside, he motioned that he could not speak and was given a piece of paper on which to write a message. "By the order of the Father," he wrote, "I have been struck dumb for three days so that I might properly receive God's vision" of what lay ahead for Münster.

For three days the city did nothing but wait and talk about the vision that Jan would describe to them when he awoke. He was not yet the appointed successor to the fallen leader, Jan Matthias, but he had succeeded in making himself the only candidate. His vision, it would turn out, was a full one indeed. Earlier, Jan Matthias had replaced the old city council and packed it with his own men, making it a rubber stamp but retaining the formal structure of local government. Now it had been revealed to him, Jan said, that the old city constitution itself, a mere human contrivance, was in violation of God's law. Mayors and council members were superfluous. Instead, following the custom of ancient Israel, the New Zion would be ruled by twelve Elders, under the direction of Jan himself. These would include some of the deposed members of the council, including a grateful Herman Tilbeck. Forgiven completely now for having protested the death of Herbert Rusher, Tilbeck tearfully begged God for the strength and wisdom to govern properly, "as I am not worthy of such high office." Joining him were powerful guild representatives, such as the master smith Mollenheck; a member of the hereditary aristocracy; and a number of the new immigrants.

Pastor Bernard Rothmann, who had said little since the arrival of the two Jans, now preached a powerful sermon as Jan van Leyden watched, declaring that God Himself was the author of the new constitution. The Elders were summoned by name and told to kneel before the preacher, who handed each man a naked sword. "Receive with this sword," Rothmann said, "the right of life or death, which the Father has ordered me to confer upon you, and use the sword in conformity with the will of God." The ceremony concluded with the singing of "Gloria in Excelsis Deo," in German.

Bernard Knipperdolling, who had been the co-mayor, was not one of the Elders. Instead, he was assigned a special title, that of *Schwertführer,* or chief enforcer and executioner. With his own bodyguard, the former cloth merchant now had the right and the duty to strike the head from the shoulders of any who lived in the New Zion and questioned its justice. He would have much to do, for the Elders were soon to announce a new table of commandments. "Mercy and peace to all who fear God!" began the announcement: "We have gathered together for you what you must and must not do."

Among the crimes now punishable by death were blasphemy, attempts to flee, impurity, avarice, theft, fraud, lying and slander, idle conversation, disputes, anger, envy, and disobedience to the commands of the Elders (women were also warned not to disobey their husbands). Inasmuch as nobody could pass a day without committing at least one of these offenses, everyone's life was now forfeit—only the mercy of Jan and the cloth merchant kept them alive at all. Two two-hour court sessions were held daily, at seven in the morning and at two o'clock in the afternoon in the Market Square, at which time the Elders would pass judgment on violators of any of these laws. Knipperdolling alone would later admit to executing personally "eleven or twelve people" during the reign of terror that now began in Münster.

Following the list of possible offenses was another, longer, list of more than thirty items, covering such practical matters as animal husbandry, nail manufacture, and fishing restrictions, as well as procedures for gathering tin, lead, copper, and oil, and for organizing community vegetable gardens. Many of these rules were sensible and reveal a secure sense of community and of organization, independent of theology. For example: "One man, to be selected, will be responsible for sugar and spices"; and "The Elders themselves will be responsible for beer and bread, in order to avoid any possible quarrels." Other rules follow logically from their adherents' central ideas: the people were to dress modestly, but not in rags. Because no private property remained, there was no need for money, though coins were struck for symbolic purposes and for necessary trade with outsiders. Any who had previously been paid in cash for their goods or services now contributed these to the common whole; in return they received the food, clothing, and tools they needed from city storehouses. Thus one needed to own very little. When "a Christian" died, "either killed by the enemy or from other causes, his possessions and his weapons" were brought to Bernard Knipperdolling, who then decided, with the Elders, if they had been promised to anyone and sent them to the storehouses if they had not been.

Every aspect of individual life was now subsumed in the group identity and mission of the Company of Christ. Children were encouraged to confront and reproach those who dressed ostentatiously. Homes were to be left unlocked, doors ajar so that anyone might enter at will. Every meal, not just those eaten by guards on watch, was taken in common; all brothers and sisters ate at separate tables without complaint whatever was placed before them, keeping silence so that they might listen more closely to the Old Testament as it was read to them by the Elders. Any reports of misbehavior by friends or family members were to be taken to the Elders, who then judged them for their infractions.

As Jan's grip on the city tightened, the Bishop's army prepared for its first assault. In March his military engineers had recommended draining the outer moat to allow the storming of the outer wall by the Judefelder Gate and the taking of the "roundel," or tower, that supported it. Von Waldeck wanted to begin the digging immediately, but had to assign several hundred men to defend his powder magazine in Wolbeck: a recent rebel assault on the village suggested that the storehouse there was in danger, and its loss would leave him without the means to continue the siege. Digging finally did commence on April 29, with a company of Saxon miners directing the efforts of three hundred farmers every night for a week.

The moat before the Judefelder Gate had been selected because the city, despite appearances, was not perfectly flat; the elevation there was about eight feet higher than elsewhere, meaning the moat, fed by the river Aa, was shallow enough to allow a drainage ditch to divert the flow temporarily and expose the bottom. This was a major engineering effort; moreover, it had to be done under the guns of the defenders, which meant work was limited to the cover of night. After a week it was apparent that more men were needed; the Bishop requested help from his neighbors, and two thousand additional farmers were forced to leave their spring planting to dig the Bishop's drainage ditch.

Jan's men struck back on May 16 in a surprise attack that destroyed sixteen cannons and decimated a supply convoy sent by the Archbishop of Cologne. Thirty soldiers were killed, and the wagons were destroyed along with a quantity of gunpowder. This setback forced the Bishop to delay his planned artillery barrage for three days, during which his commanders made a final written demand to the Anabaptists for their surrender. On May 20 came the first of two replies, which sounded surprisingly receptive: "We, the Elders of the Company of Christ in Münster, have received your message and given it our consideration. You say that you would like a sincere exchange of views, so that the world will be able to recognize the truth and this matter may be concluded in the peace of God." They were sure, the Elders said, that a solution could be reached once the princes realized whom they were fighting and why. The questions now were where they should meet—how far from the city gates?—and what solutions were to be suggested. The commanders' written response was requested, and they were enjoined to "fear God and honor Him." There is no record of a response. A second message, sent directly to the Bishop, closed the door on further talks: "Because the truth can never be known on earth, we are content to let God who dwells in heaven be our judge."

On Friday, May 22, the attack began in earnest. For each of the next four days, thirty-five cannons would each lob twenty shells per day toward the city's gate towers and defensive walls, a total of seven hundred cannonballs made of stone and iron a day—it was impossible for any defensive positions to withstand such a barrage, the Bishop's commanders said. In Telgte, twelve heavy wagons and a hundred horses were gathered to carry munitions, grappling hooks, and eighty-five storming ladders to the battle site. The foot soldiers who would take the walls after the bombardment (for double their usual pay) were backed up by the cavalry, which would drive through the gates once they were opened. On the afternoon of May 25, before the attack scheduled for the following dawn, soldiers readied huge bundles of straw, to be placed after dark over the spongy earth of the drained area of the moat. The soldiers would pass easily over these mats to attack the now vulnerable outer wall.

The Bishop was so confident of his plan's success, wrote Philip of Hesse to the King of Denmark, that he was sure he could re-lease all of his soldiers within two weeks. The defenders, to be sure, were not idle. Teams of women assembled heaps of earth and manure to patch the holes in the walls that enemy cannon would create. The old men and boys in the fire brigades practiced passing leather buckets of water to smother the flames started by burning arrows shot over the walls. Hundreds of armed men patrolled the walls and waited by their cannons at each of the ten city gates. But the men capable of battle were hugely outnumbered by a profes-sional army that had been preparing for months for an attack. As the sun began to set on the evening of May 25 and his troops gathered themselves in readiness for the coming attack, the Bishop's optimism seemed to be well founded.

It was severely shaken when he sat down at the end of the next day to write a report to Philip of Hesse. Because of a few drunken soldiers, he said, the attack had been a disaster. The soldiers had begun drinking early in the afternoon of May 25, it appeared, then had lapsed into an alcoholic stupor. On awakening they saw the thin edge of the sun on the horizon—they had slept through the night, they told each other with alarm, and the designated moment of attack had arrived! The soldiers, still drunk, raced through the camp crying "Charge!" Before the commanders could intervene, an attack was in full swing, uncoordinated and unled, other than by half a dozen drunks who could not distinguish between a sun setting in the west and one rising in the east. Stumbling into the swampy moat, where there had not yet been time to place the straw mats, the soldiers were easy targets for the alerted defenders. Two hundred died or were wounded in the short battle that ensued. The Anabaptist shopkeepers suffered virtually no casualties, and the city's reputation as an unconquerable citadel under God's protection received a healthy boost. The soldiers, thoroughly humiliated, were "beginning to be rebellious," wrote von Waldeck.

The incompetent attempts of the Bishop to destroy the Anabaptists were a dramatic contrast to the military order and imagination that had so far marked their resistance. Jan clearly had a talent for psychological warfare; his taunting of the Bishop and his men humiliated them and endeared him to his followers, who could now see the justification for his stringent discipline. Religious enthusiasm, however, was by definition hard to control; even as it made the Anabaptists so difficult to conquer it sometimes led them into disaster. On the same evening as the Bishop's misbegotten assault, a chimney sweeper called Wilhelm Bast received his own vision: he was to go forth and burn everything he could within the Bishop's realm, beginning with the powder storehouse in Wolbeck. He was captured soon after setting a few huts ablaze and condemned to die by fire in the most painful manner conceivable. Wood was piled around an iron post, at the top of which was a short chain, a few feet long, on a swivel. The victim's wrist was secured to the chain and the fire was lighted. He had enough room to run around the fire, but not enough to escape being slowly roasted alive. A song about Wilhelm Bast later noted that he had received what he had hoped to give to the town of Wolbeck.

While Jan no doubt found it useful to have a martyr in Wilhelm

Bast, he also had only fifteen hundred fighting men under his command and could ill afford useless sacrifices. As spring edged into summer, his situation was beginning to deteriorate, even as the Bishop's forces began to regroup for another attack. Ultimately, Jan hoped enough support would arrive from the Netherlands, despite the earlier disaster at Hasselt, to let him break out of Münster. United under his leadership, the Anabaptists could effect a reprise of the Peasants' Revolt of nine years before; only this time the princes and bishops would die, not the rebels. In the meantime, he must have regretted the loss of an able-bodied man. But there were plenty of women who, if they chose to offer themselves up as martyrs, need not be dissuaded. In mid-June he approved the suggestion by a fifteen-year-old Dutch girl, Hille Feyken, to save the New Zion from the evil Prince-Bishop by reenacting the biblical story of Judith and Holofernes.

The story that inspired Hille Feyken began in the sixth century before Christ. Judith was a wealthy and devout young widow who had hidden her beauty under the sackcloth and ashes of mourning since her husband's death a few years earlier. Her home was the small city of Bethulia, in the mountains of Gilboa north of Jerusalem. Several years earlier, the Assyrian King Nebuchadnezzar had waged war on his rivals, the Medes, and demanded the support of all the subject peoples in his realm. Many refused to help Nebuchadnezzar; accordingly, when his conquest of the Medes was complete, he sent his greatest general, the magnificently powerful and ruthless Holofernes, on a mission of punishment throughout the region. Holofernes's army of one hundred and twenty thousand men and twelve thousand cavalry terrified most of the offending nations into submission and utterly destroyed those that resisted him. Only Judea remained to fall, and only Bethulia, guarding the pass above the Valley of Esdraelon, prevented him from conquering Jerusalem.

Rather than attack the Jews in their mountain fastness, Holofernes settled in to starve them into submission. Within a month the defenders were dying of thirst and hunger and ready to sue for peace. They agreed among themselves that if God did not rescue them within five days, they must abandon their resistance and their faith. Judith,

who as a mere woman had not been consulted on this decision, rebuked the people, saying God would not be "threatened or cajoled,"
and that they were not being punished but tested. The chief magistrate
thanked her sarcastically for her advice and told her to pray for them.
She would do more than that, Judith said; she had a plan. But they
must ask her nothing about it.

That night Judith prayed for God to give her, a woman, the courage
she would need to embark on her plan and the wit she would need
to carry it out against a fierce enemy. "Observe their arrogance and
bring your fury on their heads. Put into my hand—a widow's—the
strength I need . . . Break their pride by the hand of a female! For
your strength does not depend upon numbers nor your might upon
powerful men. Rather, you are the God of the humble; you are the
ally of the insignificant, the champion of the weak, the protector of
the despairing, the savior of those without hope."

Judith now took off her ugly widow's weeds and bathed in
warm scented water. Her maid dressed her in her finest clothes
and the jewelry she had not touched for three years, since her husband's death. The two women, carrying enough simple food to
sustain them for several days—roasted grain, dried fig cakes, un-
leavened bread, a jug of oil, and a skin of wine—passed through
the city gates in the dead of night; the guards were struck silent by
the widow's great beauty as they watched her pass by them and
disappear into the silent desert.

The soldiers of the Assyrian patrol that shortly intercepted the two
women took Judith to Holofernes, who lay "resting on his bed under
a canopy, which was woven of purple, gold, emeralds, and other
precious stones." He rose and came toward her, "preceded by silver
lamps," and Judith prostrated herself before him. " 'Courage,
woman!' " he said " 'Don't be afraid. For I have never hurt anyone
who chose to serve Nebuchadnezzar, king of the whole world. . . .
You are safe now. Don't worry; you will live through this night and
for a long while to come, for no one is going to hurt you.' " Judith
responded that she was not afraid and that she had valuable advice to
offer the general. His siege, she said, had driven the defenders to the
verge of great iniquity: they were prepared to drink the blood of their
cattle and to eat unclean food. Her own loyalty was to her God more

than to her people, and for this reason she had fled. Within three days God would reveal to her that the citizens of Bethulia had violated His laws and thus forfeited His protection. " 'I will then come and report it to you,' " Judith promised Holofernes; " 'and you shall march out with your whole army. . . . I will guide you through the heart of Judea until you reach Jerusalem. . . . You will lead them like sheep that have no shepherd! Nor will a dog so much as growl at you! I have been given foreknowledge of this; it was announced to me, and I was sent to tell you.' " She knew that Holofernes had the "wisdom and adroitness" to heed her words, she told him: " 'The whole world knows that you, above all others in the kingdom, are brave, experienced, and dazzling in the arts of war.' "

Holofernes was entranced by Judith's beauty, her wisdom, her piety, and her courage, not to mention her keen appreciation of his manly attributes, and was not offended when she refused his offer of food and wine lest she offend her God. She had brought her own provisions, she said. For the following three nights Judith and her maid were passed through the soldiers' lines into the desert, where they bathed beside a cool spring and prayed. On the fourth day Holofernes complained to Bagoas, his servant, that his patience had reached its end; he would become a laughingstock if he did not bed this beautiful woman, who, after all, was his captive and his slave. Bagoas diplomatically conveyed the general's message: " 'May this lovely maid not hesitate to come before my lord to be honored in his presence and to enjoy drinking wine with us and act today like one of the Assyrian women who serve in Nebuchadnezzar's palace.' " Judith accepted the invitation with alacrity: " 'Who am I that I should refuse my lord? I will do whatever he desires right away, and it will be something to boast of until my dying day.' "

When Judith arrived in her finest gown, her servant preceded her "and spread upon the ground opposite Holofernes the lambskins which Bagoas had provided for her daily use to recline on while eating." Watching her lie down next to him, "Holofernes was beside himself with desire, and his brain was reeling; and he was very eager to have relations with her." Judith gladly accepted his invitation to drink with him, " 'for today is the greatest day of my whole life.' " The evening wore on pleasantly. Holofernes drank "a great deal of

wine, more than he had ever drunk on a single day since he was born."
The servants after a time left the two alone. Holofernes, the great
moment of his long-anticipated conquest within his grasp, fell sound
asleep.

And so "Judith was left alone in the tent with Holofernes sprawled
on his bed, dead drunk." She rose and stood beside his bed and prayed
silently: " 'Lord, God of all power, look in this hour upon the work
of my hands for the greater glory of Jerusalem, for now is the opportunity to come to the aid of your inheritance, and to carry out my
plan for the destruction of the enemies who have risen up against us.'
She went up to the bedpost by Holofernes's head and took down
from it his sword, and approaching the bed, she grabbed the hair of
his head and said, 'Lord God of Israel, give me the strength, now!'
Then she struck at his neck twice with all her might, and chopped
off his head. Next, she rolled his body off the bed and yanked the
canopy from the poles. A moment later she went out and gave Holofernes's head to her servant, who put it in her food sack." The two
women passed through the guards as they had for the previous three
nights, carrying what appeared to be their food and clothing for their
regular evening of prayer in the desert.

Within the hour they were inside the gate of Bethulia. " 'Here
is the head of Holofernes,' " Judith declared, " 'and here is the
canopy under which he lay in his drunken stupor. The Lord has
struck him down by the hand of a woman!' " The head of Holofernes was then nailed to the city gate, where his men saw it in
the first rays of the morning sun and fled in panic. The entire
army was soon destroyed. It took the Israelites a month to loot the
Assyrians' rich camp. When they were through, Judith was presented with everything that Holofernes had owned, and the
women of the city crowned themselves with olive leaves and
danced and sang in her honor. Judith composed a song of thanksgiving about her conquest that told "how the Assyrians had made
frightful boasts about what they would do to Israel and how God
had foiled them by the hand of a female." Not the strong army of
a mighty warrior had brought the great man down, but the beauty
of a slender woman: "Her sandal ravished his eyes; her beauty captivated his mind. And the sword slashed through his neck!"

We need for a moment to think ourselves into the mind of the devout young Dutch girl who hears this story for the first time in her life. How precise the parallels are! Here they are, the Company of Christ in the New Zion, besieged by an army afraid to attack and trying to starve them into submission. Here is Franz von Waldeck, the Prince-Bishop, notoriously brutal and corrupt, a man of the sword who kills the pious without compunction, a Catholic "priest" who has never taken orders and who suffers so from burning lust that he has a mistress as well as a wife. And here is she, beautiful, as she has been told, with the full breasts and sensuous appeal of a woman, but also clever and brave. Why should the Prince-Bishop not be susceptible to her wiles, as Holofernes had been to those of Judith?

Hille proposed her plan to Jan, Knipperdolling, and Rothmann, who seem to have regarded it as unlikely to succeed but worth a try—and to have been utterly without regard for the risk it involved for the girl. Certainly Judith's story had elements of theatricality and melodrama that must have appealed to Jan, and even of comic farce as the general drinks himself into insensibility at the moment of his assignation. If Hille could emulate the sinister yet comic punishment of the great Holofernes, the siege would surely collapse and his, Jan's, fame would be immeasurably enhanced. If she failed, little was lost save her life.

A contemporary portrait of Hille, with an inset illustration of Judith carrying a sword and the head of Holofernes, shows a pretty young woman as she presumably appeared on the evening of June 16, 1534, when she was met by the Bishop's men outside the walls of Münster. She had, Kerssenbrück tells us, "enhanced her already generous attributes of beauty" with fine clothes and jewelry provided by the city treasury. She wore a pearl necklace and three rings, two set with diamonds, and carried with her twelve guilders. She also carried a beautiful shirt for the Bishop, made of the finest linen. It had been soaked in poison that would kill him instantly; according to one report, it had also been taken from the body of a man who had recently died of leprosy.

Hille was taken to see not the Bishop but his high bailiff, Dirk von

Merveldt. He took her money and her jewelry and asked her why she was leaving her fellow believers behind in Münster. Hille said that she had married a man she loved despite her parents' objections; they then had been forced to leave Holland for refuge in Münster. Now they were disgusted with the false teachings of the Anabaptist preachers. Hille knew that if her husband tried to leave he would be killed either by Jan or by the Bishop's men, so she had come to ask for asylum for them both from the Bishop. In return for this and for her husband's life, she was willing to reveal to Bishop Franz all that she knew of the city's defenses, which she had learned about from her husband. She would even be able to show them a secret entrance into the city that would allow the Bishop to conquer it without the loss of a single man. She would only convey this information to the Bishop himself. As a sign of her good faith, she showed the bailiff the fine shirt she had made for von Waldeck.

Von Merveldt asked Hille how she had come to own such fine clothes and especially her expensive jewelry. She answered that her husband had been on guard at the city treasury and had advised her to take the jewelry and money in order to buy her safe passage. Hille must have been persuasive, for the bailiff finally agreed to take her to Iburg to see the Bishop in two days.

On June 18, another refugee was led into von Merveldt's tent. It was Herman Ramert, the citizen of Münster with whom Jan Bockelson had stayed two months during his first visit there in 1533. Ramert also sought asylum, claiming that he had been forced to convert and had fled for his life. To show his good faith, he now wanted to warn the Bishop of his danger: Hille Feyken's entire story was a lie, beginning with her supposed husband. Hille was not married, she was hardly fifteen years old. She had been supplied with the fine clothes and jewelry by Jan and Knipperdolling. And she was on a mission to assassinate the Bishop with her poisoned shirt.

Hille was immediately tortured and soon revealed that she had intended to become a second Judith in order to save the city from the Bishop. She was now ready with calm courage to suffer her punishment, she said, knowing that it was for the glory of God and that her soul would never die. After further torture on the wheel, Hille faced her executioner with a smile and assured him that he had no power over her. "We shall see about that," he answered, and struck off her head.

Very little changed as the result of Hille's efforts or her death. Herman Ramert was allowed to go free for his treachery and was promised that his wife and children would not be harmed when the city fell. Hille was soon forgotten in the rush of events that followed her death, and even later scholars have often ignored her story as an irrelevant intrusion. Judith herself has always been something of an anomaly or an embarrassment for Jews and Christians, achieving as she did a righteous end through treachery and violence. Hille never had a chance to emulate her model fully, and was either ignored or dismissed as pathetically weak-minded or insane.

Friedrich Reck would later say that Hille's story begins as poetry and ends in prosaic realism, and that the Anabaptists as a group were more naive than Adam and Eve in the Garden of Eden. The chief indication of naïveté is that, although it may have flashed into Hille's mind with enlivening freshness, the story of Judith was well known in Germany at that time, especially since Luther had given it his close attention. The fact that the historical accuracy of the story was questionable (to begin with, Nebuchadnezzar was the king not of the Assyrians but of the Babylonians) had led Luther to see the story as a poetic allegory, a passion play in which Judith is the people and Holofernes "the heathen, the godless and unchristian Lord of all ages." Many artists had been drawn to the story as well. In addition to the well-known paintings by Michelangelo and Botticelli, there were others by Albrecht Dürer, Hans Shäufelein, and Hans Baldung. Schäufelein even made a wall-size mural for the Nördlingen City Hall in southern Germany, and in northern Germany the Schmalkaldic League, of which Münster was a member, adopted Judith as one of its symbols.

It is a certainty, then, that the Bishop's bailiff von Merveldt knew the story of Judith. Why did he not see at once that Hille was following in her footsteps? He may have been misled by her thespian ability, but it seems more likely that the subtle minds of educated people find it impossible to imagine simpler folk finding moral lessons in the Bible and acting accordingly. As with Hille, at least potentially, it was the Anabaptists' undeviating insistence that the Bible meant what it said and was to be closely followed that made them such formidable opponents.

Friedrich Dürrenmatt, the Swiss playwright who won the Nobel Prize for Literature in 1978, would recognize the dramatic potential of the opposition between naïveté and cynicism in his 1946 play about the Anabaptists, *It Is Written (Es steht geschrieben)*. Dürrenmatt credits Friedrich Reck with the inspiration for his play, which is not only one of his earliest works but which, like Reck's book, is intended to be read as an allegory of the Nazi rule that had so recently been terminated. Most of the play is a kind of bloody fantasy, which has Knipperdolling and Jan skipping hand in hand over the rooftops of Münster as the city burns below. One of its more compelling scenes is the Bishop's interrogation of Hille after her capture. Dürrenmatt has turned the Dutch girl into Knipperdolling's daughter, who has married Jan van Leyden (as she did, in fact), and named her Judith. The Bishop, a very old man in this version, questions "Judith" kindly but says, "You poor child, you have sinned" in marrying Jan. She responds meekly that she is aware of her sin. The Bishop says, "And why have you come to see me now?" She is silent. "Not to repent, I think," he says. "You are very beautiful. You have read much in the Bible. You have read the story of Judith and the evil Holofernes." "You know everything, Reverend Father," she says. "You cannot lie to me, Judith," he says, "and that pleases me greatly." He kisses her on the forehead and says, "I must allow you to die."

More recently, feminist and "new historical" criticism has brought poor Hille back to life, in a sense, not as a naive victim or a unique aberration but as a strong woman, one of many during the late Middle Ages who had the courage to die for their beliefs. The author of one such work, Marion Kobalt-Groch, notes that Hille was in fact married, to a man she identified only as "Psalmus." "Psalmus" may have been Peter Simons, who was later killed in an attack on a monastery in northern Holland. Peter was also the brother of Menno Simons, the pacifist leader who opposed Jan vigorously and who became the leader of the faction that still bears his name today, the Mennonites. Perhaps, this author suggests, Jan saw in Peter Simons a threat to his own leadership; additionally, given Jan's attitude toward women, he may have also seen Hille as a threat to his rule. Her death, then, would not have unduly troubled him. Other women would soon fare little better at his hands.

6

COUNTERREVOLUTION

Sacrificial killing is the basic experience of the sacred.

—Walter Burkert, *Homo Necans*

THE TEXT FOR his sermon, Pastor Bernard Rothmann announced one morning in mid-July, was from Genesis 1:22, in which God commands all creatures to "be fruitful, and multiply." It is the continuing duty of every man and of every woman therefore to have children, within the sanctified confines of marriage. The husband's charge is to command and the wife's to obey, following Paul, who had said, "The head of every man is Christ, and the head of every woman is the man." Through her husband, the weaker sex finds not only protection but the path to God.

Rothmann's congregation would have found nothing to object to in this. The hierarchy of authority and submission had been long established in Catholic and Protestant theologies, even radical ones. But Anabaptist women did not consider themselves oppressed; throughout Switzerland and Germany they had in fact achieved an unprecedented degree of independence and equality with men, becoming their "peers and companions in the faith, [and their] mates in missionary enterprise and readiness for martyrdom," in the words of the great historian of the Reformation, George H. Williams. Freedom of conscience underlay the concept of re-baptism for all adult believers, not just men. For Williams this signified a major departure from patriarchal authority in favor of women's emancipation.

Hille Feyken's martyrdom was the most dramatic evidence of the important roles women could play in Münster. The conversion of the nuns from the Overwater Convent suggested that they saw Anabaptism as a release from virtual slavery to the Roman Catholic Church; no longer the submissive brides of Christ, they were now equal partners with their sisters and brothers in the Company of Christ, their voices heard, like those of the other women, in elections and public debates, their physical contributions noted not just at the cooking pots but on the defenses of the city walls. Women also outnumbered men three to one. All of this suggests that women played a major role in the Anabaptist movement, and that the resistance to the Bishop's attack on Münster could not have been carried out without them. In practical as well as spiritual terms, the women of Münster were the ballast of this theocratic ship of state; without that ballast, Jan's ship would soon founder.

Such at least had been the general perception. Now, however, it appeared that the men who saw themselves as chief among the Elect, the Anabaptist preachers led by Jan, had charted a new course, reactionary rather than revolutionary. As Rothmann's sermon continued, he warned that those women who indulged in sexual congress outside of marriage were no better than whores and were condemned in the eyes of God. It was commonly the case that many men were so "richly blessed" by God that they could have children by more than one woman. These men had a double obligation, first to be fruitful and multiply, and second to protect the poor unattached women from whoredom and the fires of hell. The way to achieve both of these goals was simple: one man, several wives. We have only to look to the Bible, Rothmann said, for the stories of the great Hebrew patriarchs, Abraham, Jacob, and David, each of whom had many wives. So it would now be in Münster. Every woman above the age of fifteen who was not already married would now have a husband and a protector; the first wives of the men would greet their new sisters in Christ with the warmth and generosity that the Lord required.

The preachers justified the new order of marriage not only by Scripture but for spiritual and practical reasons. Of all the sins that flesh is heir to, they said adultery and fornication were the most pernicious. Women were morally weak and would fall victim to their licentious impulses if not restrained. Medical science lent its support to religious doctrine in the writings of the influential alchemist Paracelsus, who explained, "It so happens that God has always created many more women than men. And He makes men die far more readily than women. And He always lets the women survive and not the men." God had ordained marriage as sacred and commanded fidelity to the marriage vow, but He had not prescribed the number of wives a man could or should have. If the sanctity of marriage was to be preserved and adultery and fornication avoided, then, given the imbalance of numbers, it was clear that some men should have more than one wife.

Within a few days of Rothmann's sermon the particulars of Jan's new policy became known. They were sweeping and wide-ranging. To begin with, all existing marriages were tainted with having been approved under the old order and were therefore invalid until approved anew by the preachers. All single women were obliged to take a husband; but so also were those whose husbands were no longer present—many had remained behind to look after the children or elderly relatives when their husbands had been expelled during the great purge of the previous February. Even those women past the age of child bearing were required to find husbands, so that, Jan said, they would have protectors.

Unfruitful marriages could be canceled without prejudice to either party, and the woman reassigned to another husband. If a man impregnated one wife, he had the right and the obligation to repeat the act with a second, and a third, or, theoretically at least, as many as possible. He also had the right to dismiss any of his wives, so long as he followed the proper procedures. The preachers and the elders would decide the merits of whatever cases were presented to them. Stubborn opposition to their findings would be punished with death, as would a wife's resistance to her husband's commands.

Rothmann's sermon was one of many preached during the month of July, but his ardor was at least partially feigned. Neither he nor the other preachers had been enthusiastic about the idea when Jan had broached it to them in late May. Until now there had been much to unify the men and women of Münster: the expulsion of the unbelievers; the appropriation of their property; the common tasks of feeding, clothing, and housing thousands of people; the shared fear and exhilaration attendant on defying the evil Prince-Bishop. . . . Now Jan proposed to sow the seeds of violent discord among a people who, no matter how radical their religious and political inclinations might be, were centered on the idea and the fact of family.

The preachers argued with Jan that women who had been drawn to Anabaptism because it freed them would now see themselves doubly enslaved, and men who had tired of their old wives and lusted after their neighbors' lissome daughters were all but commanded to indulge their wildest sexual fantasies in the name of the Lord. There were also men whose wives had preceded them in coming to Münster, and who were expected to arrive at some time soon in response to Jan's call for support. How would they react when they found their spousal beds occupied by other men? Within these new households of one man and several wives, where giving birth meant favor and barrenness could mean expulsion and death, how many newborn babes would die unexplained deaths at the hands of vengeful first wives too old to bear children?

During the years before Münster many enemies had condemned the Anabaptists for undermining the four foundations of all civil and religious order. The more familiar of these were the attacks on property, on infant baptism and other sacraments, and on the duty to obey Church and secular authority, and they were all bad enough. But they were all to some extent matters of theory. Polygamy, however, was attacked as a direct assault on the institution of marriage in particular and on women generally. Anabaptist or not, women found nothing theoretical about sharing their husbands' beds with one or more other "wives."

Furthermore, while most Anabaptists could find merit in the first three areas of disputation, differing mainly in approach and degree of their commitment, almost all of them condemned the "many-wives" doctrine. Menno Simons, who would later lash out at the "blasphemy" of Jan van Leyden, attacked polygamy at its source: it was true that some of the patriarchs had many wives—"Abraham had his own sister for wife; Jacob had two sisters for wives, Leah and Rachel"—but this was before the Law was handed down by Moses, after which such practices were strictly forbidden in Israel. Moreover, "under the New Testament we are not pointed by the Lord to the usage of the patriarchs before the Law nor under the Law, but to the beginning of creation, to Adam and Eve. Therefore we teach, practice, and consent to no other arrangement than the one which was in vogue in the beginning with Adam and Eve, namely, one husband and one wife, as the Lord's mouth has ordained."

Menno's reputation for piety and goodness even within the ranks of the Anabaptists in Münster was unquestioned, and many of the preachers doubtless shared his reservations about polygamy. Had he been on the scene to provide a counterweight to Jan, he might well have dissuaded the preachers from their folly (though it seems more likely that he would have been murdered). In his absence, however, Jan persuaded most of the preachers to go along with his decision. Some remained stubborn until he finally ordered them to appear before him in the City Hall. There he tore off his cloak and threw in on the floor before him; then he held before him the New Testament and shouted that it had been revealed to him here that he was ordered to do as he had ordered the preachers. He slammed the Bible to the floor on top of his cloak: did the preachers want to disobey the word of God?

The preachers went along, but there was growing resistance within the city. The real reason for the decree, it was whispered, was not divine at all—it was simply Jan's ungovernable lust. Although Jan had married Knipperdolling's daughter and moved into his house within weeks of arriving in Münster in January, the couple had soon separated. Rather than Jan moving out, the daughter had left. Then Jan had announced that he would protect and ultimately marry the mysterious Divara, the widow of Jan Matthias, after the Prophet's untimely death in April, though as yet they lived in separate quarters. Now one of the Anabaptist soldiers who was on guard at the Knipperdolling residence reported having seen Jan slipping up every night to the maid's room. His behavior could be explained no other way except as rank betrayal of both the merchant and his daughter, not to mention Divara.

Looked at objectively, the spiritual leader of the Anabaptists in Münster had already deserted one wife and his two children in Holland; married a second time in Münster and driven his bride out of her own house; and even, it was widely rumored, incited the mad Prophet Matthias to seek his own death so that he could inherit his widow and his leadership. Now he dallied with the farmer's daughter who served as Knipperdolling's wife's maid. Jan offered the man a bribe to hold his tongue but the word was out, he feared.

As Max Weber might have noted, the leader's charisma was by now severely tattered. If Jan was widely perceived as simply driven by physical desire, he would be a common (though extraordinary!) hypocrite, neither more nor less worthy than a dozen other men, and quickly deposed, if not killed. He was like a circus rider perched barefoot atop two charging horses. One horse kept its course—his revolutionary zeal and genius for organization had led him to great victories over the Bishop; but the other—his unbridled passion for dominance over women—threatened to lead him out of the ring entirely and into a fatal split. The only way to salvage his movement was to institutionalize his own perversity, to make adultery, bigamy and fornication the law of his strange land because he declared that it was the word of God.

One of Jan's most important supporters until this time had been the city's leading blacksmith, Henry Mollenheck. Leader of his guild and a resident of Münster since his birth, Mollenheck was an imposing figure physically and widely respected as honest and fair. Capable both of directing his half dozen apprentices and of fixing anything that came to his hand, he had been designated the city weapons master in March.

Mollenheck and his wife Elise lived in a house on Magdalen Street with their twelve-year-old son. Deeply devoted to his wife and the sacrament of marriage, yet a true believer in the Anabaptist cause, Mollenheck was now forced to choose between them. Earlier, when his friend and colleague Herbert Rusher had been killed so brutally by Jan after challenging Matthias, Mollenheck had apparently persuaded himself that Jan was nevertheless acting according to the will of God and had not wavered in his support. Now he decided that he had to take a stand against the leaders who would impose polygamy upon him and his city. Encouraged and aided in his planning by three leading citizens, a notary named Johann Oykinkfeld; Henry von Arnheim, a nobleman from Frisia; and a deposed councilman, Herman Bispinck, Mollenheck planned his counterrevolution.

On the evening of July 30, the horn of the watchman in the tower of St. Lambert's Church signaled nine o'clock. It was an hour when worthy folk should be in their beds, but at least two hundred armed men were gathered in groups of twenty and thirty around the city. Mollenheck waited with his group under the linden trees in the Cathedral Square; another group waited behind the City Hall, still others behind St. Michael's Chapel, the Agidii Church, and the Overwater Church. . . . In the lingering twilight of a northern summer evening these groups now converged on the City Hall, where Jan and his lieutenants were meeting in the great room on the second level. The guard at the front door challenged Mollenheck and was quickly taken into custody as the rebels rushed up the stairs, swords at the ready. Jan, Knipperdolling, and Bernard Rothmann were placed under arrest and locked in the cellar of the City Hall.

One of the most despised leaders, Herman Schlachtscape, was not with the others that evening but home in bed with his four wives— "two beside him and two in a roll bed underneath him," according to Gresbeck. Schlachtscape was Jan's vice-chancellor, responsible for order and discipline, a task he notoriously enjoyed. Now he was dragged to the stocks outside City Hall, where angry women pelted him with stones and clods of manure. "Do you have enough women now?" they taunted him, promising that more would soon be present. Mollenheck rescued the chancellor and ordered him locked up with Jan and the others.

So far the counterrevolution had gone smoothly, but now the leaders faltered. Mollenheck seems to have made three false assumptions: first, that if he and his wife, who had been such strong supporters of the New Zion, could now reject it, then almost everyone else must feel the same way; second, that everyone was as prepared as he was to act on his principles—that his bold rebellion would lead to a popular uprising against the Anabaptists; and third, that once Jan was shown to be vulnerable, his almost supernatural sway over the people would be broken.

Whatever the reason for his actions, or for his inaction, Mollenheck clearly had no plan beyond placing Jan in custody and then waiting for instructions, presumably from a city council that had regained its influence and its senses. While the blacksmith sat pondering in the second-floor chamber where the deposed leaders had met, Knipperdolling, Rothmann, and Jan were free to shout their plight through barred windows to supporters on the street. They were unhindered by the rebels, who broke open the wine casks in the main cellar and then lounged drunkenly around the Market Square, after which they looted the treasury and passed around the money and jewelry that had been forcibly taken earlier.

If Jan and his men had been remarkable for their discipline, Mollenheck and his were notably lacking in it. Many of the blacksmith's men were indeed soldiers, but not the kind to stake one's life on; they were deserters from the Bishop's army who had been lured by Jan's promise of regular food and pay, at about the same time as Hille Feyken had been captured the previous month. Their leader had been an earlier defector, Gert von Münster, a local mercenary and previously one of the Bishop's chief lieutenants. Nicknamed "the smoker" for his addiction to tobacco, still a novelty, Gert and half a dozen other renegades had gotten obnoxiously drunk on free beer and schnapps in the tavern of Evart Riemensneider—"the old preacher," in Kerssenbrück's words, "and his secret whore," a former nun. When it was nine o'clock and time to close, the soldiers refused to go. *"Du Galgenstrick! Du Halunke!"* he said: "You gallows-bait, you treacherous rogue! You're not the master of your own house!" Reimensneider and his wife left while their servant ran to the cellar to fetch more beer for the soldiers. In a few minutes the landlord returned with armed guards, who took Gert and the others into custody. Thinking they would be allowed to sleep it off in jail and then be punished with no more than a fine or a whipping, as drunk and disorderly soldiers were customarily treated, the men went without protest.

The following morning Gert and his men were led into the Market Square and summarily sentenced to be executed. The punishment, according to Kerssenbrück, was a novel one. The men were taken to the Cathedral Square and their heads pushed through metal collars that hung from the branches of a linden tree; they hung there, their hands tied behind them and their toes barely touching the ground, as the Anabaptists riddled them with arrows and musket shots until "the divine will of the heavenly Father had been done."

This incident had occurred only a few weeks earlier, in mid-June, almost at the same time as Hille Feyken's death was reported. Clearly the brutality on both sides of the wall was increasing. Now the renegade soldiers who had been intimidated and angered by what happened to Gert the Smoker had joined Mollenheck's band, moved by thoughts of revenge and drink and booty. Perhaps if Gert had been alive and sober, he would have suggested to Mollenheck that he should try to capture the city gates, but no such attempts were made, and they remained firmly in the hands of Jan's soldiers. Gert probably would not have been eager to call in the Bishop's army that he had deserted, but according to Helmut Paulus, Mollenheck never even considered appealing to the Bishop: "He is the enemy of the city," Paulus has him say. "What have I to do with him?"

As Gresbeck's laconic but fairly thorough account makes clear, Mollenheck had badly misjudged his current situation. Aside from Jan, Knipperdolling, Rothmann, and the manure-covered Chancellor, Henry Schlachtscape, none of the other Anabaptist leaders were rounded up until Herman Krampe, a businessman who was now one of Mollenheck's lieutenants, protested that they could not be allowed to remain free. At the same time, Mollenheck's own chief advisers, Oykinkfeld, Arnheim, and Bispinck, the three men who might have given some direction to the coup, had themselves been mistakenly arrested by Mollenheck's men and confined. When they were finally released, toward dawn, and allowed to see their leader, they all knew it was too late. Herman Tilbeck, the former mayor who should have been arrested immediately, had remained at large; he rallied some three hundred armed men and was directing the placement of cannon outside the City Hall. More men would arrive within the hour. The three men left Mollenheck alone to confront his fate and returned to their homes.

Shortly after dawn, Tilbeck's force had grown to nearly six hundred men, many of them Hollanders, who surrounded the City Hall and aimed their cannons at it. Although the City Hall was one of the revered buildings of the city, foreigners would have no qualms about destroying it if that was the only way to defeat the heretics inside. Some of Mollenheck's men had already been captured or had vanished; about one hundred and twenty remained with him in the three-story City Hall, posted at the windows with heaps of bricks to throw at the attackers—Mollenheck the weapons-master had neglected to secure enough power for their firearms. Mollenheck stood under the arcade with Herman Krampe and twenty other men, watching Tilbeck's forces as they assembled and listening to the cries of the Anabaptist women as they shrilled, "Death to the traitors!"

A shot rang out from a nearby house and Krampe fell dead, a bullet through his heart. Mollenheck and the others bolted the doors and retreated to the second floor, leaving on the stairs a barricade of benches, chairs, and desks. Two men used a church bench from St. Lambert's to break down the door, then ran down to the cellar to release Jan and the other prisoners. The young Prophet emerged at the head of a group of about forty men to confront the cheering crowd of men and women. He raised his arms to command silence and cried, "No mercy toward the enemies of the Lord! No mercy for Mollenheck!"

The battle was soon over. Jan and his men remained under the arcade, protected from the bricks of the defenders, while Tile Bussenmeister led the firing from adjoining buildings and poured bullets through the windows of the City Hall. Mollenheck must have seen the heavy cannons that he had helped to make pointed at the top floor of the City Hall. There was nothing to do but surrender. He stuck his old hat on a sword and waved it slowly out of the window. The counterrevolution had failed.

Given what had already happened to Rusher and Gert, it seems unlikely that Mollenheck expected to survive, but he may have hoped that by surrendering he might save the lives of some of his followers. All of the men were pummeled as they left the building, most viciously by Jan's women supporters, who stripped the clothes from their backs and cursed them. Nicolaus Dettmar was found to be carrying coins stolen from the treasury and was saved from immediate death only when Jan stopped the beating. Ask him, Jan commanded the women, if it was true that Mollenheck had ordered him to steal the money. Yes, it was true, the terrified man agreed. Then Jan said, ask him if it was true that Mollenheck had sent a message to the Bishop offering to open the city gates to his army. Yes, that too was true, Dettmar agreed.

Now that Jan had established that Mollenheck was motivated by personal greed and treachery, not by revulsion against Jan's perverted policies, little time was wasted on ceremony. There were no trials, only announcements of condemnation. Mollenheck and two dozen of his men were led out to the Cathedral Square the following afternoon. Each was given a shovel and ordered to dig. Then they were shot and tumbled into their graves. Over the next several days, twenty-five more were killed, including Dettmar, but not so quickly. To let the Bishop's men hear the noise of gunshots would be unwise, leading them to suspect an uprising; and besides, powder was in short supply.

The Dutchmen, Gresbeck reports, had wanted to kill all one hundred and twenty of the captured men immediately. Forty-seven were condemned out of hand, and the rest were told they had to prove that they had only joined the rebellion that morning, not the night before. Of those, most escaped with their lives, after being advised by the egregious Schlachtscape that they should consider themselves fortunate to be taken back into the arms of the Lord. Years later Kerssenbrück was still pained by what he had to recount: "No pen can describe the rage with which their adversaries fell upon them, and the refinements of cruelty to which they became victims," he writes. After being "overwhelmed with blows and curses, [the rebels] were imprisoned," but the Anabaptists, in Baring Gould's translation of Kerssenbrück, "continued inflicting upon them such horrible tortures that the majority of these unfortunates would have a thousand times preferred death." When death did come, it was gruesome; Bernard Knipperdolling, the erstwhile cloth merchant, now sword-bearer of the Kingdom of Zion, took personal charge of the executions. In the passionless but compelling words of Henry Dorp, the contemporary Lutheran historian sent to Münster after it fell to write the official report, Knipperdolling beheaded "several" men; others he cut in half at the waist; still others had their arms lopped off, after which they were tied to posts and shot point-blank. Others were bound together around gravestones and shot. Gresbeck describes how one man was cloven in two as he begged only to be allowed to return to his house to say good-bye to his wife and children. Dorp reported a total of forty-nine killed, and concluded sadly that the devil was truly revealed in Jan van Leyden to be not merely a liar but a murderer.

In the midst of this carnage, knowing full well what would happen to them, three men gathered a crowd around them in the Cathedral Square to denounce the killings. They were imprisoned for several days, chained hand and foot without food or water under the roof of a house baking from the August sun. Then they were beheaded by Knipperdolling for their courage. They were Johann Oykinckfeld, the notary, who had earlier, Kerssenbrück asserts, "burned many official documents and consequently bore a considerable share of the blame for what had transpired"; and Henry von Arnheim, a Frisian noble-man, and Hermann Bispinck, the former councilman, both of whom had failed earlier to oppose the "uproar" caused by the Anabaptists. Belatedly, but with great courage, they had paid in full for their misdeeds and for their failure to help Henry Mollenheck when he needed it.

Now only the prudent, the terrified, and the fanatical remained at large in Münster.

7

KING JAN

Behold how good and how pleasant it is for brethren to dwell together in unity.

—Psalm 133:1

"NOW THAT NO-ONE remained to offer opposition" to Jan's decree, Kerssenbrück writes, "the Prophet took as his first wife" the widow Divara, the former nun who would rule over his ultimate harem of sixteen wives. The men rushed to follow his example, including such formerly upstanding citizens as Tilbeck, the hot-tempered little co-mayor Kibbenbrock, and Rothmann himself, apparently now converted to the cause. Many of the nuns, both noble and common, willingly gave "themselves over to license and debauchery." "One took a soldier, one a shoemaker, one a fast talker; one a laborer, one a farmer, one a burgher, one a noble—they went where the spirit led them." The prurient details are omitted by Kerssenbrück, who, in Baring Gould's entertaining translation, says, "We must draw a veil over what took place, for we should scandalize our readers were we to relate in detail the outrageous scenes of immorality which took place in the town, and the villainies which these maniacs committed to satisfy their abominable lusts. They were no more human beings, they were foul and furious beasts."

Henry Gresbeck's account is both more personal and less heated than Kerssenbrück's, concentrating more on resistance by women to the new decrees than on license. For his own part, he married a young woman named Clara Clevorn for her protection, as he represents it, and moved her in with his mother in their small house near the Over-water Church for a time, before moving the entire family into the Clevorn house for greater security. Even though he was a guard and a minor official within the Anabaptist hierarchy, Gresbeck, like every-one else, had to leave his door not only unlocked but ajar. Anyone who wished to enter could do so at any time. The foreigners from Holland and Frisia were particularly demanding, according to Gres-beck, barging into houses and demanding that all the females line up for their inspection. Girls as young as ten and eleven were taken away as wives by men old enough to be their grandfathers. The more wives a man had, Gresbeck wryly noted, the better a Christian he must be. Many of the young girls resisted and were beaten so badly that their arms and legs were broken. Some of the older women tried to help, including a "woman doctor" who brought fifteen injured girls back to health. One woman was thrown fully clothed into the river Aa and held under water until she drowned. Her body, kept afloat by her billowing skirts, drifted down the river toward the moat.

Even as Jan performed forced marriages during open-court sessions three times weekly in the Market Square, he annulled others of long standing: "The wife complained about her husband, the husband about his wife, and divorces were granted to couples who had lived together in peace for twenty or thirty years." Women who refused to marry or to accept divorce were taken to the Rosenthal Church, now a prison, and warned they would be beheaded if they continued to disobey.

But the outraged protests persisted through the month of August, and the preachers were finally forced to establish some rules for hus-bands in search of supplementary wives. The situation was getting out of hand, they said: "Dear brothers, you should enter a house alone and ask your sister if she wishes to join you in marriage. If she has chosen another, you should leave her and seek elsewhere." The woman as well as the man should have the right to choose, so that the unions formed would be fruitful in the praise of God.

The uproar subsided momentarily, due less to the preachers' calm-ing advice than to the renewed threat of attack by the Prince-Bishop. After the first unsuccessful attempt to take the city had failed in May, the Bishop's soldiers and even some of his commanders, like the unfortunate Gert the Smoker, had begun to desert, and those who remained were disinclined to attack again so soon. Moreover, the outer moat, repaired and full of water again, frustrated the commanders at every turn. Some suggested filling the moat with dirt instead of again attempting to drain it, but the officer in charge of the attack refused to press it unless the moat was drained. Now several refugees from the city who were familiar with the moat assured the Bishop's engineers that this could be done in four or five nights, in front of the St. Mauritz Gate. The commanders doubted and dithered. They preferred to build blockhouses instead, and shoot flaming arrows into the city from them.

In June Queen Marie of Burgundy, concerned that the assault on Münster was taking too long and thus breeding discontent and rebellion in her own lands, offered the Bishop whatever help he needed to end the affair. The leaders of Trier, Cleves, and Cologne grudgingly agreed to provide more soldiers and money for the Bishop to hire farmers to dig trenches for the anticipated assault and to disable the moat. The digging began in earnest on June 7, when twenty-eight hundred farmers began to work; they were joined on June 13 by another four thousand men. However, the continued cannon fire and sniping from the city walls was devastating the morale of these impressed laborers, and the soldiers were constantly terrorized by the night raids of the Anabaptists.

In mid-June the officer in charge of construction recommended a change in tactics. The new plan would require the step-by-step construction of a moving earthen wall that would be shoved up against the dam controlling the flow of water through the moat. The Bishop hoped that some nine thousand farmers could be drafted for this immense project, assuring his confederates that the lives of their subjects would be protected behind the high mounds of dirt. A much smaller number actually showed up, following the lead of their masters whose reluctance to get involved they more than shared. The work progressed, but slowly. At night the soldiers would put in place huge screens of straw, behind which the farmers worked from sunup to sundown, at a pace of no more than a few feet per day. By the end of July it seemed as though it would take another three months to reach the moat. Finally the Bishop's desperate appeals for more laborers were heeded; the dam, near the Hörster Gate, was reached by mid-August, and the moat at the Judefeld Gate had again been drained.

Following established custom, the Bishop's war council now, on August 25, formally declared a three-hour truce with the Anabaptists in order to offer them a chance to surrender. A small delegation was allowed to enter the city. They saw few people on the streets, and those whom they did see turned away from them fearfully, they reported upon their return. It was forbidden on pain of death for anyone other than Jan himself to speak with the Bishop's representatives. Jan's message to the Bishop was a vow that "he was ready to fight until his last drop of blood if that was what it took to honor the word of God." The messengers had the impression that Jan was certain of help coming from the Netherlands.

When the Bishop learned that his offer had been rejected, he had several hundred copies of a message made up for the defenders. He promised mercy to any of the innocent citizens of Münster if they would now leave the city, and threatened them with great punishment if they remained and came into his hands after the city fell. He extended the period of truce for three days to give them time to decide. The Bishop's archers tied the messages around blunted arrows and shot them over the walls. Jan, however, had learned of the Bishop's ploy and threatened instant execution for anyone found with an arrow or a message. No one left the city.

The attack began at dawn on the twenty-eighth of August, in the midst of a late-summer thunderstorm that would turn into a three-day deluge. The great cannon loaned by Philip of Hesse, "the Devil," lofted iron and concrete balls into the city, its concussion breaking windows in the nearby villages and its roar resounding for miles around. The main gate, St. Maurtiz, was nearly shattered and the walls were broken in a dozen places. The defenders responded with cannon fire from the platforms they had constructed beside the roundels, preventing the besiegers from following up on their advantage. Jan rode through the rain on a white horse, fully exposed and indifferent to the arrows, bullets, and cannonballs. The day ended in a stalemate. That night the women repaired the walls with earth and dung and stone from desecrated tombs while Gresbeck and the other carpenters worked to fix the gate.

The rain continued without ceasing, inch upon inch. The farmers who had continued to work on the protective bulwarks behind which the soldiers would advance could do nothing in knee-deep water and soon melted away to their farms. The loose dirt they had so laboriously tossed before them dissolved under the deluge; the bulwarks became useless mounds of mud. Months of hard labor costing the Bishop a small fortune and not a few deaths had gone for nothing.

Cavalry and foot soldiers could barely move in the mire that surrounded the city, and the moat that had been successfully drained was beginning to fill again. But the cannons could continue to fire, and after two days the outer wall near the St. Mauritz Gate had been broken and the inner walls and gates were so severely battered that if the Bishop's men could cross the moat they should be able to take the city. At dawn on the last day of August, the Devil belched a mighty blast as a signal for the final assault. Then the lesser cannons, including the Devil's Mother, chimed in. The rain had ceased. Through the silence that followed the cannon fire the defenders could hear the trumpets blare and the reedy tremolo of the flutes that accompanied the stately procession of the cavalry. Massed squares of several thousand soldiers spread across the plains, ready for the attack.

At a signal, hundreds of men carrying bundles of straw before them streamed through the breach in the outer wall and launched themselves into the moat. The rain-swollen river Aa had brought the moat back to its previous level of more than ten feet, but the improvised straw rafts let the men cross quickly, with only token opposition.

The Bishop's men were confident that their overwhelming numbers and the long bombardment must have terrified the Anabaptists. Within minutes the attackers had sent across scaling ladders and grappling books, set explosive mines against the gates, and established a position at the base of the inner wall. Soldiers hoisted the long heavy ladders into place and scrambled awkwardly up them, encumbered by their armor and their weapons.

These men were hardened professionals, veterans of campaigns in Spain, Italy, and France, and accustomed to violence and hardship. Their opponents were only shopkeepers, smiths, tailors, and housewives; but they were fighting both for their lives and for God. The hapless mercenaries could not have anticipated the fury they would encounter on this summer morning. Some had their hands hacked off as they grasped the top rungs of their ladders, some were battered through their helmets with heavy notched clubs, some were cloven with broadswords, some run through with spears. Those climbing behind the leaders looked up to see the strong arms of two men on either side of their ladder, holding posts and tree limbs between them which they dropped together, stripping the ladder of five or six men at a stroke. The women who had for months stirred their cauldrons of boiling pitch and quicklime in anticipation of this day dashed the caustic liquid in the faces of the enemy soldiers and poured it down their armor, or made lighted necklaces which they threw upon the men as they scurried frantically around the base of the wall. The men on the ladders fell backward into the moat, and some of those waiting below jumped into it, hoping to escape the quicklime that dissolved their flesh or the pitch that seared it, only to find the weight of their armor dragging them to their deaths.

The surviving soldiers managed to make their way back across the inner moat and through the breached outer wall to the second moat. There, in a narrow defile of thorn hedges, hundreds of the Company of Christ were hidden in the bushes, lying in wait to slaughter the soldiers as they retreated in panic from the horror they had faced at the walls. As night fell, the Anabaptists retreated into the city and raised their voices in song: "A Mighty Fortress Is Our God." Jan and his followers were delirious with self-satisfaction, assuring each other that "if God had not been with us this day, we should surely have been lost." Outside the high inner wall, the dead and dying lay in the thorn hedges while their women shrieked their grief. The survivors crawled and dragged themselves to safety through the thorns and across the outer moat.

Jan had been brilliant in his defense. His dead amounted to only fifteen men, while the Bishop had lost forty-two officers and hundreds of soldiers. It was not simply a defeat but a humiliating rout for the Bishop; had Jan followed up on his triumph immediately, he might have decimated his oppressor's army as Judith had that of Holofernes. It would have taken von Waldeck months to persuade his skeptical allies to send him yet more men to be misled into destruction—time enough for Jan to break out and join the other dissident bands throughout northern Germany or to draw supporters to him from that same region. Perhaps he had not thought beyond mere survival; perhaps it was simply that he was more effective at improvisation than at serious planning.

Whatever the reason for Jan's uncharacteristic lack of aggression, the Bishop was off the hook. He refrained from any more direct attacks, determining to starve the city into submission. By late December 1534, half a dozen blockhouses had been built to anchor a cordon around the city, with plans being developed for connected redoubts between them, to be patrolled night and day.

In their euphoria, the Anabaptists scoffed as they perceived the Bishop's plan. They were stronger than ever, having overcome first the treacherous counterrevolution of Mollenheck and then a frontal attack by an enemy several times their number in terms of fighting men. Their young leader's courage under fire and his brilliant planning had become famous throughout the region and were already drawing new supporters to his banner.

One of these was the lame goldsmith Johann Dusentschur from nearby Warendorf. Scorned by Kerssenbrück as a deformed charlatan, Dusentschur had a powerful talent for arousing his listeners to a fervent pitch of enthusiasm. Not even Rothmann or Krechting or Knipperdolling praised Jan so effusively. Did Jan's fortunate people realize, Dusentschur said to growing crowds, that they had a truly biblical hero in their very midst? Jan was no mere Prophet—he was the one prophets anticipated; he was more than a man, he was a veritable David, returned to be their king.

The twelve Elders called Dusentschur before them to explain what he meant. As Gresbeck records the event, the goldsmith said God had told him in a vision that Jan of Leyden, famous as a soldier and a prophet, was to be their new David. He will cast the mighty down and raise the lowly; he will seize the crown and the scepter and the throne of Saul. He will take in his hand the sword of justice and bring the divine word to all the peoples of the world.

Dusentschur took a sword and handed it to Jan, saying that with that sword Jan would rule until God himself took it from him. He commanded Jan to bend his head and anointed him with oil, declaring that Jan was the true inheritor of the throne of the great King David. Dusentschur then reached into a bag by his side and withdrew a gold crown and a golden chain emblazoned with the apple, the scepter, and the sword, symbols of devine majesty, and rings for each of the king's fingers, fashioned by the goldsmith from the confiscated treasures in the city hall. All of these he reverently bestowed on the young man who stood silently before him.

The newly anointed king reacted with becoming modesty, throwing himself to the ground in prayerful humility. He rose and looked out upon the people. He was too young for such a heavy burden, he said. But he would do his best to bear it well and wisely. "In like manner," he reminded his new subjects, "was David, a humble shepherd, anointed by the Prophet, at God's command, as the King of Israel. God often acts in this way; and whoever resists the will of God calls down God's wrath upon himself. Now I am given power over all nations of the earth, and the right to use the sword to the confusion of the wicked and in defense of the righteous. So let none in this town stain himself with crime or resist the will of God, or else he shall without delay be put to death with the sword."

A swelling of uneasy protest from the crowd drew a sharp rebuke. The bravest among them had died with Mollenheck, but it did not require courage to see that the appearance of a stranger who declares that their young leader has been elevated to king might be less providential than it appeared. Jan's theatrical flair was well-known, and his political shrewdness might have reminded some of their recently deceased Italian contemporary, Machiavelli. How came it that he required a stranger from another city to see his kingly qualities, rather than the preachers in Münster and the local leaders like Knipperdolling and Tilbeck, who knew him so much better? And why did these worthies appear, despite themselves, as startled and distressed as the populace? If Dusentschur's revelation concerning Jan were as spontaneous as they both represented it as being, why did he have crown and jewels ready at hand? If Jan was so overwhelmed by the new charge laid upon him, why did he recover and accept it with such alacrity?

Jan responded immediately to the swelling unrest. "Shame on you, for complaining against the ordinance of the Heavenly Father! Even if you all joined to oppose me, I will still rule, not only over this city but over the whole world, for the Heavenly Father has said it should be so. My kingdom which begins today shall never fall!" Cowed into submission, the people retreated and, for the next three days, listened to the sermons of the newly enthusiastic preachers on the royal virtues of the tailor's apprentice from Leyden.

King Jan's first duty was to establish a court worthy of him. No castles were available, but the splendid residence next to the Cathedral of the evicted Bishop's representative, Melchior von Buren, with its grand salon and its courtyard, would serve for the time being. Among King Jan's chief attendants would be some familiar faces: Bernard Knipperdolling was now the prime minister, his duties as chief executioner taken over by one Master Niland. Bernard Rothmann was the royal spokesman, charged with the important task of communications and propaganda. The Krechting brothers whom Jan had known since he stayed with Henry, the surveyor, several years earlier, now assumed important positions in his court—Bernard Krechting as his chief of staff and Henry as his chancellor. Herman Tilbeck, the former mayor who had rescued Jan from Mollenheck, was rewarded with the office of the royal marshal, responsible for maintaining civic discipline among the merchants and guilds.

The king and his ministers were attended by a retinue of more than a hundred lesser officials and servants. The royal tailors made King Jan a splendid scarlet robe that he now wore constantly; silken gowns adorned his queen, the Lady Divara, and she and Jan's other fifteen wives were all housed in a separate wing of von Buren's mansion. There were a designated keeper of the royal cellar, a chef with a staff of several dozen cooks and scullery maids, a jeweler, a riding master, a butcher and a baker, a keeper of the royal wardrobe, and a chief armorer, who made for Jan a magnificent suit of armor. In a royal chapel the royal organist accompanied the court in stirring renditions of Anabaptist hymns. Most important of all, Jan now had a royal bodyguard, a score of stalwart young men, each with his own horse, who rode recklessly through the city streets to clear the way for the king and who had sworn on their lives to protect him against all harm.

Among these privileged guardians was a young aristocrat called Christoph von Waldeck. He was the Bishop's illegitimate son by his well-born north-German mistress, captured in June after the first abortive attempt to take the city. Some believed the youth had been compelled to join Jan in order to save his own life. But nobody had forced the nobleman to marry, a few weeks after his capture, the daughter of one of Jan's chief advisers, Christian Kerckering. Now the Bishop might anticipate an Anabaptist grandchild! In the meantime he could see his ancient name listed for all the world to see among the servants of the bastard tailor who had already humiliated him so terribly—Jan did have a cunning sense of irony.

Certainly that ironic sense was at work when he ordered his subjects to eschew all earthly vanity and pride of possession. They had, it was true, already given all of their valuables in the form of money and jewels to the city treasury; but many wore clothing that was far grander than their needs. It was to be delivered immediately to the city warehouses. No true brother in Christ needed to own more than a single coat, two pairs of trousers, two vests, and three shirts; the sisters in Christ must make do with two blouses, one fur, two collars, two pairs of sleeves, two skirts, and four chemises. Their best clothing—all that was not needed at court—would be kept for the day of their final salvation.

King Jan explained that the stringent vow of poverty his subjects were to keep could not apply to himself or his court. He was entirely dead to the appeals of the world and the flesh, he assured them solemnly, but the glory of God required appropriate manifestations of pomp and splendor. The common people were not admitted to the feasts in the palace, served on von Buren's silver platters. However, the young king knew how necessary it was to offer them bread and circuses to keep their minds from their growing privation and isolation, so he commanded that various games be played. Frequently there would be jousting, which Jan always won, accompanied by much playing of pipes and trumpets. Some days he led his followers into the despoiled Cathedral for a mock Mass; it would be introduced by tossing detritus onto the altar, such as cats' heads, dead rats and mice, and horses' hooves. After this would follow a play by the king, a mocking satire of Catholic rituals that often featured "monks" lifting their robes to bare their naked posteriors and farting on command. At its conclusion Bernard Rothmann would appear on stage to say, "Dear brothers and sisters, all the Masses in the world are exactly as holy and sanctified as the one you have just seen."

The laughter of the people was uneasy, for they frequently saw King Jan as their final judge on earth. In the Market Square a crew of carpenters had constructed a throne that, covered with a cloth of gold, loomed over benches for the officers of the court and their attendants. On September 25, as on other days, the fanfare of trumpets announced the imminent arrival of the king and his court. Riding his white stallion, preceded by Knipperdolling and Krechting on foot, all enclosed within a moving box of bodyguards, Jan rode slowly into the square and took his place on the throne. On one side of the throne a young boy, a page, held a copy of the Old Testament; on the other, an older and stronger boy held a naked sword. A young woman was led before the throne, her head bare and her hands tied before her. Her name was Elizabeth Holschern. She was charged with having three times denied her husband his conjugal rights. The young woman said she had been assigned to her "husband" against her will—despite the preachers' earlier assertions that no woman should be forced to choose a husband—and she did not regard him as having any rights over her at all. She said, in James Stayer's translation, "Heavenly Father, if you are almighty, see to it that I never more in my life have to climb into this marriage bed." With that, King Jan decreed that she must pay with her life for violating the will of God. The two guards who had led the woman before the throne forced her to kneel, and Bernard Knipperdolling, though he was no longer the official sword-bearer, cut off her head with a single stroke.

The next day, September 26, Katherine Kockenbeckin was executed in similar fashion because she had taken two husbands: in the Company of Christ, as Stayer aptly says, "polygamy was the Lord's will, polyandry the Devil's."

Regimes based on intimidation and terror frequently collapse not from the bottom but from the top, as presumably loyal supporters are revealed to have ideas and ambitions of their own. But nobody, certainly not King Jan, could have expected that his first serious challenge would come from the erstwhile cloth merchant Bernard Knipper-dolling, who had been wielding the sword of justice with seeming alacrity, even against young women.

Knipperdolling has always been the greatest conundrum in the story of the Anabaptists in Münster. He was the man who had everything: a wife and daughters and a network of his own and his wife's relatives who had lived in the city for generations; a position on the city council that he had used effectively to force the previous Bishop to grant the city an unprecedented degree of independence, and later the honor of being co-mayor; a successful business that rewarded his enviable qualities of acumen and initiative. Nothing in his first five decades of life suggested that he would be capable of such murderous deeds as he had performed for the young stranger from Leyden. Now it was Jan's turn to be surprised.

Henry Gresbeck, who gives several pages of his book to this epi-sode, is not inclined to psychological explanations of why Knipper-dolling acted as he did; he simply says that "when the spirit took him, he was not right in the head." Herman Kerssenbrück, a sophisticated student of human nature by the time he came to write his account many years later, sees envy and jealousy as probable reasons. Knip-perdolling was, after all, what we would now call a merchant-prince, one who had challenged the Prince-Bishop as a true equal in his own eyes. Now this foreigner Jan Bockelson, "a bastard, a pathetic rhyme-spinner, an adulterer, a tavern-keeper, a former tailor, a newcomer and stranger to Münster," had elevated himself to the position of King, with royal garments and a kingly retinue who praised and pro-tected him, while Bernard Knipperdolling, the foremost citizen of the city, was scorned and mocked as nothing more than an executioner—and even this despicable duty had been taken from him.

Whatever the cause, we can be certain that King Jan was shocked when, on a day in late September while he was passing his customary judgments on sinners, Knipperdolling appeared in the Market Square, spittle dripping from his chin, crying, "Repent! Repent of your sins, all of you, for the Lord sees and knows of your evil ways!" He rolled in the muck and dung of the street before the astonished court and the crowd of townspeople who were gathered to witness the king's decisions. He rose and leaped like a hare over the heads of some bystanders, according to the rather implausible story picked up by Kerssenbrück, and began to roam through the crowd. He had the ability to cure blindness, he cried; he spat upon his fingers and rubbed them across the sightless eyes of some old people, saying, "You are chosen! You are holy! You will see!" When they failed to respond, he began to crawl on all fours like a dog, then jumped up and began to dance in a grotesque and lascivious fashion, saying, "I have often danced this way before my women, and now the heavenly father commands me to do the same before my king." He danced around, his face pale, his breath gasping. He stood on his head. He jumped between the wives on the bench beside the king and went among the men and women of Jan's court and blessed them, kissing them and saying, "You are saved! God has saved you!" He said to the king, who was struck dumb by this apparition, "Good day to you, my king! It was revealed to me last night that I am a fool!"

The king, Kerssenbrück says, was so astounded that he "fell from his throne, as did the scepter from his hand, and he clasped his hands and sat where he was" in silent wonder, as if he had been struck dumb. The wives were all thrown into a panic as well. When Knipperdolling saw that the king had fallen, he ran toward him, wrapped his slender body in his big arms, and lifted him upon his throne again. He grabbed a halbard from a nearby guard and raised it high, saying, "Courage, brother! We go together, the king's fool and the fool-king, to do battle with the world!" The king, as Gresbeck puts it, regained some control of himself and said, with a quavering voice, "Dear sisters and brothers, you should all go home and pray"—but then losing control of his glib tongue, in unprecedented fashion, he began to stutter so fiercely that it sounded as though he was saying "g-g-g God knows, g-g-g-God gives you l-l-l-leave to g-g-g-go to your h-h-h-house." Knipperdolling, unabashed, reproached the king insolently, saying Jan should have said "brothers and sisters," not the other way around: "That's not the way I taught you, is it?" The crisis was momentarily averted, though, as the people obeyed Jan's feeble command, wandering off muttering to themselves.

But on the king's next judgment day, Knipperdolling (unaccountably left at large by Jan) resumed the same act, much more aggressively than before. This time he pushed in front of Jan and sat himself on the king's throne. "By rights I should also be a king," he said to Jan. "I made you king!" Jan turned and walked away from the Market Square, in full view of the crowd. Baring Gould has a lively but fictitious reading of what then followed. Turning back to Knipperdolling, "John of Leyden sprang at him, dragged him from the throne, beat his head with his golden scepter, and administering a kick to the rear of his lieutenant, sent him flying head over heels from the platform, and then, calmly enthroning himself, he gave orders for the removal and imprisonment of the rebel." What actually happened, according to Gresbeck, is that Jan left the throne and the Market Square to return to his palace. The confused cloth merchant remained on the throne, but stepped down quietly when Jan soon returned and asserted his rights. As his guards took his former right-hand man off to the Rosenthal prison, presumably to be executed, Jan told the people that such rebellion could not be permitted; the merchant had taken leave of his senses and would be confined until a decision as to his fate had been reached. Knipperdolling remained in prison for three months, kept alive by virtue of his former eminence in the city. He was released finally and reinstated in Jan's court after he made a public acknowledgment that an evil spirit had taken possession of him, and he knew well now that Jan had been chosen as the King of the World.

A recent scholar argues that Knipperdolling was taking a calculated risk, trying to overthrow Jan and to assume the leadership himself because he could see that the King's course was leading them all to destruction. This seems possible. However, a modern perspective on Knipperdolling's peculiar actions would have to include the possibility of a rare form of epilepsy. This violent form of the disease has been known since ancient times as "the falling sickness," with the falling preceded by wildly erratic physical movements and foaming at the mouth and followed by deep states of unconsciousness. It often involves wild mood swings and temper tantrums, resulting in "misconduct of varying degrees of seriousness"; the misdeeds are often forgotten entirely by the victim, leaving him puzzled as to the reactions they have provoked. It also is frequently linked to mystical, visionary, and religious experiences. Both Knipperdolling and Jan Matthias had exhibited these forms of behavior earlier, as had King Jan, though rather less convincingly.

ANABAPTISTS BATHING. Sexual license and profligacy were among the most deadly charges against the Anabaptists, especially after King Jan instituted polygamy in Münster and himself took sixteen women as wives. This ambiguous portrayal of an Anabaptist bathing scene was adapted by a later artist from an illustration by Heinrich Aldegrever, a sympathizer. A combination of innocent domestic images seems to celebrate the joy of the body in an atmosphere of communal bliss, even as more suggestive actions occur in the foreground and perhaps among those leaving by the stairs at the rear.

FRANZ VON WALDECK. The Prince-Bishop Franz von Waldeck (1491–1553) was not only not ordained but was married, and had a mistress as well; like many so-called "prince-bishops" in Germany during this period, he owed his station to politics rather than to religion, and was if anything more sympathetic to the Protestant cause than to the Catholic. But when the city of Münster, in the heart of his realm, openly defied him he had no choice but to bring it to heel, though that task took him more than a year and drove him deeply into debt. The menacing militance of the prince's sword and the armor are clearly more significant than the bishop's regalia.

KING JAN. The dominant element in the painting other than the face of the king is his coat of arms, a globe pierced by the two crossed swords symbolizing revenge and spirit, with a cross above. The pierced globe appears at the end of the large gold chain above Jan's left wrist and again, much enlarged, in the upper left corner, beneath his crown. The inscription above Jan's head reads, "Jan van Leyden, King of the Anabaptists in Münster, truly rendered." The inscription beneath the painting is a mixture of Latin, Greek, and Low German, and says, "This was my image and these my royal vestments when I held the scepter, I, the King of the Anabaptists, though only for a short time./Heinrich Aldegrever of Soest did this in 1536./In God's power is my strength."

THE SIEGE OF MÜNSTER, 1534. Other than depicting hills, this is a reliable approximation of the siege, according to the Münster Catalog description. Note the double moat and the defensive palisades; the cannon shot emanating from the Cathedral tower; and even the execution of the Mollenheck rebels in the Market Square. Outside the walls we see a

confusing but rich display: tents, wagons, marching soldiers, burning
windmills, cannons protected by round screens woven from rushes, wives
cooking—even, in the lower right corner, a soldier attending to some private business.

BERNARD KNIPPERDOLLING.
In addition to his painting
of King Jan, Heinrich
Aldegrever's other celebrated
portrait is of the cloth
merchant Bernard
Knipperdolling, Münster's
leading businessman, who
became Jan's sword-bearer
and second-in-command.
The title reads, "A True
Likeness of Bernard
Knipperdolling, one of the
twelve princes of Münster,"
an incorrect statement
according to a later com-
mentator. The subtitle reads,
in effect, "This is how I,
Bernard Knipperdolling,
appeared, when I was at my
peak. Heinrich Aldegrever
did this picture in 1536."

KNIPPERDOLLING CAPERING
BEFORE KING JAN. Jan van
Leyden's story was retold for
many years in Holland. This late
seventeenth-century representation by a Dutch artist describes
the episode when Knipperdolling
plays the fool to Jan's king, perhaps as a challenge to the young
usurper of his authority—a vivid
contrast with the characterization
above.

Berend Knipperdolling tantzet und prophezeiet vor
dem Könige.

THE MOLLENHECK REBELLION. In July 1534, Jan's decree of polygamy provoked Henry Mollenheck, a prominent guild leader and long-time citizen of Münster, to lead a revolt against the king. He captured Jan and some of his followers but then surrendered after a counterattack. He and about fifty of his men were publicly murdered as depicted in this powerful rough drawing and buried in a mass grave.

König Johann enthauptet sein Weib.

KING JAN EXECUTES
ELIZABETH WANDSCHEER.

Near the end of his reign one of Jan's wives, Elizabeth Wandscheer, rebelled against his authority. He beheaded her in the Cathedral square, then danced around her body with his other wives, singing Anabaptist hymns. These illustrations by the Dutch artist Lambertus Hortensius are typical of the many that depict this notorious episode.

THE KING AND HIS OTHER
WIVES CELEBRATE THE
DEATH.

*König Johann tantzet mit seinem Kebs Weib umb den
Cörper seines enthaupten Weibes.*

Sigmund Freud's disciple Ernest Jones, in his book *On the Nightmare,* provides a related insight. Less well known than nightmares, Jones wrote, are "daymares," which cause their victims to behave in extraordinary ways completely at variance with their normal behavior. One of the many examples Jones provides describes a patient who says "daymares" are worse than nightmares, "stealing upon me while in perfect possession of my faculties; . . . [I] have undergone the greatest tortures, being haunted by specters, hags, and every sort of phantom—having, at the same time, a full consciousness that I was laboring under an incubus." If ever a man seemed to be "laboring under an incubus," it was Knipperdolling.

Whatever the cause of Knipperdolling's behavior—jealous rage, madness, physical illness, political calculation—it must have seemed symbolic to some of those who witnessed it of a deeper disorder, not only in him but in the Company of Christ. He had been a moral anchor in years past, a good man, generous to the poor, brave in opposing injustice. Now he had become first an executioner and finally a pathetic yet dangerous madman. Similarly, everything in the world of the Anabaptists in Münster had become reversed, inverted, turned upside-down, with a new version of the Ten Commandments in force: Thou *shalt* kill, thou *shalt* bear false witness, thou *shalt* commit adultery.

And thou shalt give up thy life for suggesting that this new order is not God's way.

8

THE RETURN OF HENRY GRAES

I send an Angel before thee, to keep thee in the way.

—Exodus 23:20

THE LAME PROPHET, Johann Dusentschur, had begun to preach in early October that soon the Company of Christ would hear the Lord sound His trumpets three times; this dreaded yet longed-for signal would summon the people to gather in the Cathedral Square, or Mount Zion, to be taken to the Promised Land.

An hour before dawn on Saturday, October, 23, all the men, women, and children of Münster were called from their beds not by trumpets but by the hollow, mournful sound of a cow horn blown from the tower of St. Lambert's Church by the limping prophet, then repeated as he and others ranged through the streets with horns and flutes. The people responded with fearful yet practiced haste. The men dressed for battle, many wearing light chain mail fashioned in the city's forges, while their wives dressed and comforted their frightened children. Thousands of people then stumbled through the dark streets, most of them heavily burdened. The men carried every weapon they owned—swords, knives, pikestaffs, halberds, harquebuses, longbows, and quivers of arrows—while the women shouldered whatever they could manage of their meager possessions, suspecting they would never see their homes again. Many of the women carried nursing babies and were trailed by whimpering, terrified children. The aged, the lame, the infirm limped tentatively over the frosted cobblestones, importuning gray-robed preachers like Henry Graes, the schoolmaster, and Johann Shaffer, who had been a wooden-shoe maker, for explanations. But the preachers only responded with brusque shakes of the head to anxious questions about what was happening; they knew no more than any other humble member of the Company of Christ what was afoot.

In the Cathedral Square, the people clustered around the dozen bonfires that eased the morning chill and waited for instructions from King Jan. They had been told many times to expect this day, the Day of Judgment, when they would go forth to do battle with the Bishop's army and either destroy it or be themselves taken into the Kingdom of Heaven. They had been warned to bring with them no more than they could carry, for if they succeeded in their holy battle they would leave the city behind to carry the truth into the world. If they failed, they would not need earthly possessions.

In practical terms, the men knew that now might be the best time to challenge the Bishop. His mighty army had drifted away after the great defeat in August, and fewer than three thousand men now stood between the Chosen Ones and freedom. The threatened blockhouses and their linking fortifications had not yet been completed, and would not unduly hinder their departure. But the city's fortifications were stronger than ever, and it frightened all but the boldest to think of leaving them to attack a force twice their own number of fifteen hundred battle-ready men. What did Jan have in mind?

The king kept his subjects waiting in fear and trembling for more than an hour, until just after the sun rose. Then the sound of trumpets announced his arrival; from the courtyard of the von Buren mansion slowly marched the royal procession. At its head was Jan's white stallion, its golden reins held by a purple-liveried page. The king sat straight and stern, wearing full armor and holding his sword erect in his right hand. In lieu of his helmet, which along with his spear was carried by another page who rode behind him, he wore his golden crown. The twenty young men who formed the king's bodyguard rode slightly behind him on either side, spreading out in a protective wake. Queen Divara followed in an open coach, attended by her ladies in waiting and the fifteen lesser wives.

The people waited for Jan to speak, but he sat in stony silence. A company of soldiers galloped into the square, escorting two flagbearers who carried pennants emblazoned with the king's crest, the world pierced by a sword. The captain of the troop, Gerlach von Wullen, approached the king and begged permission to speak to the people. Permission was granted. It was, everyone knew, the dashing young nobleman von Wullen who would lead the charge against the Bishop, and they anticipated now that he would order the men to their posts for the attack. "Our Lord, the just King of Kings," Gerlach shouted, "has ordered you to prepare for the final battle, and He is pleased to see that you are ready. But today is not to be the day. The Lord has revealed to King Jan that such is not His will, that today has been a test of your will and your readiness to obey. The Lord is well pleased with you," von Wullen continued as sighs of relief spread through the multitude at their deliverance. "As a sign of His pleasure, He has ordered that a great feast be prepared for you." The people were told to return to their houses and make themselves ready for the feast which would begin at noon in the Cathedral Square.

During all this time King Jan had not spoken a word. Now he nodded to his page, who turned the white stallion toward the palace, and was led silently from the square.

The feast began as promised. Everyone except for those on guard sat down to the tables assembled in the square. The sun blazed from the blue autumn sky on men and women hoisting tankards of dark beer as the court musicians played lively drinking songs and the cooks turned roasting pigs on their spits. All of these people had been spared from probable death only hours before, and their relief was almost palpable. The king himself, earlier so stern and distant, now strolled among the crowd, a warm and kindly smile on his face, looking like the youth he was but wearing his golden crown and his scarlet robe. His darkly beautiful queen walked beside him, her fingers resting lightly on his arm.

As they completed their passage through the square, Jan called his preachers to him and called for silence. He wished the people to hear that he, King Jan, and his royal court and the Elders would now serve the people with their own hands. And this they did, through the warm afternoon. Boiled beef and turnips made up the first course, followed by ham and green beans, and at last the roast pigs. Beer and wine flowed unceasingly, and by the end of the afternoon the Company of Christ was fully sated.

As the evening approached, the mood turned more solemn. It was time for communion, one of the Roman Catholic sacraments that had often been parodied by the Anabaptists. The preachers brought wafers on silver plates to the King and his court. Jan took a wafer and ate it, saying, "I eat this and show forth the death of the Lord." Then he drank from the silver chalice handed to him by Queen Divara, saying, "I drink this and show forth the death of the Lord." All of the adults in the square filed before Jan and Divara and the preachers and participated in this surprisingly devout and traditional communion.

When the communion was concluded, Jan climbed upon the table where he had been seated and slowly, with great deliberateness of movement, removed first his crown, then his golden chain, and placed them next to his scepter at his feet. Shorn of his royal symbols, he looked out upon his people and began to speak, in a broken voice and with tears running down his cheeks. Shocked into silence, the people heard Jan say that he was not worthy to be their king. He had been remiss in his duty to wield the sword and to punish the godless and the evildoers. He had failed them as their king.

Johann Dusentschur pushed his way through the crowd and climbed with difficulty upon the table. "Listen to me," he said; he had just had another vision from God. Before this day should end, the Lord had told him, the New Zion must send forth its apostles to all four corners of the land to oppose the enemy and to spread His word. The Lord had called out the names of the twenty-seven chosen messengers, his new apostles, and told Dusentschur to write them in the register that the crippled goldsmith now held before him like the tablets of Moses.

Spontaneous though Dusentschur's performance may have seemed, it shared the qualities of calculated melodrama that marked virtually everything that happened in Jan van Leyden's peculiar playhouse. It seems likely, given the composition of the list of names, that Jan was hoping to accomplish two ends, both related to keeping and extending his power. The first was to stir up support for Münster from nearby cities. The second, less obvious, reason, may have been to rid himself of competition for leadership and influence—Dusentschur himself, so instrumental in elevating Jan to the throne and consequently a figure of growing powers, was among the named messengers.

The meticulous planning that preceded the announcement was evident in the preciseness of Dusentschur's instructions. Eight men, including Dusentschur, would depart by way of Servatii Gate south toward Soest; six, including the schoolmaster Henry Graes, through the Hörster Gate north toward Osnabrück; eight through the Virgin Mary's Gate west toward Coesfeld; and five through the St. Mauritz Gate east toward Warendorf. They were all to leave the city before dawn and should announce their joyful presence wherever they were sent.

One after another, the men whose names God had told Dusentschur to write down in his register came before him for instructions and to confirm their allegiance. He then tore the register of their names into four pieces and scattered them to the wind. If those to whom they carried God's message refused to hear and obey, he said, they would be scattered to the flaming winds of hell just as these flimsy parchments were now carried away by the evening breeze.

But the limping prophet had one more service to perform before his departure. "Jan van Leyden," he called out, "where are you? I call upon you!" Jan, who was now sitting, head bowed, at Dusentschur's feet, slowly lifted his head and said, with renewed vigor, "I am here!" The prophet said to Jan that he could not lay aside his kingly duties. The Lord had revealed to him, Johann Dusentschur, that Jan must continue to punish the ungodly without mercy. He picked up the crown that Jan had put aside and placed it on the young man's head; he hung the golden chain about his neck; and he placed the discarded scepter in his hand. The end of the present evil time was at hand, the prophet said; the time of the thousand-year kingdom was about to begin, under the guidance of King Jan.

As the twenty-seven apostles left to bid their wives farewell—one hundred and thirty-four wives in total!—Jan announced to the crowd, resuming his stern manner, that they had now eaten and drunk their fill, and had heard the word of God. They should accordingly return to their work and their homes. Something of the confusion these people must have felt comes through in Gresbeck's narrative of the day's events. They had been threatened with death at dawn; at noon they had been grandly feted; at dusk their king had declared his un-worthiness, only to be reinstated by the strange goldsmith from War-endorf, who had exiled himself and much of the leadership of the Company of Christ to virtually certain death. The king himself had changed before their eyes from fierce warrior to gentle lamb of Christ to self-doubting wretch and, finally, back to stern master of their fates.

Now, as the chosen ones prepared to leave the City of God, the king sat down to a new banquet with his queen, his main advisers, including Knipperdolling, the Krechting brothers, and Bernard Roth-mann, and a few minor functionaries. The bare tables that had been used earlier were covered with damask tablecloths brought from von Buren's mansion, and silver candelabra were placed upon them. An-nounced by trumpets, servants brought heaps of steaming meats on golden platters and poured wine from the Bishop's cellars into golden cups.

Strangely, the king's mood seemed to darken as the festivities wore on, and for a long time he sat staring straight ahead, without expres-sion. Then he beckoned abruptly to an aide. "Go to the prison where the unbelievers are kept," he said, and bring one of them, one of the Bishop's Landsknechten, to him now. He must also bring him his sword, Jan said, for it would soon be used in judgment.

Here the two accounts of this incident by Kerssenbrück and Gres-beck differ interestingly. In Kerssenbrück's version, as elaborated by Helmut Paulus in his novel, the prisoner is first given a heaping plate of food, which he devours without hesitation; a beaker of red wine disappears and is refilled several times. After watching the drunken soldier gorge himself, Jan turns to him with contempt and asks, "What is your faith?" "Why ask me such a question?" the prisoner replies insolently. "I'm a soldier, not a preacher." The king asks the soldier why he is not properly attired for such a holy ceremonial repast. "I wasn't invited to this whore's feast but forced to come with a sword at my back," the soldier says. "Now that I'm here I'm happy to eat and drink my fill, even if a tailor's dirty mouth has touched the cup." Jan turns to his court. "I have received a sign!" he says. "Just as I will strike the head with its lying tongue from this soldier, you may strike my head off or burn me at the stake if I have not saved this holy city from the Bishop by Easter! Get up from the table and kneel before me!" he orders the soldier, who laughs drunkenly and says things have come to a fine pass when a tailor becomes a king. "I have a hole in my breeches, tailor. Will you sew it up for me?" Enraged, the king orders the soldier's arms to be bound and strikes off his head.

Henry Gresbeck, who had been a soldier himself, has a less heroic version. There are no preliminaries—the soldier is hauled before the king and told to kneel. He refuses. Jan says he will cleave the soldier in two where he stands unless he obeys. The soldier begs for mercy and falls upon his knees. Jan cuts his head off without further ceremony.

The original accounts agree on at least two important points: that Jan himself performed the execution, with a sword like the one that today hangs next to his suit of armor on the wall of the City Museum in Münster; and that the headless corpse was left where it lay in the middle of the banquet until dawn while the party continued around it.

Nothing was heard from or of the apostles for days after their departure. Rumors, however, abounded of successes near and far. The mighty King of England, Henry VIII, had been re-baptized into their faith and now recognized King Jan as his sovereign. An Anabaptist army was about to invade Rome, the citadel of Satan, and overthrow the Pope. In the Netherlands thousands of supporters were arming their ships for an expedition shortly after the new year to rescue the besieged city of Münster.

More prosaically, and a good deal closer to home—for none of the four cities to which the apostles had been sent was more than a day or two away—circumstances were less promising. In Soest the irrepressible Dusentschur and his men gathered some followers and approached the City Hall, where the council was in session. They forced their way in with swords drawn. The council stared at the intruders and demanded to know their business. "Here is our sign," Dusentschur said, and tossed a golden coin at the feet of the council president. The coin, newly minted in the New Zion, bore the likeness of King Jan and was imprinted with the king's vow: "In God's Power Is My Strength." Dusentschur demanded the right to preach openly in the city, on pain of death at the hands of King Jan if they denied him. All of the intruders were seized immediately, jailed, and executed within days at the city gate. In an eerie echo of the death of Hille Feyken, Johann Dusentschur, "the boldest and least abashed, told the executioner he did not believe that he could die, that his neck would be unharmed by the sword. The executioner answered that he had expected trouble, and swung his sword with such force that it would have separated three heads from their necks."

In Coesfeld there were already many Anabaptists and the potential for an uprising, but the Bishop frightened the city fathers with dire punishment if they did not turn over the preachers; all eight were executed, after pitifully complaining that they had been misled by the prophet Dusentschur.

Warendorf, though much smaller than Münster, was a walled city barely fifteen miles from the heart of the insurrection and consequently a matter of great concern to the Bishop. Jan's five apostles, led by a former soldier from Cologne, Johann Klopriss, were greeted enthusiastically by a sympathetic council, and more than fifty men and women were baptized. The Bishop sent a written directive to the council. They must not let themselves "be blinded by the juggling tricks" of the Anabaptists, or misled from the pure teachings of the Church by these disturbers of the peace, but hand them over to him for his mercy or his punishment.

When the Warendorf council staunchly replied that they supported Münster, the Bishop sent cavalry and foot soldiers to demand entry into the city. The intimidated citizens opened the gate, after receiving assurances that the city would not be plundered. When the troops entered the city, all the cannons were gathered in the market place and fired at the same time, their concussion breaking all the windows in town. The citizens handed over the preachers; the Bishop locked them up, along with the recently baptized citizens, whose names a council member had written down. The citizens had to give up their weapons and could not leave their houses. In addition to the weapons, the soldiers took the documents that guaranteed the rights of the city.

Most of the newly baptized men and women were imprisoned in Sassenburg and Iburg until their families could ransom their freedom. The instigators of the unrest did not escape so easily. On October 24, three days after the surrender, on a scaffold hastily constructed from planks and beer barrels, four of the preachers from Münster were beheaded; each of the four gates was then adorned with the head of a heretic. Also executed were the city counselor who had allowed the apostles to enter; a burgher who had destroyed a gilded statue of Christ in the churchyard; and the guard for the east gate who had vowed to tie a hair rope to the Bishop and drag him through the city if he dared to show his face there. These three were, however, granted the mercy of having their bodies buried in the church cemetery. All of the dead men were luckier than Klopriss, the apostles' leader, who languished for three months in prison until he was burned at the stake, in February 1535.

The adventures of the apostles to Osnabrück were equally disastrous, but there was one who returned to tell the tale to the king and his court: Henry Graes, the schoolmaster. As reconstructed by Helmut Paulus from the accounts left by Kerssenbrück and Gresbeck, shortly after midnight on October 23, the Anabaptist guard at the Ludger Gate heard noises—chains rattling, a man's voice calling out piteously for help. A cold, sleeting rain was falling, obscuring all vision. The guard called the captain of the watch, who said they could not open the gate door for fear that it was a trick of the Bishop's to gain entry. Whatever was out there would have to wait until morning.

At dawn five men exited quietly through the small door of the gate to investigate further. The thin grass was iced with sleet and covered with a heavy frost that had descended after the rain had stopped. Under a naked, glistening thornbush lay the body of a man whose hands and feet were bound with heavy iron chains. The captain peered at the gray, stubble-bearded face; the man's cheeks were sunken, his thin lips were blue; he was unconscious, more dead than alive, and barely recognizable as the apostle from Borken, Henry Graes. The men carried the schoolmaster into the city and before a gathering crowd rubbed his limbs vigorously. After a time Graes opened his eyes, looked around at his old friends, and sighed, "The great Lord has had mercy on me, and I am with you again! Take me to the king, for I have a message for him."

Still in his chains, barely conscious, Graes was carried to Jan's court, accompanied by a crowd singing psalms of praise for his deliverance.

When he had recovered sufficiently to eat and drink, he told King Jan and his advisers what had happened to him and his brothers in Osnabrück.

After their departure on the evening of the great feast, Graes said, he and Dionysus Vinne and their four companions had made their way safely through the enemy's lines and arrived at Osnabrück the following morning. They asked a man in the street for directions to the house of Otto Spieker, who they had been told was a strong supporter of the cause. Spieker greeted the apostles warily. Graes dropped one of the gold coins at Spieker's feet. Spieker thanked him for the gift but said Graes was misinformed; he was not an Anabaptist and they could not stay in his house. Dionysus Vinne looked at him suspiciously and said they had no fear, because they were under the Lord's protection, and that Spieker should know that whoever lied about or betrayed even one of them was betraying the will of the Heavenly Father.

The apostles marched onward to the City Square, where they quickly gathered a crowd that seemed receptive to the sermon preached by Vinne, but soon a company of soldiers arrived to seize them. Spieker was at their head. "There they are!" he cried; "those are the men who boasted that they have come from Münster to preach the Thousand-Year Kingdom of King Jan!" The crowd boiled angrily around the soldiers, but Vinne shouted that they should stand back, that he and his companions were not criminals or disturbers of the peace but men of God. They would go with the soldiers without protest. And so they did, singing hymns and surrounded by admiring followers, as they were marched to the Bock Tower prison. The captain of the guard told Vinne that it was not right to treat men of God in this way, and he was sorry. Vinne responded that the captain was a true brother in spirit, and that God would remember his kindness in the hour of judgment that was so close at hand. For the rest, who would so mistreat the children of God, they could expect only the harshest of punishment.

When the crowd heard this, they turned with such fury on Otto Spieker that the traitor was forced to flee for his life. The jailer, like the captain of the guard, treated the prisoners well, laying out a thick bed of straw for them and bringing food and wine. Vinne's group had great support among the council because they had so clearly wanted to avoid violence; the traitor Otto Spieker had been driven from the city, probably to Iburg to seek refuge with the Bishop. When he heard this, Dionysus Vinne, far from comforted, began to pray.

Early the following morning, long before the sympathetic council could meet to debate the fate of the apostles, a dozen of the Bishop's soldiers forced the guard to open the cell door. They tied the hands and feet of the prisoners and threw them bodily into heavy carts by the city gate. Spieker had sold them out to the Bishop, into whose dungeon at Iburg they were cast before noon. Over the next few days they were all tortured, some with red-hot-glowing tongs that tore pieces of flesh from their bodies, others with thumb-presses turned by heavy screws, and, on the rack, Dionysus Vinne, with so much weight and pressure that his back was broken and he was paralyzed. But none of them had lost his faith in the Lord, Graes said, despite all of their torment.

Even worse than the physical torture for the apostles was their isolation from each other, in separate cells, chained hand and foot, hearing each day from their keeper that their brothers in Soest, Coesfeld, and Warendorf had all been taken and killed. Their cruel warden did not know that his most crushing news, that Dionysus Vinne had died of his great and painful injuries, was seen as a sign of God's mercy. But Graes's faith began to waver when he heard the sounds of a scaffold being constructed in the courtyard of the Iburg palace, and when he was told that he and his brothers were to lose their heads in the morning, he did not think he could stand any more.

Gresbeck does not tell us how Jan and his retinue received this dreadful news, though Paulus shows the king as impatient and curious to hear how Graes had managed to evade death himself. The answer to that question was, indeed, a tale to inspire wonder and awe.

The schoolmaster told Jan that as he lay in his cell, cold and hungry and in irons, he called out aloud to God for strength at the moment of his coming martyrdom. When he opened his eyes after prayer, a bright, shimmering shaft of light appeared before him, and a voice called his name: "Henry Graes!" "I am here!" Graes cried, "I am here!" And then the light dissolved and the angel of the Lord stood before Henry Graes, a glowing sword in his hand. "Rise up!" the angel said. "How should I stand?" Graes replied. "You must see how miserably I lie upon the earth, bound hand and foot with chains!" The angel took him by the hand, and the chains became as light as twine and he felt strength flowing again into his limbs. "Come with me," the angel commanded. "The scaffold is ready; all my brothers must die. How can I leave them now?" Graes pleaded. "Leave me with them, I beg of you." The angel's eyes burned into his heart, Graes said. "The Lord has chosen you to return to the Holy City of Zion," the awful voice said. "You must bear witness before the king and his people. You must let your faith be an example to them that the Lord Almighty will save those who stand firm in their faith, even while the weak must die without His help." The voice was like thunder in his ears, so loud that Graes fell backward in his chains, hitting his head on the stone floor and losing consciousness.

When he awoke, it was to find himself nearly frozen under a thornbush, gazing upward at the faces of his brothers in Christ. Truly, he had been saved by the grace of his Lord.

9

RESTITUTION AND REVENGE

The most dangerous follower is he whose defection would destroy the whole party: that is to say, the best follower.

—Friedrich Nietzsche

HENRY GRAES RECOVERED quickly from his terrible ordeal and soon became revered in Münster as a living symbol of divine mercy and hope. As an apostle he now occupied a position of power equivalent to those of the two Bernards (Rothmann and Knipperdolling) and was thus a member of the king's inner circle, privy to his plans and problems alike. Kerssenbrück tells us that not everyone believed his strange story. But those who doubted it could not do so on the ground that it was fantastic. The Bible offered many stories of similar rescues—of Daniel in the lions' den, of Jonah from the whale, and particularly that of Peter, rescued from his chains in Herod's dungeon by an angel who said, "Arise up quickly," and led him from his cell. To deny Graes's miraculous salvation out of hand would be to cast doubt on the literal truth of the Bible as the revealed Word of God. Moreover, Jan himself occupied his position as the result of his own visions from God and those of Johann Dusentschur. He could hardly have denied Henry Graes's tale, then, on grounds of implausibility— though he might have thought it peculiar that Graes alone of the twenty-seven survived to tell it.

The schoolmaster's survival was in fact due not to angelic intervention but to his excellent education, his quick mind, and his suddenly flexible moral philosophy. The story he told Jan's court was true up to the moment when he and his fellow apostles were taken to the prison in Iburg, the Bishop's seat. When the prisoners were herded before the Bishop, von Waldeck heard one of them whisper to him, in Latin—a language that only the two of them would know—this plea: "Does the Bishop have no power to set a prisoner free?" The Bishop gave no sign that he had heard; but later Henry Graes was brought from his cell to be questioned further, not under torture but with wine and bread.

He told the Bishop everything he knew about the beleaguered city, but that alone would not have saved his life—he would have revealed the same information under torture, and the Bishop had other spies to pass on such details. What kept Graes alive was his offer to return to the city as the Bishop's man. He had been highly placed before; now he realized that he had been in the service of Satan, and he had no hesitation in seeing the devil defeated. He would become, if his plan worked, a privileged spy for the Bishop. He knew what he had to do to convince the fanatics there of his fidelity. He proposed to let himself be bound with chains and left before the city gate. When the guards discovered him, he would declare that an angel had miraculously delivered him from his imminent execution.

It says much for Graes's power of persuasion that he could convince a hardened cynic like Franz von Waldeck to agree to such a ludicrous plan. Then again, the Bishop must have regarded it as a risk-free proposition. If Graes failed in his masquerade, his friends would take care of him in ghoulish fashion. If he succeeded, he might well be useful. As for Graes, it could not have been a part of the plan that he should nearly freeze to death after being deposited before the city gate, but even that bad luck had worked to his advantage, providing proof of real danger.

The Bishop's frustrations with the Anabaptists in Münster, always intense, had peaked with the capture of the so-called apostles, bent on stirring up more trouble in his shaky realm; hence their extermination—excepting Henry Graes—virtually on the spot, without trial or hearing. He accepted Graes's outlandish proposal because everything was working against him. He was anxious to avoid further military clashes, which seemed always to end badly for him, and to get out from under the expenses of the siege, which were mounting heavenward. Queen Marie of Burgundy had, it was true, recently offered the Bishop the loan of a few thousand guilders, as had the Bishop of Lüttich. But these sums were a pittance compared to the several hundred thousand guilders he had spent during the past eight months, and the patience and support of his fellow princes, never reassuring, now seemed to be tangibly lessening. The Roman Catholic Bishop turned in desperation for advice to the Lutheran Landgraf Philip of Hesse for help.

Count Philip was no less eager than Bishop Franz to see the Münster fiasco come to a peaceful end; it was tarnishing the reputation of all Protestants and setting the stage for a counterreformation. He told the Bishop he would send his pastor, Dietrich Fabricius, to him for a last-ditch attempt to persuade the rebels to come to terms. A few days after the return of Henry Graes, on November 2, the Bishop sent a messenger under a flag of truce to Jan, asking for safe passage for Fabricius, which was granted.

On his previous, similar mission, before the mass expulsion the previous February, Fabricius had been bullied and badly frightened by Rothmann's followers, but he was nevertheless a good choice of ambassador. In earlier days he had been one of the more rebellious intellectual young advocates of the Reformation, and not hostile to some of the concepts of the Anabaptists. After study under Melanchthon, Luther's disciple, Fabricius had been appointed to teach Hebrew in Cologne in 1526. His reputation as a radical almost lost him the post, and he grew more restive at the failures of the Reformation in the years that followed. He formed a close bond with a number of men who would become the most radical Anabaptists, including the doomed apostles sent out with Henry Graes, Dionysus Vinne, and Johann Klopriss. It was true that Fabricius had pulled back from the brink of religious radicalism, becoming instead the pastor of Philip of Hesse. But if anyone should be able to talk to Jan and his preachers, to persuade them to avoid further bloodshed and to "plant the seed of proper belief" among them, in Kerssenbrück's phrase, it was Fabricius.

Fabricius was met at the city gate by a delegation of twelve Anabaptists. Walking toward the City Hall with his armed hosts, he found the streets quiet—so little-used that grass was growing in the alleys—and the people subdued, apparently "pressed down and sad," though he was not permitted to speak to any of them. After waiting for a few minutes in the City Hall, Fabricius heard a lively drum salute. Twenty young men dressed in satin and velvet marched through the wide doors; the king's bodyguard, they took up positions around the long room and stood at attention. Two young pages followed, one bearing the king's sword, the other the book in which his judgments and decrees were recorded. Finally the king himself entered, wearing a black velvet robe and a white silken cloak against which glittered a golden chain; at the end of the chain was the king's coat of arms, through which a golden dagger was thrust. As the king was seated on his throne, Knipperdolling, Rothmann, and the Elders entered the room and took their seats. Rothmann then addressed the visitor. If he was a member of their brotherhood, he said, he could remain seated. Otherwise, he must stand. Fabricius rose and said that he came in peace and in the hope the Bishop's just cause would be recognized. Several of the Elders rebuked him for his words, saying that the Bishop desired the king's death.

After a while Jan, bored with the scene, ended the royal audience and conducted Fabricius on a tour of the city's defenses, obviously hoping to convey their solidity. Noting the many ruined churches, including the truncated Overwater Church, Fabricius asked Jan why their destruction had been necessary. "Sooner than let them be abused by the Papists," Jan replied, he would pull them all down, just as he would "sooner eat the children in their mothers' wombs than let them live to be unbelievers."

That night the shaken Lutheran slept uneasily at the King's invitation in his palace, where he saw four of the sixteen wives but recorded no further conversations. The following morning he presented the Bishop's case, in its strongest light, to Jan and the court in the City Hall. They should know, Fabricius said, that their war was no longer with Bishop Franz alone. Besides Marie of Burgundy, the Prince of Saxony had promised support. His own master, Landgraf Philip, had been disgusted by the Bishop's murder of Dr. von Wyck but now was certain that the rebellion had to be crushed. Emperor Charles V had

ordered the Spanish rulers in Holland to vigorously suppress any Anabaptist movements there, which meant that their long-anticipated
salvation from Dutch supporters was doomed. Finally, Fabricius said,
the Archbishop of Cologne had appealed on behalf of Bishop Franz
to the Emperor for added support. If Charles failed to help defeat
Münster, the Archbishop had said, not only the neighboring cities in
northern Germany would be threatened, but all of Germany; indeed,
all of Christendom would be at risk.

Surely Jan must see, Fabricius concluded, that the Bishop was not
at liberty to do anything but crush the Anabaptist kingdom; his own
survival depended on it. Even as they spoke, the guards at the city's
walls could watch the seven blockhouses under construction within
arrow-shot of the city; if seven were insufficient, seventy would be
built. Jan and his kingdom were doomed. They could surrender now
and hope for mercy, or maintain their resistance and be sure of destruction.

The twenty-five-year-old innkeeper and tailor's apprentice was
threatening not only the Empire but all of Christendom! Jan's vanity
must have been hugely gratified, but he did respond temperately at
first, after his fashion: he would be willing to talk further to some of
the princes who were not directly involved in helping the Bishop.
But under no circumstances would they turn the city over to von
Waldeck. They were all prepared to die first.

Fabricius returned safely to the Bishop and gave him a written
report of his discouraging findings. He recommended that the blockhouses be finished as soon as possible, and that the connecting walls
between them, which the Bishop had been resisting because of their
cost, also be completed. He had seen many signs of easy passage into
and out of Münster, even two weeks after the unnoticed departure of
the twenty-seven apostles and consequent attempts to tighten the cordon.

It is no easy matter to seal off a city with a circumference of three
miles, opening into vast fields threaded with drainage and irrigation
ditches and hedgerows and trees. Nothing short of another virtual city
of some three thousand soldiers nearly four miles long, completely
enclosing it, could be expected to work, and the expense and labor
of such a project were enormous. Seventy woodcutters were brought

in, along with eighty-five carpenters, to finish building the block-houses, and two thousand farmers for incidental labor. Several of the blockhouses were massive and all were formidable: one of the smallest was a square of which the sides measured 225 feet, about 60 feet per side. It was surrounded by its own moat, ten feet deep, and a rampart twenty-five feet thick and ten feet high; it rose ten feet above the rampart and had two cannons and six musket-slots. Several others were three times as large. By the end of December the blockhouses were complete; so too, finally, were the connecting ramparts, sturdy and broad and secure—so much so that a seven-horse wagon loaded with powder and ammunition could safely pass along it, in full view of the helpless rebels. By January the city was tightly sealed; a few men might sneak in or out, but the serious potential threat of a mass breakout was foreclosed.

Autumn declined into winter, the cold, wet winter of northern Germany. Increasingly isolated behind their own walls and moats as well as by the Bishop's surrounding wall, the Anabaptists could do little but reassure themselves of the righteousness of their cause and lay plans for securing relief from abroad. They turned again to the man who had provided the intellectual engine-power for their revolution, Pastor Bernard Rothmann, for inspiration and spiritual guidance.

Jan's contemporaries often derided his kingdom as a carnival of fools and Bernard Rothmann as a redheaded heretic and adulterer. But Rothmann was not a fool. He wrote serious arguments that are discussed with respect today by religious historians and that forced responses from the greatest minds of his time, including Melanchthon, Luther, and Zwingli. One of those works, "Restitution," was published in October, before the departure of the twenty-seven apostles, and doubtless reinforced their sense of divine mission.

The title "Restitution" refers to the restoration of the original or primitive Church, a goal that the Anabaptists shared with Luther and Zwingli. Rothmann did not disparage the accomplishments of these men but put them into a broader context. There had not been, as George H. Williams explains Rothmann's argument, just one Fall from Paradise, that of Adam and Eve in the Garden of Eden, or one restoration of God's grace in the birth and life of Jesus. Rather, there had been a series of falls and restorations: first, "the fall into bondage in Egypt and the return to Canaan, [followed by] the exile into Babylon and the restoration"; then another in the second century; and more recently "a final restoration, begun by Erasmus and Luther and climaxing" in Jan van Leyden.

The Anabaptists parted from Luther and the other Protestants in their refusal to limit or divide their vision of the truth of God, either by turning the biblical accounts into allegorical "stories" or by constructing new bastions of churchly authority. Their slogan, stamped on their medals and on the coins that the apostles threw at the feet of their antagonists, was "The Word Has Become Flesh and Dwells in Us: One God, One Faith, One Baptism." Church and state were the same; an absolute theocracy was the only structure of government possible.

In early January 1535, Jan sent copies of "Restitution" and of another work, "On the Secret Significance of Scripture," to Philip of Hesse, to Luther, and to Melanchthon, among others, in an obvious effort to lessen their opposition. Philip responded with some temperance that "if the thing depended only on me," he could help them plead their cause where it was just. But the rebels should have "addressed the princes of the empire" before, not after, they took the law into their own hands, "flying to arms, erecting a kingdom, electing a king, and sending prophets and apostles abroad to stir up the towns and the people. Nevertheless, it is possible that even now [the Anabaptists'] demands may be favorably listened to," if they called back those they had expelled and returned their property and restored the city's proper government; for all government was derived from God, and the rebels had acted against this basic truth from the beginning.

The response from Luther, either written or approved by him, was addressed to the Anabaptists in Münster as a group. Notoriously hot-tempered and prone to hyperbole, Luther nevertheless provides a sense of the passions stirred by Rothmann and Jan among those who might be presumed at least marginally sympathetic to their position. "Since you are led astray by the devil into such blasphemous error, and are drunk and utterly captive to your delusions, you wish, as is Satan's way, to make yourselves into angels of light and to paint in brightness and color your devilish doings." Earlier Luther had joked that if the devil was involved in the carryings-on in Münster it must be through the efforts of an incompetent "schoolgirl apprentice," inasmuch as what the Anabaptists were proposing was so shockingly revolting that they could never hope to find support among the people. Now Luther was forced to take the rebels more seriously, for they were using "Holy Scripture as all heretics have always done." Almost plaintively, Luther continues, "What shall I say? You let all the world see that you understand far less about the kingdom of Christ and than did the Jews . . . for the Scripture and the prophets point to Messiah, through whom all was to be fulfilled, and this the Jews also believed. But you want to make it point to your Tailor-King, to the great disgrace and mockery of Christ. . . ." Even worse than denying and supplanting Christ, Luther continued, speaking now of himself in the third person, "you have cast away all that Dr. Martin Luther taught you, and yet it is from him that you have received, next to God, whatever sound learning of the Scripture you have. You have given a new definition of faith, after your own fashion," which has not only "darkened" but "utterly annihilated" its true meaning.

The modern reader is struck by the extraordinary heat and violence of the responses from recognized Protestant leaders who might be expected to have some sympathy for protesters. It is the Anabaptists advocating "Restitution" who by contrast look almost measured and thoughtful; from their perspective they were engaged in a brave and principled attempt to recapture the purity of the Christian faith that had been lost, in the face of determined opposition by a corrupt and powerful religious and political establishment. It was this kind of appeal that must have originally attracted such men as Henry Graes— and, for that matter, Bernard Rothmann—to the Anabaptist cause: not fools or villains, but seekers after truth in a corrupt world.

But the darker side of the story fatally undermines any pretensions to idealism—the story that, among many others, Herbert Rusher, Henry Mollenheck, Gert the Smoker, Katherine Holscher and Barbara Butendinck, and the headless banquet guest could have told, if they had been allowed to live. It was the story told in the second pamphlet Rothmann was writing at this time, entitled "Revenge."

If "Restitution" showed the Company of Christ in its better aspects, "Revenge" explained why they were feared. Rothmann begins softly, with the beautiful words from Ecclesiastes 3:1, "To every thing there is a season, and a time to every purpose under the heaven." But this does not mean passively waiting for God to "come with his angels from heaven to wreak revenge on the godless. No, dear brother, this is not so. He will come, that is true, but the revenge must be executed first by the servants of God." He recalls in order to deny them the words of Isaiah, 2:4: ". . . they shall beat their swords into plowshares, and their spears into pruninghooks; nation shall not lift up sword against nation, neither shall they learn war any more." On the contrary, Rothmann now says—it is time for them to turn their plowshares into swords so that they and their leader, King Jan, wearing "the armor of David," might seek "revenge with the help of God [against] all Babylonian power and extinguish all godlessness. . . ."

Like "Restitution," "Revenge" was a powerfully persuasive piece of writing to those who were sympathetic to its arguments and its rhetoric. It was intended to rouse its readers not to meditative speculation but to action. On Christmas Eve, 1534, a thousand copies of "Revenge" were handed to one of Jan's most militant Dutch supporters, Jan van Geelen, along with a large amount of gold. There were Anabaptist supporters in Deventer, Groningen, Amsterdam, Delft, and in King Jan's home city, Leyden. With three companions, van Geelen was ordered to use "Revenge" to rouse the faithful and to use the gold to buy weapons for them. Sometime before Easter, they were then to gather for a march on Münster, where they would attack the Bishop from the rear while Jan and his men broke through his lines to freedom.

Henry Graes, who had been given a special robe, colored green for persistence and gray for gratitude to God, was by now a privileged member of King Jan's inner circle. However, the life of a secret agent is never a comfortable one—he was only on parole by the Bishop in return for useful services, and he must have wondered constantly when he would somehow be exposed to Jan as a traitor, with consequences that did not bear thinking about. He knew that Jan van Geelen's mission was no trivial threat, and that the Bishop would reward Graes with his life if he could get the information to him. It was time to separate himself for good from the Company of Christ.

On New Year's Day, 1535, Graes revealed to his brothers and sisters in Christ that he had been visited yet again by a commanding vision: he was to leave Münster immediately and to raise support throughout southern Germany. With this aid, in addition to that brought by van Geelen, the City of God would be delivered from the oppressors. Jan obligingly gave Graes a letter that began, in grandly regal fashion, "We, Johann, the just king of the new temple and servant of almighty God, do hereby advise all who are bound up with us that the bearer of this letter, Henry Graes, is a prophet blessed by God," and ended with the injunction that all who can do so must help him in whatever way possible. It was signed "Pronounced in Münster, the city of God, and under our seal in the 26th year of our life, the first year of our reign, and on the second day of the first month after the birth of Jesus Christ, the son of God, in the year 1535." Jan also provided a diversionary attack on the night of January 2, enabling Graes to make his way easily through the enemy lines.

Once out of the city, Graes immediately rode to the Bishop's palace in Iburg, where he made a full report of everything he had seen, as of the first of January. In addition to his news about the van Geelen mission, Graes revealed that the Bishop's blockade was having an effect. Münster's prosperity had been based on trade, farming, and the Church, all now canceled, and for the past ten months it had been consuming its dwindling resources. As winter settled in, there was not enough fuel for heating, as most of the wood set aside for fires had been used to shore up the city walls after the August attack. There was little meat to eat—they had only three hundred head of cattle left, which they were trying to save for later—and only enough rye and wheat for another month.

The mood of the people was mixed, Graes said. The fifteen hundred armed men who controlled the city were well fed from provisions set aside for them; they had in many cases several wives to tend to their every need; and they remained certain that God was on their side. The people, however, were beginning to fall into a deep melancholy. Trapped between the Bishop who called them heretics and their king who alternately inspired and terrified them, they were too frightened to do more than struggle from one day to the next. The women and children were suffering the most and had the least power to change their situation. In sum, Graes said, privation and hunger would render the city helpless in another two or three months, and it would fall like a rotten apple into the outstretched hand of Bishop Franz.

The Bishop, having no great incentive to move against an enemy that would inevitably succumb, relaxed in his comfortable castle in Iburg and left the Anabaptists to freeze and starve behind their walls for the rest of the winter. Henry Graes, who presumably had expected to be allowed to return to his home in Borkum, remained as an uncomfortable guest, in complete seclusion: he had, it would turn out, two more services to perform.

The first of these would occur in March, when the Bishop grew impatient with growing unrest in the small city of Wesel. Like Warendorf, Wesel had been outspoken in its support of King Jan, and reports had reached von Waldeck that hundreds of armed Anabaptists were gathering there to march on Münster. Late one afternoon near the end of March, the faithful in Wesel were overjoyed to find in their midst none other than Brother Henry himself, King Jan's most famous apostle, the only one of the twenty-seven to survive, the man the angel had plucked from the scaffold before the very eyes of the Bishop himself (the legend had acquired a few embellishments). Nothing had been heard of Graes since his departure from Münster in January, supposedly for southern Germany, but now he was among them, with two tough-looking assistants, to provide them with inspired leadership.

Graes demanded to know what the people of Wesel planned to do to help King Jan in his hour of need. They would do whatever he asked, the people said. Graes suggested that they march on Münster the next week, but that first they gather their weapons together for safekeeping in the city arsenal. This was done according to his instructions. On April 5, Graes sent one of his two "assistants"—both of them the Bishop's men assigned to watch Graes as well as to protect him—with a message to Count von Jülich, the knight in whose domain the city lay. The count's men, several hundred in number, stormed into town and secured the armory. Without weapons the rebels had to surrender immediately. Six of the ringleaders were beheaded. The rest were allowed to live, but had to appear in church to beg for mercy, wearing white gowns of repentance.

The schoolmaster's final contribution would be revealed at a particularly difficult time for King Jan. At the conclusion of the murderous banquet the previous October, Jan had vowed, on the head of the profane soldier he had killed, to see the city free by Easter Sunday 1535. Otherwise, his own life was forfeit. That day, March 28, was now imminent and the city was still under siege. Although we can be certain that no one was brave or stupid enough to remind him of his promise, Jan knew he had to account for it. He went into a long seclusion, while the city waited anxiously for him to announce his decision. He was haggard and humble when he finally appeared in the Market Square on Good Friday, March 26. For the past three days, he revealed to the assembled crowd, he had wrestled with the problem not only of his fate as their king but of his subjects' fates as well. Finally, God had told him that he, King Jan, had erred in his great compassion. He had taken the sins of his people unto himself, and thus he had accordingly been confused and misled. God now told Jan that when he had promised their deliverance by Easter; he had meant their *souls* would be delivered into true righteousness by that time. Because of Jan's efforts, God had told him, they had achieved this happy condition: the souls of all who listened to Jan this day had been freed into righteousness. Therefore it was not necessary for their king to sacrifice himself; indeed, it was positively forbidden.

Jan's ingenuity and stagecraft had saved him for the moment from his own folly. But almost immediately he had to deal with an almost equally mortal threat—a letter from Henry Graes, found nailed to the city gate. How it came there, under the eyes of the guards, is a mystery. Even stranger is Jan's decision to make it known to all his people; he had executed several of them who had been found carrying leaflets from the Bishop offering rewards for leaving the city. The common supposition was that the first guard to see it had read it and was so thunderstruck by its revelation that he had given it to another; each man who read it passed it along like a hot potato to the next, fearing for his life if he had to be the bearer of such terrible news to King Jan. By the time it reached Bernard Knipperdolling, the only man who had the courage to hand it to the king, too many people had seen Graes's letter for it to be kept secret, or for those who knew the secret to be killed.

There was never any question that the letter was genuine, for it bore the apostle's own seal. Graes had written it earlier, in January, before his mission to Wesel. Now the Bishop saw no reason for holding it back, knowing what a potent assault it would be. The letter begins with a prayer for God to "protect us all in His loving mercy." It continues:

> Dear fellow-citizens. God has opened my eyes so that I now see how what we have wrought in Münster is false and poisonous; He has commanded me to hold up for you the mirror of your wickedness, as He has held it up for me. I beg you to open your eyes—it is high time!—and to see that what you have done is against God and His divine command. All the prophets are only men like me. You poor, stupid fools have been deceived, betrayed, and misled. I know everything. You may still save your lives if you will turn from your path and leave this godless business behind. This is God's command. So that you will be sure to believe that this letter comes from me, Henry Graes, I have sealed it with my signet ring, which you all know.

The schoolmaster's parting admonition was written in what Friedrich Reck termed "honest medieval Westphalian dialect" and had the ring of truth. Coupled with the proof of the seal, it could not be denied. King Jan could only rage and bitterly remind his followers that false prophets abounded in times of trial: they would have to redouble their efforts to guard against further treachery.

10

FLIGHT

For want and famine they were solitary, fleeing into the wilderness
in former time desolate and waste.

—Job 30:3

JAN WAS WISER than he knew—traitors were indeed all around him, including the carpenter Henry Gresbeck, who had been an apparently loyal Anabaptist since his arrival in Münster more than a year earlier. Now Gresbeck had written a letter, smuggled out of the city by yet another traitor, to his former master Count Robert Manderscheid. Written in mid-April, shortly after the turncoat apostle Henry Graes's more public letter had appeared, it begins directly with an admission of error:

"Honored and noble sir: When I departed from you last year with your permission for leave for fourteen days to visit my poor mother in Münster, I had not intended to stay here, but it proved impossible to leave, especially in that I have taken a wife and she and I and my mother are now living with her mother and father and her brothers." He has married to protect the young woman, Gresbeck implies; "had I not done so, strangers would have moved in with them, or the house would have been burned." He has had to stay in Münster to protect his new family and his mother, though the warning words of his master's mother still ring in his ears: "She spoke truly when she said, 'Master Henry, if you return to Münster, you will have to let yourself be baptized,'" which would put him beyond the possible forgiveness of the Bishop, as Henry was still a devout Catholic.

"I did not want to believe it," Gresbeck now admits, but his mistress had been right; it had happened as she said, and he now has to beg his master's forgiveness: "I have always been your loyal servant and will be again for the rest of my life." But his life will be a short one unless he can escape and help to bring an end to the terrible siege, for his mother and his wife and her family, like almost everyone else, are dying from hunger. He has only two choices: "I must either stay here and starve or escape and risk death from the Bishop's soldiers."

Gresbeck asks Manderscheid to see that mercy is granted to his mother and to Clara Clevorn, his wife, and to her parents and her two brothers, Albert and Wilhelm, whatever happens to him. He pleads for patience: "My dear master, my heart is too sore to tell you now of all that I have seen, but I hope the day will come when I can explain it to you." In the meantime, whether he lives or dies is up to God, but Gresbeck hopes his master will assure the Bishop that he is a good and true man. "I am ready to leave the city to cross over," Gresbeck concludes. "I am assigned to the watchtower opposite the Cleves Blockhouse, by the Holy Cross Gate. If someone will call out this name, Hans von Brielen, from the blockhouse, I will know that this message has been received and will cross over at the nearest opportunity. In heaven's name, though, do not let me be called by my own name, or my head will leave my neck. Please, my dear master, do your best for me. I will be your true servant for as long as I live. Master Henry, Carpenter of Münster."

It is hardly fair to stigmatize as "traitors" those who tried to flee or to undermine Jan's kingdom of terror and privation. Some, like Gresbeck, had entertained doubts about Anabaptism from the beginning. Others, like the oddly named young Danish nobleman Turban Bill, were spies for the Bishop. And still others were hapless former believers who made fatal errors.

Turban Bill had allowed himself to be captured during the attack of the previous August. After "converting" to Anabaptism, he had worked his way into the confidence of the young king, who, born a bastard to a peasant woman, must have retained a primitive awe of inherited as opposed to self-administered nobility. In April Bill disappeared without warning, arousing Jan's suspicions; these were confirmed when a young woman who had been a prostitute, Margaret Tunneken, admitted under torture that she had stolen money from the city chancellery for Bill and had given him a letter to the Bishop begging for mercy for herself. Another young woman, Anna Hoenes, said she had given Bill eight guilders for assistance. And a third, Else Drier, admitted that she had known of Bill's activities.

The three women were taken to the Cathedral Square. The first two were beheaded by Master Niland, who declared with satisfaction that God had chosen the right kind of work for him. The third woman, however, was a special case. Else Drier was the mistress of Bernard Knipperdolling—not one of his five wives, as she would have been if she had not been a prostitute before her conversion, but the woman to whom he turned for comfort and support as well as for sexual favors. Accused now and condemned to die for treason, she turned on Knipperdolling, who stood beside the executioner. It was he, she shouted, he, the great Knipperdolling, who was the traitor, since he had been her lover and was now prepared to watch her die. Knipperdolling had earlier ordered his first—that is, his original—wife, Martha, to stand in the Cathedral Square for two hours holding a sword above her own neck for displeasing him. Now, hearing himself publicly exposed and reviled by a whore, the enraged merchant tore the sword from the hand of Master Niland and cut off the head of his mistress himself.

The carnage continued as treachery, real or perceived, was punished. Jan's queen, Divara, inadvertently caused the death of a young man in her retinue, Sander Busch, by giving him a ring which, when the king saw it and learned its source, cost the boy his head. Another of her servants, called Tall Albert, was responsible for tending the few remaining cows in the city herd. The herd was pastured in a meadow beyond the outer moat, safely under the guns of the roundel during the day and brought each evening back into the city. Albert tried to purchase his freedom and forgiveness from the Bishop by driving the cows toward the nearest blockhouse. Jan personally executed him. Henry Graes's wife, who had, surprisingly, not suffered after his treason was revealed, was now put to death, with another woman, on charges of stealing bread.

A tailor, Claes Northorn, was executed because a letter he wrote to the Bishop offering to reveal a secret entrance to the city was intercepted. Northorn was tortured until he revealed the extent of his plans, then condemned to die. He had sufficient courage, according to Gresbeck's account, to taunt Jan, saying, "Who selected you as king? What about your promise to die if we were still under siege by Easter? You'll soon sit yourself for God's judgment, you damned bloodhound!" "Do you think you will be there to see that happen?" Jan scoffed, and struck off his head. The rest of Jan's followers then leaped upon the body and cut it into twelve pieces, which were nailed on the city gates. The head was placed on a long stake on top of the Cathedral. "The heart and liver," as might be expected, Gresbeck scornfully says, "were eaten by a Hollander."

Jan's terror tactics were relatively selective, directed mostly against the few who had the courage or the folly to resist him openly. The hunger that could drive people to cannibalism was far more widespread and even more difficult for Jan to deal with than treason. Already, in addition to Henry Graes's wife and her friend, a woman had been executed for taking more than her allotted portion of horseflesh from the public butcher shop, and a ten-year-old boy had been hanged—twice, because the rope broke the first time—for stealing apples from a fruit stall in the market.

By mid-May, thousands of people were facing starvation. The king and his court continued to dine well, however, because all the produce from the private plots had been appropriated for the palace and for the approximately eight hundred armed men assigned to the city's defense (all that were left after deaths, illness, and, in particular, desertion). For everyone else, even the coarse barley used for making bread was now almost gone. The cattle that had cost Claes Northorn his life had been eaten. The remaining horses had been killed and butchered, a sure sign that the promised escape through the enemy lines was no longer even conceivable. During the preceding summer, when one hundred and twenty horses had been slaughtered, their heads and tails and innards had been buried. Now everything was eaten, including hooves and intestines. Every cat and dog had long since vanished into the cooking pots, and the mice and rats that would have gone to the cats were caught and fried in the tallow from candles. River snakes, hedgehogs, sparrows, anything that moved was devoured. People ate the green bark and tender shoots of the willows that grew by the river Aa, and they ate grass. They ate chalk. They ate dried cow dung. One woman ate her still-born baby.

"Terrible maladies" resulting from famine, according to Kerssenbrück, afflicted the starving people; "their flesh decomposed and rotted" on their bones; "their skin become livid, their lips withdrawn; their eyes, fixed and round, stared from their sockets; they wandered around town, haggard and hideous, like mummies, and died by the hundred in the streets. The king had the bodies cast into large common graves, where they were dug up at night and devoured by the starving. Night and day the houses and streets resounded with moans and sobbing cries. Young men and old, women and children sank into the darkest despair."

In this dreadful emergency, King Jan tightened his hold on the allegiance of his true supporters and found ways to rid himself of the rest. He accomplished the first goal by announcing a reward for his most faithful followers: he divided up the whole of Germany and gave it to a dozen men who until a year before had been simple folk. The shopkeeper Johann Denker became the Prince of Saxony; the tailor Bernard Moer now owned Braunschweig; Herman Redeker, the shoemaker who had been one of the first citizens of Münster to support Jan, would replace Count von Juelich as the ruler of Cleves; a coppersmith named Leddanus would become the new Archbishop of Cologne; and so on. Each of the dozen new princes and archbishops and counts was given command of twenty-four men for the final defense and ultimate battle with the Bishop and the current holders of those positions, after which they would be free to claim their rewards.

There is an almost whimsical quality of make-believe to Jan's behavior at this point that some later apologists, especially the Communists in the nineteenth century, would find perversely appealing. What a clever parody of the very system that he was attacking! And *quelle justesse!* How different, after all, were King Jan and Emperor Charles V in their talents, their principles, their behavior? What did Jan van Leyden do that was worse than the deeds of the Prince-Bishop? Give the devil his due, they say; he did not lack for inventiveness or courage.

The most vivid illustration of the antagonists' essential sameness in one critical respect is provided by their approaches to the problem of dealing with starving people. Jan's solution was to tell those who wanted to leave that they were free to go. But they had to understand that he could not forgive them for deserting his holy cause; under no circumstances would they be permitted to return to Münster, no matter what the Bishop did to them. Despite his warning, hundreds of people, beginning in mid-April, passed through the city gates toward the Bishop's army.

But the Bishop was not eager to receive the refugees. He had ordered the entire city to surrender, not just a part of it. Besides, he knew that these hungry mouths would deplete Jan's supplies and shorten his resistance if he could not get rid of them. The Bishop ordered his soldiers to shoot the men and turn the women and children back into the strip between the city's outer wall and his own cordon. Four miles in circumference and a few hundred yards wide, what a few months before had been a pleasant medieval tapestry of farms, woods, and tiny villages was now a stripped and ruined wasteland of shattered trees, rain-filled wagon ruts, and debris from months of shelling.

The Bishop's chief commander, Count Ulrich von Dhaun, protested. It was against all conscience to kill these unarmed men, and pitiful and terrible beyond words to let women and children die of hunger before their very eyes. He wanted to send Jan a message that he would be permitted to take the refugees back within the comparative safety of the walls, even though Jan's men had already barred the doors to the refugees and fired on them when they pleaded to be allowed to return. The Bishop ignored von Dhaun, instead executing several prisoners and tying them to posts and wagon wheels that were placed in front of the city gates as a message and a warning: if the rebels surrendered immediately, the innocent would be spared. Otherwise, they would all end up as these had. On April 26, four more refugees were beheaded and their bodies displayed in a similar manner.

By early May, up to three hundred people had left the city; by June 3, the totals were an estimated four hundred men, four hundred women, and a great many children. The Bishop's soldiers were killing between twenty to fifty men per day, as well as a total of fifty renegades from their own side who had deserted to the Anabaptists, only to find conditions there intolerable. The women and children huddled against the barricades, where some of the soldiers' wives and mistresses took pity on them, throwing them bread, and bringing a number of the children into the blockhouse. The soldiers themselves, full of bitter memories of earlier humiliations at the hands of these same people, were less inclined to show mercy.

Von Dhaun begged Philip of Hesse for advice. Act according to your conscience and your reason, Philip advised the general; perhaps the Bishop could be persuaded that refugees could be held safely in small groups, and some of them might be able to impart valuable information if they were allowed to live. But the Bishop was now absent from the scene, having taken to his bed with a fever. Von Dhaun asked the Bishop's council for advice; like Philip, the council left it to the general, as a man of honor, to make the right choice.

Finally, in early June, the refugees were released from their purgatory between the antagonists' walls. All of the women were brought to the Wolbeck house of the Bishop's most reliable man, Eberhard von Morrien, to be held until a decision could be reached concerning their fate. The foreign women would be sent home after the local authorities had been alerted, to keep them from making trouble, while the rest—local women and those from other German cities and states—would be held under guard until the city fell. Philip declined to offer advice, other than to suggest that von Dhaun accept the word of the women that they would cause no more trouble and let them go free. The council insisted on giving the responsibility for the refugees, including the possibility that some would be condemned to death, to the Bishop. As for the men, it had to be determined if they had been forced to join the Anabaptists or had been willing volunteers, but this process would have to wait until after the conquest.

In all this time there had been no response to Gresbeck's letter to Count Manderscheid, and by late May the young carpenter was desperate. He had been able to keep his mother and his wife and her family alive by pilfering extra rations from the guards' allotment. Although the captain of the guard, formerly one of the Bishop's men, was friendly and seemed sympathetic to his plight, Gresbeck was afraid that if he was found stealing soldiers' rations he would be executed. Already the terror had reached into the lives of all, even as the once meticulous discipline on the watches began to disintegrate.

The erratic nature of the terror, mixed as it was with odd moments of lenience, was especially frightening. One of the soldiers had approached Jan as the king sat on his throne in the Cathedral Square, his head in his hands in obvious though uncharacteristic melancholy. "I must have food!" the soldier cried, clutching at Jan's arm, and those watching were sure the man would die on the spot. But Jan only smiled wanly and walked slowly into his palace. To Gresbeck this sudden change of character was more alarming than the king's previously predictable fury. He determined to leave the city with or without a sign from the Cleves Blockhouse.

He must have somehow signaled his intent to the captain of the guard—who himself, as he then confided to Gresbeck, was planning to go back to the Bishop he had deserted the previous autumn. They would go together; half of the twelve men on his watch, a total of six, including themselves, were ready to take their chances with the Bishop rather than stay with the blood-drenched king and his zealous apostles. Gresbeck must have felt reassured, for this young professional soldier from Frankfurt was clearly a man who knew how to stay alive. His given name was Johann Nagel. Though small, less than five feet in height, he was aggressive and hot-tempered, and his behavior belied his childish nickname of Hansel Eck, "little Hans in the corner." Little Hans was constantly in trouble for gambling, drinking, and brawling. Fortunately, he was also very good at his job, constructing von Dhaun's siege ramparts; and, though not formally a cavalryman, a *Reiter*, he sat a horse like a dwarfish centaur and could lance a coin-sized ring on the first pass.

The previous October Hansel had started a brawl while playing dice in a tavern and "knocked a comrade bloody." Thrown into the stockade, he escaped the same night and fled toward the city gate, pursued by shouting soldiers. The guards fired on the pursuers and allowed Hansel to enter. He told King Jan that he would rather live with the wildest beasts in the forest than return to the Bishop's army. He had valuable information for the king about the Bishop's plans for the blockhouses and their linking cordon, and he could help the king improve his own defenses. Jan approved of the little man's spirit and was heartened by his desertion of the clearly weakened Bishop. His great skill in the medieval jousts in which the tailor-king was prone to indulge that autumn and his cocky charm led the king to make Hansel Eck a member of his inner circle, and until recently the young turncoat had lived very comfortably as a part of the king's palace entourage. Now, though, he had been reassigned to guard duty, which was boring and dangerous at the same time, and he had had enough.

Shortly before midnight on Sunday, May 23, Henry Gresbeck, Hansel Eck, and four other renegade watchmen quietly left their posts on the outer wall at the Holy Cross Gate and slipped into the moat. The other six men on watch were dozing in the earthen bunker that they had fashioned near the base of the outer gate. Though this was forbidden on pain of death, the long period of somnolence on the Bishop's side of the wall and a feeling of lassitude and indifference had undermined the once formidable discipline of the guards. Especially in bad weather they burrowed into their bunkers and left it to the next guard post to sound the alarm, if one was needed. Spring thunderstorms had swirled around the region for days, and clouds now obscured the moon. As the men paddled across the moat, the wind came up and shredded the clouds; shouts from the city walls revealed that they had been seen: "Come back, brothers, come back!" "They've discovered us!" Hansel said to Gresbeck as the other four soldiers began scrambling through the grass toward the nearest part of the Bishop's ramparts. "In that case," Gresbeck replied, watching them go, "I'm not going that way. I will make for the Cleves Blockhouse. Come with me if you like." They heard the trumpets announcing the changing of the Bishop's guard, a time when the watchmen were always distracted and movement was easier. Hans disappeared with the other soldiers, leaving Gresbeck alone.

The wind died, and the night grew so dark that he became lost; cold and frightened, he groped his way toward the Cleves Blockhouse. An hour before dawn he thought he had found it, a dark bulk dimly outlined against the black sky. He waited next to the deep ditch that surrounded the blockhouse for the sun to come up. Behind him lay the kingdom of Jan van Leyden, and certain death if he now tried to return. Before him lay the soldiers of the Bishop, who had already killed hundreds of men who, like himself, had tried to surrender. In a masterpiece of understatement, Gresbeck says he was "lonely and afraid."

At first light he stood upright to reveal himself to the unseen guards he knew were watching. "Come forward!" ordered the guards. "Come back!" shouted the Anabaptist guards from across the moat. Gresbeck descended into the ditch that surrounded the blockhouse and climbed painfully through thornbushes toward the soldiers, whose weapons remained fixed on him. When he reached the top, he could see two soldiers waiting outside the blockhouse by a barricade at the top of the ditch. Crouching before them in a thicket of thorns, half-dead from hunger, cold, and fear, he could see the guards looking curiously down at him and hear them talking. They were discussing his future. "Let's shoot him," one said. No, the other replied, they would "take him prisoner to see what he had to say. He's just a youngster; we'll let him live."

"Dear comrades," Gresbeck pleaded, "I was a soldier once too, like you. I beg you to take me to your captain." First tell us, they said, how things were in the city. Very bad, Gresbeck replied; everyone was starving and the Anabaptists were going crazy, killing people right and left. That was why he had escaped. "Please," he begged the soldiers again, "please take me prisoner." The guards thrust their long spears downward. "Take hold," they commanded. He did so, each hand grasping a spear just above the sharp pointed blade. The soldiers yanked him up through his thornbush cover to where they could grasp him by both his hands and by one leg and heaved him over the barrier.

Now they will surely kill me, Gresbeck thought, and he waited on his hands and knees for the fatal blow. "Get up," the older guard said, "we're not going to kill you." But they made him strip, to be sure he carried no hidden knives, before they led him inside the block-house. They summoned the captain of the guard and said they had captured this fellow and chosen not to kill him because of his youth. "Let him enter," the captain said, looking at Gresbeck. "You can thank God that you are here and that you are still alive. All the others who have tried to surrender have been killed." He ordered food and beer to be brought for Gresbeck. After he had had his fill, Gresbeck begged permission to speak to the captain. Another man had escaped with him, he said, a former soldier who had been captured. He was called Hans Nagel and Gresbeck hoped they would take him prisoner and not kill him. The captain sent some men out to search; one of them came back shortly to report that he had asked around about Hans Nagel and the word was out that he was a traitor. If he was caught, he would be sliced into a hundred pieces.

Before noon two senior officers appeared and conducted Gresbeck to the command headquarters at Wolbeck, where he was taken to see Count Ulrich von Dhaun and Count Oberstein. It was a cold reception; since Hille Feyken's attempt to kill the Bishop, all purported turncoats from the City of Zion were regarded as potential murderers. These two august commanders loathed the sight of the Anabaptists who had so long resisted them. Young Henry Gresbeck, we can be sure, was shaking with fright as he tried to persuade them that what he said was the truth. Indeed, he said, he knew a way through the city wall through which the soldiers might enter. The disciplined watches that had kept the city safe had broken down under the press of hunger and terror. It would take no more than a few men to overpower the guards and open the gate to the entire attacking army.

Gresbeck never learned, or at any rate does not tell us, exactly what had happened to his letter to Count Manderscheid, but then everything happening was confusing, including his own situation. The narrative that describes his actions is written in the third person about an unnamed "citizen" who escapes with Hansel Eck. Written several years after the events in Münster, it remained anonymous for centuries, until a nineteenth-century scholar put all the pieces together and confirmed Gresbeck as the author. Count Manderscheid, who saves the "citizen," is presumed to have been the former master addressed in Gresbeck's signed letter, but he is not named in it and he never saw it—or, at least, he was not the first to see it, the Bishop was. These are not the inevitable confusions that arise from the passage of time but deliberate obfuscations built into Gresbeck's narrative to protect himself. His Victorian editor likes the personality of the adventurous young carpenter that shines through his story, finding in him the voice of the people, full of common sense and shrewd observation, much of it confirmed by other sources. That such an inherently straightforward person felt compelled to take such precautions indicates the hazardous complexity of his world.

Presumably Count Manderscheid had by this time vouched for Gresbeck, but the commanders were still unsure they could trust him. They had him taken to a large cell, where he was given a quantity of mud and sand and edged tools. He had the next two days, he was told, to construct a scale model of the defenses of Münster. Every gate, every protective ditch, every gun emplacement, every guard position had to be represented. Henry Gresbeck had grown up in Münster and had been involved in the city's defense for more than a year. He was, as his narrative reveals, keenly observant. He had made his living as a carpenter, shaping cabinets, benches, and chairs out of raw wood. And he was doubtless very eager to please. He worked for two solid days on the model, after which the commanders questioned him on its various aspects. Of special interest to them was the approach by way of the Holy Cross Gate where Gresbeck had stood guard.

In order to be certain that he was telling the truth, Wilhelm Steding and another officer, Lenz von der Horst, took Gresbeck, still under close guard and in chains, to the moat that night. The chains were removed and, while the others waited, Gresbeck "lowered himself into the moat, swam across it, and crept through the underbrush to the wall." None of the Anabaptists on the watch detected him; he disappeared through the wall and in a few minutes came out again. He swam across the moat and stood before Steding and the others. "If we were armed and ready for an attack with enough soldiers," he said, "we could take the city right now." The officers concurred with his judgment. "And thus did the citizen climb out of the moat yet a second time toward the blockhouse," Gresbeck records; but this time it was finally and abundantly clear to the Junker Wilhelm Steding that he was telling the truth, and that he had all but delivered the city to the Bishop. He did not have to put the chains back on, and was no longer a prisoner.

A few days later Gresbeck rode with Steding to Bevergen for a conference with the general staff. As they approached the meeting site Steding asked Gresbeck if he knew what had happened to his friend Johann Nagel. He had heard nothing of Hansel since they had escaped two weeks earlier, Gresbeck said. "Where do you think he might be?" Steding asked. "I barely know where I am myself," the sorely tried young carpenter replied with some asperity, "or where I'm heading. How should I know where Hans has taken himself, or whether he's alive or dead?" Then Steding said, "I will tell you the truth now. We are going to meet him in Bevergen. Hans has already recommended the same plan of attack as you have." The two of them would meet with the general staff and between them confirm the approach they had independently recommended.

So "little Hans in the corner," far from being sliced into a hundred pieces, was now involved with the general staff in planning the final attack on the New Zion. How did this come to be? According to one version of his story, Hans had been a double agent from the beginning; his fight, imprisonment, and flight from the stockade to Münster had been part of a plan concocted by Wilhelm Steding after the failed August attack, in order to get another man inside the city walls. But it seems more likely that he was just one of those rogues who usually find a way to survive. Kerssenbrück, who knew nothing of Gresbeck or his narrative when he wrote his own account thirty years later, says simply that Hans escaped with another man and made his way to his former commander, Count Meinhardt von Hamm, and gave him the information necessary to take the city with only a few men.

And so it was that at the end of May 1535, after fifteen months of expense, humiliation, and frustration, Franz von Waldeck was handed the virtual keys to the city and the destruction of the Company of Christ. His army was not at its earlier strength, numbering now only three thousand men. But his effective enemy amounted to fewer than a thousand men, burdened by thousands of starving and dispirited old people, women, and children. He had the certainty of surprise. And yet he would linger for nearly another full month before launching his final and long-awaited attack.

11

ATTACK

Then shall they deliver you up to be afflicted, and shall kill you: and ye shall be hated of all nations for my name's sake.

—Matthew 24:9

THE PRINCE-BISHOP, HAVING been twice burned in attempts to take the city, may have delayed now in launching his attack because of news brought by Henry Gresbeck of a formidable final weapon developed by the Anabaptists—at the suggestion of none other than Henry Graes, the schoolmaster of many talents. Graes, when he was still a true believer, had persuaded Jan that he should order the city's blacksmiths and wheelrights to build a "rolling fortress" of armored wagons with which the Anabaptists could break through the Bishop's lines to join up with the supporters still anticipated from the Netherlands. The prototype for the wagons had been completed the previous autumn. It was big enough to hold six men. The wheels were rimmed with iron, their spokes turned from ancient, rock-hard oaken flooring from city houses. The shafts, staves, and side panels were wrapped and covered in flattened iron. The wagon was large enough to carry a small cannon, as well as a new weapon designed to allow six or eight of the gigantic, primitive muskets called *Hackenbüchse* ("arquebus" in French; "harquebus" in English) to be stacked like a horizontal pipe organ and fired at the same time. Special protection was designed for the six horses needed to pull the wagon, but even if they were disabled the smiths had designed a portable spiked metal fence that could be thrown up around it.

By April 1535, there were sixteen wagons standing ready to go in the Cathedral Square. These were, as a later account records, "dangerous war machines, fully armored as they were, behind their protective walls, with cannons, artillery pieces, and their frightening organ pipes. It is hard to imagine that soldiers and horsemen faced by these machine could keep their wits about them or that their own artillery could keep these moving targets in their sights long enough to have an effect." Henry Gresbeck, overwhelmed by the war wagons when he first saw them, had been convinced that if God did not take a hand against the Anabaptists, nobody could stop them from making their escape.

It was true that escape was no longer a possibility. The supporting armies from the Netherlands that the wagons were to meet would never appear. Thanks to the information provided by Henry Graes, Jan van Geelen had been killed in Amsterdam, and three shiploads of other militants had been intercepted by the Duke of Guelders. And in any event, the horses needed to pull the wagons had all been eaten. The wagons remained as formidable weapons of defense, however, a veritable fortress within the city, King Jan's potential last redoubt.

The Bishop continued to hope for surrender in lieu of an expensive assault, but his own behavior toward those who had already surrendered, or tried to surrender, could not have been encouraging. Von Dhaun, seeing how ruthless the Bishop intended to be, had finally tried in vain to persuade the Anabaptists not to expel any more of their people. Jan replied that they were not forcing anybody to leave, and that the Bishop could do with them as he pleased.

Final estimates of the numbers involved were fifteen hundred men and women expelled or departed from Münster, not counting numerous children. Of these, between six hundred and seven hundred unarmed men were killed in the field or executed in a four-week period. The Bishop had far too much work for his own executioner to handle, including killing fourteen women, so he engaged the services of executioners from Osnabrück and Arnsberg. They came willingly. But a third man, from the city of Bielefeld, was repelled by von Waldeck's evident lust for blood. He responded to the Bishop's command to report for duty by saying he would rather give up his job entirely than participate in such a shameless bloodbath.

Being faced with a Bishop so brutal that he is rebuked by a professional executioner understandably hardened the resistance of Jan and his supporters; as rebels and heretics they could expect no mercy. Neither were they inclined to grant it to their own disenchanted followers, as the story of Elizabeth Wandscheer, perhaps the most famous to emerge from the long saga of the Company of Christ, would vividly demonstrate.

Elizabeth was the blond and beautiful daughter of Bernard Wandscheer, a blacksmith. She had been married at nineteen years of age by force after the king's decree of polygamy to a man named Reiner Hardwick and had tried unsuccessfully to run away from him, through the city gate. Hardwick had then died, and her father had arranged for her to be married to an old man, cadaverous, pockmarked, and bald, one August Cloterbernd. One day in the late fall of 1534, as the king was holding court in the Cathedral Square, Elizabeth was brought to him for judgment, arms bound behind her, by her father and her new husband. Bernard Wandscheer complained that his daughter had been disobedient to him and that he should be allowed to punish her. August Cloterbernd went further. He said that Elizabeth, though she was his pledged wife, had told him she would sooner sleep in the bushes than with him. He asked that King Jan pronounce on this rebellious woman an appropriate judgment. Jan asked Elizabeth if she had married Cloterbernd of her own free will. She asked, according to Helmut Paulus's version of the story, how anybody could think that a young woman might want to marry such a stinking old goat; she would rather be three feet under the ground. The king reprimanded the old man and the girl's father for imposing their will on her unfairly, and had her imprisoned in the Rosenthal for disobedience. A few days later she became his tenth wife. Beautiful, spirited, and brave, Elizabeth was Jan's favorite wife, after Queen Divara.

But in early May, Elizabeth had grown difficult. Accounts varied. Some said she had been disturbed by the sad fate of the refugees Jan had turned away from the city gates. Others said she had protested the starvation that was evident all around them while she and the other members of the court were allowed to eat all they wished. Whatever the cause, the various accounts agree that Elizabeth reproached Jan for his inhumanity and demanded to be allowed to leave him and the city. Outraged at her ingratitude and her temerity, Jan led her to the Market Square and, before the other wives and the assembled throng that had been summoned, condemned her to death.

Helmut Paulus, adding a novelist's insight to the documents describing this incident, imagines Elizabeth's last moments as she hears the king say, " 'God has commanded that you must die. This is the same test that Abraham faced; I cannot escape it.' How strange those words sound to the young woman. Her lips draw back in scorn, but her eyes are shocked when she looks into the face of the king who stands before her, his back to the crowd. His eyes gleam with animal savagery; his lips are pulled back from his teeth. In great fear she tries to stretch out her hands against the truth now revealed in his face that a mask had previously hidden, but her hands are bound behind her. She wants to scream, but she is gagged. She sees how the king takes the sword from the hand of Master Niland. Her hands are unbound and she is lifted with inhuman strength and forced to kneel with her head on a block. She clasps her hands before her as she hears King Jan reproach the other wives. 'Why don't you sing? Sing!' She hears the frightened voices of the women, weakly, like an exhalation, singing 'In Excelsis Deo,' 'Glory to God in the highest'. She sees a flash of light, feels a terrible pain, and drops into a dark sea. All now is peaceful and dark."

Several graphic sketches of the king dancing with his other wives around the headless corpse of Elizabeth Wandscheer have come down to us as perhaps the most vivid documentation of his depravity, and it was this incident more than any other that led serious observers to see Jan as indeed the devil in human shape. But perhaps the true devil in this scene is the one omitted by Paulus in his reconstruction—the former Catholic priest, Bernard Rothmann, who looked on as the king and his court danced and said, "Glory to God in the highest!"

On June 8, a delegation from Prince Philip was allowed by King Jan to approach the Judefeld Gate with a final offer to settle the siege without an assault—so that, as a modern writer puts it, the Bishop could avoid appearing bloodthirsty. Jan met the delegation, accompanied by Rothmann, Knipperdolling, and the Elders. The delegation handed Jan a theological tract opposing the Kingdom of Münster and asked him if he would be willing to give up the city and beg the Bishop for mercy. "Ask me in a year," the king laughed.

Count von Dhaun ordered a final reconnaissance of the secret approach to the city by Gresbeck and Hansel, along with a dozen officers and men. Once again, Gresbeck proved that they could enter the city undetected, and the commanders began to set in motion the plans for their final attack. It would take place on the night of June 22. The officers and men were promised their fair share of the booty and told to prepare themselves for battle. This time, however, made wise by experience, Count von Dhaun announced that he was forbidding, on pain of death, the sale and drinking of liquor, including beer and wine.

All through the afternoon and evening of the summer solstice, June 22, heavy thunderstorms rolled over Münster, pounding the city with sheets of wind-driven rain mixed with hail the size of hen's eggs. The outer-wall guards were driven from their exposed positions into the earthen bunkers at the base of the wall where, cold and hungry, they huddled by a charcoal fire and slept, waiting out the storm. If they had been at their posts, the intermittent brilliant flashes of lightning would have revealed unusual activity near the blockhouses beyond the outer moat. Scores of peasants, impressed as laborers for the occasion, were unloading storming ladders and portable sectioned bridges brought from the armory at Wolbeck. Five hundred soldiers, volunteers who would again be paid twice their usual wage for daring to use the ladders, watched and waited, cold and wet but sober, for the signal to attack.

An hour before midnight, Gresbeck and Hansel Eck wrestled one of the bridges into position along the edge of the moat. Gresbeck secured one end of a rope to the bridge and slipped into the cold water. Tugging the heavy coil of rope, he paddled to the other side, climbed out, and fixed the rope with an iron hook to a post in the wall. The twenty-foot bridge, two sections hinged at the middle, had swung with the mild current so that it lay parallel to the opposite bank. Hansel pushed the end of the bridge away from him with a long spear. Gresbeck pulled it toward him and secured it by snubbing the rope to the post. Hansel ran across the bridge, carrying a ladder that he propped against the wall.

Wilhelm Steding, who would command the raid, then led thirty-five of his soldiers across the bridge, one at a time, as Gresbeck stood chest-high at the edge of the moat to keep it steady. The only sound was the creaking of the bridge and the rustle of muffled swords brushing against leather jerkins and body armor; all communication was done by sign and low whispers. The soldiers brought with them several other ladders to place beside Hansel's. Gresbeck was left behind to watch as they followed Hansel up the wall.

The guard post on the wall was empty. The soldiers climbed down and surprised the dozen sleeping guards in their bunker, killing them all instantly with quick knife thrusts. Through the pelting rain, they dashed across the stone bridge that spanned the inner moat toward a small door at the base of the Holy Cross Gate. Hansel opened this door with a key that he had copied earlier. Inside this door, which opened into a tunnel that led to the gate tower, Steding's men found only one guard, a frightened furrier named Bernard Schulte who quickly revealed the password for the day to the soldiers: "Earth."

So far no alarms had sounded. Steding sent a man back to the outer moat, ordering the rest of his force to cross over. When the bridge broke in the middle, the back-up bridge was put into service, with Gresbeck again swimming the moat. This would be his final contribution to the attack, he realized sadly as he watched the last of the three hundred and fifty soldiers disappear up the ladders and over the wall. He wanted to go with them but he was still a prisoner, not as fully trusted as he had earlier thought. He was to remain where he was, without weapon or armor, alone again between opposing forces. One of the soldiers, taking pity on the shivering carpenter, tossed him his Spanish cloak.

Beyond the outer wall waited the main force of Ulrich von Dhaun, about three thousand men. The plan was for Steding to advance silently, in three separate formations, to the Cathedral, which had been turned into the city arsenal, and to capture it. The Anabaptists, weakened from hunger and frightened, would presumably be thrown into a panic by the loss of their armory and by the sudden onslaught of four hundred assault troops—not more than eight hundred men in the city were now capable of fighting and most of them would be asleep. Anticipating opposition from no more than two hundred panicked defenders, Steding would then open the Holy Cross Gate and others to von Dhaun's main force and the city would be theirs.

Steding's men quietly made their way through the Overwater Church Square and across the small stone bridge that led to the Cathedral Square. They overwhelmed the guards at the Cathedral and secured several cannons within, which they wheeled to the entrance and aimed onto the square. It was not yet midnight—all of this had happened in less than an hour—and so far all had gone well; they had only to leave a few men behind to guard the armory and then to return to open the gates to von Dhaun. Within minutes, however, Steding heard alarm trumpets sounding and saw a large force of armed Anabaptists, more than twice their own number, charging across the square under the protection of cannon fire from St. Margaret's Chapel. Steding trained his captured cannons on the chapel but the balls bounced harmlessly from the heavy stone walls into the street.

Rather than be trapped in the Cathedral, Steding led his men into the winding streets of the south quarter, fighting a delaying action. He assumed that when von Dhaun heard the sounds of heavy fighting and saw that the gates were not swinging open, he would comprehend the advance force's danger and send his men through the tunnel that Steding had used. But Steding had erred seriously. Known as a kind and forgiving friend but a terrible enemy, he was one of the Bishop's best soldiers. He had nonetheless failed to leave a small force behind by the door to the Holy Cross Gate to aid von Dhaun's assault. The open, unattended door had been discovered, as had the bodies of the overwhelmed watchmen at the outer wall, as Steding was securing the Cathedral.

Von Dhaun, in the meantime, heard the fighting within the city but hesitated to attack. One account suggests he feared that Hansel had led Steding into a trap, and that Gresbeck was in on it. He was afraid that yet a third disastrous assault was in the making, and he refused to move without assurance that he had not been betrayed.

Steding was now indeed trapped in a blind alley off Margaret Street, but through no fault of Hansel or Gresbeck. The intrepid four hundred were cornered and desperate to escape, suffering not only the bullets and arrows of Jan's men but the indignity of pots and chairs and bed-warming bricks dropped by the women and children who lived in the apartments above them. Steding forced his way through a nearby house and out the back door; leaving half his men behind, he took the other half and surprised the attacking Anabaptists from the rear. Thinking that Steding had been reinforced, Jan's men fled. Disaster had been narrowly averted.

Steding took up a more secured secure defensive position, waiting for von Dhaun's appearance or a second Anabaptist assault. Neither occurred. Instead, he heard Jan van Leyden's voice identify himself as king; he was, Jan said, declaring an unconditional cease-fire. He wanted to negotiate. Steding considered his situation. It was now well after midnight. The storm had ended and the fighting was at an ebb; it was too dark to see without torches, and anyone carrying a torch was a sure target. In the distance they could hear the women shrieking defiance from the walls to the waiting army.

Steding agreed to the cease-fire. Jan said he would let them all go free if they would kneel before him and beg his forgiveness. Steding stalled for time, saying he needed to look after his wounded. He sent his young aide, Johann von Twickel, on a special mission while he pretended to negotiate. It was still four hours until dawn.

As first light broke over the city, Jan and Steding were still negotiating. Then, in the distance, from the vicinity of the Jodefeld Gate, both sides could hear a single voice loudly calling out. Johann von Twickel was on top of the inner wall, waving the Bishop's flag and shouting to the gray, massed forces of von Dhaun who were waiting beyond the outher moat to attack. "To Waldeck!" he yelled, "To Waldeck! Münster is ours! Charge! Charge!" Moved at last to action, von Dhaun's men easily scaled the once-formidable walls as the women left their boiling vats of pitch and lime in a panic. Steding's men, hearing the commotion at the gates, charged Jan's forces as they ran to meet the new and greater danger. Caught between Steding and von Dhaun, the Anabaptists broke and fled. The discipline that had enabled the Company of Christ to repel the Bishop for nearly a year and a half had collapsed within minutes, as though a bubble had popped. The siege of Münster was over.

But the fighting was not. Most of the noncombatants fled into their houses, but there were around eight hundred armed men to hunt down and kill, and individually or in groups they put up a stiff resistance. Tile Bussenmeister, the Cyclops, single-handedly held the Aa Bridge against an onslaught of soldiers with spears, halberds, and knives until he was finally overwhelmed and his body thrown into the river. When the Market Square was taken, four defenders held the tower of St. Lambert's Church; soldiers fought their way up the narrow tower steps and killed three of them; the fourth threw himself from the tower onto the spears of the soldiers below. As the fighting swirled through the streets of the city, hundreds of men died rather than surrender.

Finally a force of two hundred retreated behind a formidable barricade in the Cathedral Square; it was constructed out of the sixteen armored war wagons that had so impressed Henry Gresbeck, and the defenders were under the capable command of Henry Krechting, Jan's chancellor. They had enough ammunition for their cannons and their organ pipes to hold out for at least a day, and to make von Dhaun and Steding pay dearly for killing them. Steding offered to let Krechting and his men leave the city unharmed if they would give up their weapons.

Both the offer and the acceptance of it, which came almost immediately, seem surprising. Even more so is the surreptitious passing of ten gold pieces to Krechting by the Bishop's supreme commander, Johann von Raesfeld; they had once been comrades in arms in foreign wars, and had participated together in the great Sack of Rome in 1527. Krechting and twenty-five of his men were escorted to the gate and allowed to leave. The others, who presumably could have done so, chose to return to their homes to say farewell to their wives and were cut down in the streets by enraged soldiers who were killing anything that moved.

These soldiers had waited for sixteen months through summer heat and winter cold, forgoing pay and the possibility of booty elsewhere. The Bishop had required them all to swear that they would abide by the articles of war; these required little of them beyond not injuring pregnant women and those who had just delivered children, or members of the clergy—not a category intended to include the Anabaptist preachers. Any booty had to be turned over to commanding officers for later distribution and sharing in lots. But to their dismay and their fury, the *Landsknechte* found little loot besides clothing and kitchen utensils. Then one of the soldiers who had been held as a prisoner revealed the existence of a treasure trove of gold and silver in the city chancellery. After torturing the keepers of the treasury into revealing its precise location, the soldier and his friends led fifty looters to the City Hall. Steding stopped them and executed seven of the ringleaders on the spot. The rest were stripped, bound with ropes and covered with white shirts, then escorted out of the city; their clothes were returned to them and they were sent on their way, minus their fair share of the booty.

They were not much out of pocket, as it happened: the share per man, after all was said and done, was sixteen guilders per man, not much of a bonus for a year's time. (Sixteen guilders would equal about eight hundred of today's dollars.) They found no money hoards in the houses of the Anabaptists; other than some silver, most of the money had been sent out of the city with the apostles in December and with Jan van Geelen in January to raise troops and to buy weapons.

Realizing that they had wasted a year waiting to steal an empty purse, the soldiers took out their frustrations on their helpless antagonists, running wild. "The murder was too terrible to describe," in the words of one contemporary writer, Dietrich Lilie. Kerssenbrück has no such reservations, regarding what happened as poetic justice: "Bernard Swerte, who had a house full of children, Magnus Kohüs, master of the royal wardrobe, and many others were rooted out of their hiding places and run through in the alleys with knives and swords," he says. Johann Estmann from Warendorf, a heavy, gray-haired man, claimed that he had remained in Münster only because of illness, and would have been allowed to live except that his brothers in Christ betrayed him to the soldiers.

Also meeting a sad but fitting end was the former *Bürgermeister* Herman Tilbeck, the respected leader who had betrayed the city first by refusing to pass along the Bishop's offer to defend it against the Anabaptists and who later led the counterattack against Mollenheck.

Tilbeck was found hiding in an outhouse by the Agidii Cloister. He was stabbed to death and his body dumped into the cesspool, a burial fit for a dead donkey, according to Kerssenbrück.

The butcher Johann Boventorp was fixed to a pillory with an iron collar and cloven in two. The tailor Gerd Kibbenbrock, former co-mayor, the father of eight children, was dragged from his house by the Market Square and killed. Henry Sanctus, a coppersmith named recently by Jan as the Prince of Mainz, was beheaded in front of the City Hall. Evart Riemensneider, in whose tavern Jan Matthias had received the vision that sent him to his death, was found after a soldier billeted in his house discovered that his bread rations were disappearing in the night. A search found Riemensneider hiding on the roof with the former nun he had married and two other wives. He was executed the following week with one of the women and with his son, Jaspar.

The soldiers did obey the Bishop's strict orders to take the more important Anabaptists alive. The first to be captured was Bernard Krechting, Jan's chief of staff, hiding in the Agidii Cloister; despite his pleas to be allowed to die, he was thrown into prison. The nobleman Gerlach von Wullen, commander of the king's cavalry and of his bodyguard, was also captured; von Wullen had married the daughter of Christian Kerckering, whose other daughter had married the Bishop's bastard son Christoph. Christoph himself had fled in May. Von Wullen and Kerckering, recently appointed by Jan as "the Prince of Westphalia," represented special problems for the Bishop as members of the nobility, and were kept in separate confinement.

King Jan himself almost escaped, managing in the confusion of the last battle to reach the Agidii Gate. Popular accounts by the hundreds recount Jan's capture. Some depict him as cravenly deserting his people in their hour of greatest need, while Knipperdolling fought bravely in the Market Square for the entire day. Others have Jan bravely stepping forward when capture was inevitable, as opposed to the skulking Knipperdolling, who had vanished entirely, along with Bernard Rothmann. Helmut Paulus, in his modern version, has Jan pursued through his palace by a soldier on whom he turns and kills before he is captured. Paulus seems to have picked up and revised the account left by a soldier named Röchell, who later became a sexton in the

Cathedral when Herman Kerssenbrück was its schoolmaster and was constructing his account of the Anabaptist kingdom. According to Röchell, he entered the palace, von Buren's mansion, and chased Jan, waving his sword and shouting for him to stop, through the house and up to the top story. Jan closed the door of his chamber against his pursuer and hid behind it. When Röchell forced the door open and rushed into the room, Jan slipped from behind the door into the hallway and ran down a circular stairway to the street. In his panic Jan hurled his halberd at Röchell, which slowed the soldier down enough so that he lost sight of the king as he disappeared in the direction of the Agidii Gate. He was captured by Steding's men, who disregarded Jan's haughty command not to lay a hand on his royal person; then Ulrich von Dhaun, hearing of the capture, commanded Steding to turn his prize catch over to him.

Although Jan was the Bishop's primary antagonist, it was Bernard Rothmann, along with the merchant Knipperdolling, whom he blamed for inciting the city to rebellion in the first place. Rothmann's end, like his demon-driven life, remains a mystery. According to eye-witness reports, he had appeared in a white gown with a sword in his hand, like an Old Testament hero, to do battle. He was said to have received a spear thrust to the side, like Jesus. Anxious to assure himself that Rothmann was in fact dead, the Bishop later ordered the burial crews that were digging mass graves in the Cathedral Square to inspect each body before they stripped it and tumbled it into the ditch with the others. Rothmann failed to turn up, alive or dead.

A few days after the fall of the city, Ulrich von Dhaun had all the captured women, numbering more than three thousand, brought to the Cathedral Square. He told them that if they promised to abjure their heretical vows they would be free to go from the city, leaving whatever they still owned behind them. One exception was offered: if any of the women knew and would reveal the hiding place of Bernard Knipperdolling, still at large, she would receive a complete pardon. Catharina Hobbels asked von Dhaun to repeat his pledge. He promised her that if she could help him, she would be pardoned. With that, she told him that Knipperdolling was hiding in the attic of her house on New Bridge Street; she had already told Knipperdolling that he had to leave, protesting that he was putting her life and that of her husband in danger. The merchant who called himself the Just One, the fearsome sword-carrier for King Jan, was quickly found and taken to prison. Von Dhaun kept his bargain with Catharina Hobbels; she was not harmed. Her husband, however, who had been found along with Knipperdolling, was not protected by her bargain. He was brought to the Market Square and immediately, as Kerssenbrück puts it, rendered "a head shorter" than his previous height.

Some of the women refused to recant and were executed: Queen Divara, who had been first a nun, then the wife of the Apostle Jan Matthias, and finally the consort of King Jan, chose to die; so also did Tilbeck's sister, Knipperdolling's mother-in-law, Clara Brand, and his wife, Martha, whom he had forced to stand in the Market Square for disobeying him. Others also refused to recant but had wealthy families who could ransom them. Some were set free on high bail of six thousand guilders. Those who recanted were allowed to return to their native villages. Only a few came back to Münster; a year later the recovering population of Münster included only two hundred and sixteen women and nineteen men who had been Anabaptists and who had forsworn their heretic faith.

On Tuesday, June 29, Prince Bishop Franz von Waldeck's splendid coach, drawn by six white horses, was escorted through the Agidii Gate by three companies of soldiers in their finest dress uniforms. Ulrich von Dhaun and Wilhelm Steding stood at attention as the portly Bishop descended from the coach. Von Dhaun knelt before the Bishop and held out to him on a blue velvet cushion the keys to the city, which the Bishop took with solemn ceremony. Steding then knelt and offered the Bishop the true signs of his conquest: King Jan's crown, with its sword-pierced globe, his ring, his golden spurs, and his golden-hilted sword.

Jan himself was there to see his regalia handed over to the Bishop, according to Gresbeck. He had spent the last six days in his dark cell in the Rosenthal Church. Always vain of his appearance, he was now unwashed and unshaven, barefoot, wearing only heavy chains above his rags. The withering scorn in the voice of Franz von Waldeck, noble lord, as he spoke to the doomed wretch who stood before him, echoes through the centuries in Gresbeck's terse account: "Bist du ein

König?" asked the Bishop, using the familiar "du" reserved for children, close friends, and inferiors: "And are *you* a king?!"

The response was immediate and, considering Jan van Leyden's talent for public performance, inevitable. It was also, in its own way, just:

"Und bist *du* ein Bischof?"

12

Punishment

*Be not over much wicked, neither be thou foolish: why shouldest thou
die before thy time?*

—Ecclesiastes 7:17

THE TRAGEDY OF Münster always had its element of farce, as Jan's
insolent reply to the Bishop illustrates. He had also joked with the
crowd that gathered outside the dungeon in Dülmen to watch his
arrival. "Is this the king who took to himself so many wives?" they
shouted. "I beg your pardon," he answered with mock indignation.
"I took maidens and *made* them wives!"

He was no less cheeky after a month in his cell at Dülmen, when
the Bishop came to reproach the upstart king again, with "pointed
words." Did he have any idea, he asked Jan indignantly, how much
money it had cost him to crush his miserable kingdom? King Jan,
chained to the wall and wearing an iron collar around his neck,
shrugged off the complaint. He had a splendid plan, he said, that
would amply remunerate the Bishop for all his expenses. "Let an iron
cage be built," Jan said. "Put me in it along with Knipperdolling and
send us out on the road, throughout all of Germany. Charge everyone
a penny to take a look at us. You'll earn more money than you ever
spent in our war."

Considering that Jan knew full well that his fate was certain to be
as horrendously painful as the man sitting opposite him could conceive, his insouciance is remarkable. For centuries afterward, the leg-

end grew that he, Krechting, and Knipperdolling were indeed trundled around the country for six months, each in his own iron cage, as reminders of what happens to traitors and heretics. This did not happen; but it may have been Jan who gave the Bishop the idea to have three cages constructed, each large enough to hold a man, all three sturdy enough to have lasted, as they have, until today.

Jan was more serious during his extended visits with a team of inquisitors led by Antonius Corvinus, a Lutheran theologian, the record of which provides a remarkable insight into Jan's personality and into the system of justice and punishment at the time. It was not enough for either the Lutherans or the Catholics simply to defeat and execute their doctrinal opponents; they had to persuade them of the error of their ways, to allow them to recant and die in the faith.

Interestingly, Corvinus in his report calls Jan "the king," with no hint of satire: "When the king was brought out of prison, we greeted him in a friendly manner and asked him to be seated before the warm fireplace. We asked him how he was getting along in prison, and if he was cold or sick. The king answered that he was obliged to endure the cold and the sins that weighed on his heart with patience, as was God's will." By means of this amiable approach, having already determined that this was the only way to reach him, Corvinus says he was able to get Jan to talk openly about what he had done.

"Dear Jan," he begins, "we have heard unbelievable and terrible things about your kingdom. If what we hear is true—and regrettably it seems to be—we find it impossible to understand how you could have done such things in the name of Holy Scripture."

The record of Jan's answer to this and other questions—a record that Corvinus attests is "word for word" what he said—does not suggest madness or even unreason on Jan's part, and certainly no lack of intelligence or wit. Equally, there is no sense of shame or guilt. He says he will answer to God for what he did and for what he taught, and let Him decide if he had been wrong.

What about the passage in Holy Scripture where Jesus says, "My Kingdom is not of this world"?

Jan knows the passage well, and says that if he had erred in Münster, it was not so much in trying to create a kingdom in the image of Christ but in allowing himself to become king; he let it happen only because Dusentschur claimed he had a vision from God demanding it. The kingdom itself was now a dead issue.

Jan denies Corvinus's charge of "novelty" against the Anabaptists by noting that while the Catholics might make such a claim, the Lutherans had been around only a few years longer than he had. He feels kinship with Luther, moreover, in that he agrees to Luther's central idea, the necessity of justification by faith rather than deeds.

Concerning the Eucharist, which his followers had so often parodied, Jan's objection is that he considers it a matter of symbolism, not of the literal transformation of bread and wine. For Lutherans as for Catholics, the bread and wine were not merely symbols but actualities; whether those who received them believed in them or not did not affect the reality. This would mean that an unbeliever who went through the motions of the communion actually partook of the "body and blood of Christ," and Jan "cannot conceive" of how this could be possible. Corvinus rebukes Jan for being perverse: "It is clear that what we believe or do not believe cannot add to or detract from God's power." Jan says that if Corvinus is right, then "unbelievers must have partaken" of true communion, but that he cannot believe it.

Corvinus now constructs a new approach, asking Jan, "Why was the sun created?"

"Scripture teaches that it was made to rule the day and to shine," he responds, correctly.

"So, if you were blind, would the sun still shine?"

"I know of course that my blindness or yours would not keep the sun from shining."

"And so it is with all the works and ordinances of God, especially with the Sacraments," Corvinus says, proceeding to the heart of the matter, baptism. If a baby were capable of understanding his faith and professing it, that would be good; but baptism is, regardless, a "precious, noble, and holy sacrament, what St. Paul calls a regeneration and renewal of the Holy Ghost because it is ordered by God's word and given His promise." In other words, to deny the efficacy of infant baptism is to deny God; therein lay the Anabaptists' heresy. Jan does not budge on this issue.

Corvinus then asks Jan about his concept of marriage. He had always, Jan replies, "held marriage to be God's work, and that no higher or better estate exists in the world than the estate of matrimony."

Why, then, "have you so wildly violated this estate, against God's word and common order, and taken one wife after another?" Corvinus asks, continuing, almost plaintively: "How can you justify such a proceeding?"

"Why should we be denied what was permitted to the patriarchs in the Old Testament?" Jan responds. "What we have always held is this: he who wanted only one wife was never to be forced to have more than one. But we felt that a man who wanted more than one wife should be free to do so because he was obeying God's command to be fruitful and to multiply."

This would not do, Corvinus insists. The patriarchs took their many wives before the law of the land forbade them to do so, and were therefore innocent of wrongdoing. What other texts could Jan cite to justify polygamy?

Jan cleverly refers Corvinus to Paul's assertion that a bishop should be the husband of one wife. "This implies that laymen must have had more than one; otherwise, why would the bishop be specifically limited? There you have your text."

Growing impatient, Corvinus says that all agree, Catholic or Protestant, that the law of the land in this matter must be obeyed: one man, one wife. "You will have to answer for your violation of this law before God."

"I am consoled by the certainty," Jan says, "that we cannot be damned for doing what the fathers were permitted to do. I prefer to be with them and not you."

"Well, we prefer to be obedient to the state," Corvinus replies, concluding the interview.

It was not Jan who interested the Archbishop of Cologne. He was simply a criminal, and Bernard Krechting was no more than a thug. It was Bernard Knipperdolling, erstwhile leading citizen and merchant, who represented the truly serious threat to established order, for if such a man could turn so viciously against the state and the Church, all could be lost. The Archbishop sent von Waldeck an order to have Knipperdolling rigorously questioned again in order to get some answers to his written questions, such as: "How many men and women have you personally executed? Was it true that children were eaten by the starving masses while the king and his court feasted in their palace? Had the grain supplies for the people been poisoned to reduce the number of the starving? Was is not the case that your motivation for rebellion against the Bishop was derived entirely from the desire for revenge? Will you reveal the names of your confederates in Amsterdam, Wesel, Maastricht, Aachen, and Essen, in Hamm, Soest and Lippe—and, of course, in our own city of Cologne? You must answer these questions," the Archbishop wrote; "you know full well what kinds of instruments we have to force you to answer."

To all of these questions, even under torture, Knipperdolling stubbornly refused any answer, other than to deny that his motives for opposing the Bishop had been revenge. King Jan, upon receiving similar demands, had overwhelmed his questioners with the story of his life—of his mother's seduction and his illegitimate birth, his school years in Leyden, his youthful wanderings in England, Flanders, and Lübeck, his wife's complaints about his extravagance, his management of the Inn of the Two Herrings, and so on. But Jan was merely throwing up rhetorical dust, never answering direct questions about how he happened to go to Münster, other than to say he had heard there were inspiring preachers there, and frustrating by evasion and prolixity the Archbishop's attempts to uncover a wider conspiracy. He repeated his offer, on the other hand, to proclaim to all who would listen throughout the empire that he had been wrong and that they should avoid his example; all that he asked in exchange was his life.

But there was never any doubt that Jan and the others would be executed. Hundreds of their followers who were guilty of nothing save loyalty to him had already died, only Henry Krechting, granted free passage out of the city after he relinquished command of the wagon fort, and Gerlach von Wullen escaping. Young von Wullen was a special case, a member of the nobility who was spared because it was thought too demeaning to that class to place him on public display. His father-in-law, Christian Kerckering, was less fortunate. Kerckering was also the father-in-law of the Bishop's illegitimate son, Christoph, but his status as a noble and as a relative through marriage to the Bishop could not save him. He was guilty twice over of treason, having not only advised and supported King Jan but also having betrayed his class. On June 28, as the wagons bearing Jan and his court rolled out of Münster, the one in which Christian Kerckering rode turned from the highway into a "green and pleasant" place in the woods, as Kerssenbrück puts it. There he was beheaded and buried—a discreet and merciful death, as it was regarded, granted not out of compassion but because the Bishop's pride of place could not tolerate the embarrassment of a noble kinsman's public execution.

For the execution of the ringleaders of the revolution, however, more formal procedures were necessary. Both religious and secular authority had been grievously endangered; the punishment of those responsible could not be lightly undertaken. An indication of the gravity of the situation is provided by the recommendation of Luther's friend Melanchthon. Gentle and conciliatory by nature, immensely wise, learned, and humane, Melanchthon was originally sympathetic to some of the Anabaptist arguments and far less virulent in his opposition to them than was his master, Luther. Yet he now had no hesitation in calling for the extermination of the Anabaptists. Like Bernard Rothmann, for whom he had several years earlier foreseen either great good or great evil, Melanchthon went to the Bible to justify his recommendations. "The kings in the Old Testament, not only the Jewish kings but also the converted heathen kings, judged and killed the false prophets and unbelievers. Such examples show the proper office of princes. As Paul says, the law that blasphemers are to be punished is a good law. The government rules men not just for their bodily welfare but for the honor of God, for they are God's ministers." It is not for the preachers, however, to enforce these laws; "they should not use physical power under the excuse of their office. It is plain that the worldly government is bound to drive away blasphemy, false doctrine, and heresies, and to punish those who hold to these things. This sect of Anabaptists is from the devil," and it was the duty of the authorities to punish the Anabaptists with death.

Philip Melanchthon, kindly humanist, knew exactly what kind of punishment he was recommending. Two years earlier, Emperor Charles V had approved the *Constitutio Criminalis Carolina,* the new criminal code, which contains two hundred and nineteen articles describing the exact procedures to be followed in punishing those guilty of capital crimes. Many of these tortures would soon become notorious through the Spanish Inquisition as preliminaries to death, designed to wring acknowledgments of wrongdoing from the guilty and thus to let them save their souls. The method of execution selected for the ringleaders in Münster was perhaps less terrible than the drawing and quartering commonly practiced in England under Henry VIII, but it was grim enough. Heavy iron tongs were to be heated until they were red-hot. The condemned were then to be led to a public place and their bodies ripped apart with the tongs. At a designated moment a dagger would be thrust into their hearts.

On January 19, 1536, the three prisoners, Jan, Knipperdolling, and Krechting, were brought back to Münster and subjected to yet another judicial hearing, described by Antonius Corvinus later in a letter to a friend. "They judged the king first, as the greatest criminal, whom no lie could save, as was known throughout Germany. He answered that he had fought not against God but against man's authority. He admitted that he had violated the laws of the state and the king, and he was condemned" to die on the morning of January 22. Knipperdolling and Krechting, who refused to speak, were similarly sentenced.

On the night of January 21, each of the three was offered the comfort of a priest to stay with him. Knipperdolling and Krechting, according to Kerssenbrück, rejected the offer with contempt. They maintained that they had committed no sins; all that they had done was for the glory of God; they were secure in their faith in Jesus Christ. They needed no priest, for their God was with them. Jan van Leyden accepted the presence of the Bishop's priest, Johann von Siburg, who "stayed with him the entire night and found Jan greatly changed. He greatly regretted his godlessness, his murders, his looting, his lack of discipline, and his shameful deeds. He admitted that he deserved the bitterest possible death ten times over, and he renounced all his errors . . . Jan was thus comforted and consoled the whole night long by the priest."

The crowd began to gather in the Market Square after dawn on January 22, and by the time the prisoners were led forward at eight o'clock the people of Münster and the surrounding areas had filled the square where so much had happened. To one side stood Bernard Knipperdolling's grand three-story house, where he had first entertained Jan and given him his daughter to wed. A block in the other direction was the City Hall where Henry Mollenheck's abortive counter-revolution had collapsed in a shambles. And opposite was St. Lambert's Church, where Bernard Rothmann had first preached against the rule of the Bishop and where three iron cages, each large enough to contain a man's body, now waited on the stone steps with open doors.

Two companies of soldiers stood at stiff attention; no longer needed to maintain order among the cowed remnants of Münster's population, their colorful presence lent the occasion an air of dignified ceremony. Above them, in an open second-story window, sat Franz von Waldeck, Bishop of Münster, swathed in heavy ermine capes against the damp mid-winter cold.

The large scaffold depicted in numerous later illustrations was in fact simply three wagons placed side by side and covered by planks. On the middle wagon a large single post had been erected to which iron collars and chains were attached. The prisoners were led from a house off the square to the base of the scaffold and stripped to the waist. As Jan mounted the scaffold, he fell to his knees and with folded hands said, "Father, in thine hands I place my soul."

The three men were secured to the post with the iron collars, which were imbedded with spikes that dug into their necks and prevented any movement, though each could hear the others' sufferings. Jan was the first to be approached by the two executioners, one from Paderborn and the other a native of Münster. The first gripped Jan's left side with the glowing tongs; the second did the same on the right side. The executioners were versed in their art and aware that the law required the victim to be kept alive and conscious for a full hour of excruciating pain. Alternately applying the four different sets of tongs to Jan's body and reviving him when he fainted, they finally ended the matter with a dagger thrust into his heart.

Some observers said that Jan took the first two bites in silence, after which he cried out in pain. Antonius Corvinus, who probably knew Jan as well as any man because of their extended conversations, wrote about what he witnessed to a friend. He had been greatly moved and frightened by "the courage with which [Jan] proved himself, giving only once a cry against the pain"; he could only explain it by recalling that "it is certain that Satan is able to lend strength and courage to those he catches in his web."

Bernard Knipperdolling, hearing Jan's suffering, let himself slump against the spiked collar in an effort to kill himself. He was pulled to his feet and revived to suffer as Jan had. "I don't know if he said anything," Corvinus wrote. "Those who were closer than I was said very definitely that Knipperdolling cried, 'God have mercy on my sins.' Bernard Krechting died the same way, twice crying out, 'Oh Father, Oh Father.'"

"There were many here who said that this was a pleasant thing to watch," Corvinus concluded. "But to me and to others what happened here was not at all pleasant. It is true that they were properly and according to custom dealt with—which man with a consciousness of his own guilt could deny it?—but we still must remember that God will punish us similarly for our sins."

13

THE LEGACY OF THE TAILOR-KING

As Savages commemorate their great Hunts with Dancing, so History
is the Dance of our Hunt for Christ, and how we have far'd.

—Thomas Pynchon, *Mason & Dixon*

THERE WERE LAWS and procedures for plundering defeated cities. In the case of Münster, the Bishop was entitled to take all of the buildings and property that had belonged to the Anabaptists. Everything of any value—weapons, furniture, rugs, curtains, paintings, books, foodstuffs and utensils, implements and tools—was sold at auction, and the proceeds divided equally between the Bishop and the soldiers. He also discovered a treasure hoard consisting of six barrels of gold and a trunk of silver weighing four hundred and fifty pounds.

He still had huge expenses to pay, but the Bishop did his best to reduce them. He noted that the army had captured the city by subterfuge, and thus had not been required to expend much energy, money, or manpower in the final assault. Though the commanders might have reasonably expected a bonus for a job well and expeditiously done, the Bishop lopped ten per cent off of their final wages. The common soldiers received little for their efforts when their share of the loot, which did not include the gold or silver, was split up and distributed, no more than sixteen or eighteen guilders each.

In addition to being shortchanged, if not actually swindled, of their fair share of the loot, some of the soldiers had not been paid for two months, and by mid-July they were threatening to plunder Münster again for whatever little was left. The Bishop was forced to come up with another 26,000 Emden guilders to pay them off and get them out of the city; that challenging assignment he handed over to the able Wilhelm Steding, bypassing Ulrich von Dhaun because the count had complained too much about von Waldeck's high-handed manner. By the end of July the Bishop was able to tell the council at Worms, which had been pressing him for a speedy resolution to the embarrassing affair, that he was making arrangements to pay his debts.

Bishop Franz's financial obligations to the princes who had supported him were enormous—the Archbishopric in Cologne was still collecting installments on its loans as late as 1617. At the same time, he was roundly condemned for having dithered too long in crushing the revolt, supposedly because he was a secret Lutheran in his sympathies; and he has come down in history as cruel, corrupt, and incompetent. A recent, more even-handed summary is that of Karl-Heinz Kirchhoff: In an age when religious strife was the ruling condition of political life, the rebellion in Münster forced the Bishop to request help from Hesse, Cleves, and Burgundy because the burden was too great for him to bear alone. The problem was that all of these powers were competitive with each other. One must appreciate the complications entailed by the military, religious, and political elements of these arrangements in order to see why the Bishop's course of action during the long siege of Münster seemed so unsteady. He was, in the beginning, without support and without the means to force the city to surrender. He managed to engage the support of the opposing princes partly through their mutual fears that if they did not help him, others would, to their disadvantage. There was also a real fear that Burgundy, already the strongest of the principates, might in fact conquer Münster and dominate the region. Bishop Franz's dramatic entry into the conquered city, then, and his even more compelling witnessing of the final punishment of the men responsible for his troubles, amounted to a most ambiguous triumph—he had won the battle but virtually lost control of his own destiny.

Matters did not improve thereafter for the Bishop. Münster, though nominally still within his power, became the northern center of the Counter-Reformation, with considerable attention from Rome. Bishop Franz, never a devout stalwart of the Church, tried to persuade the other Catholic princes to desert to the Protestants. When they indignantly refused to follow his lead, he joined the Protestant Schmalkaldic League (several smaller cities forming a lesser version of the better-known Hanseatic League), became embroiled in regional conflicts that he lost, and had to pay a fine of one hundred thousand guilders to his enemies in lieu of seeing Münster again destroyed. He died in 1553, perhaps not, as one account has it, "of grief," but certainly in frustration.

Of the Bishop's associates and underlings, Wilhelm Steding may have fared the best, receiving as a prize a splendid house that had belonged to a businessman. The bailiff Eberhard von Morrien got some property on Agidii Street. The house of Clara Brand, Knipperdolling's mother-in-law, went to a knight. The merchant's own house on Market Square was claimed by Bishop Franz, and remained standing until it was destroyed by Allied bombs during World War II.

All told, about four hundred and thirty houses that had belonged to Anabaptists were given to the Bishop's supporters or sold at auction prices, including that belonging to Henry Gresbeck's mother, her son's services notwithstanding. Gresbeck himself finally received some money for the house upon the death of his mother in 1542, when he was living in nearby Osnabrück; otherwise his only reward from the Bishop was being allowed to live. His friend Hansel Eck, properly known as Johann Nagel, received fifteen guilders and a small house. He married Anna Kolthave; her former husband, the goldsmith Cord Cruse, had been the keeper of the city treasury for the Company of Christ and had died in the melee after the final battle. Sadly, the little adventurer's luck finally ran out in 1537, when he tried to cheat a goldsmith out of the money he owed him for fashioning a necklace and lost his head as a consequence.

Henry Graes, the Latin scholar who talked to angels, lived out his days comfortably in Borkum, a few miles from Münster, as a schoolteacher. Some of his former brothers were not yet willing to give up the fight, and throughout northern Germany and the Netherlands for the next several years splinter groups of Jan's survivors and others harassed the authorities. One of the most potentially dangerous of these survivors was Henry Krechting, King Jan's former chancellor, who made his way safely after the defense of the wagon fort in the

Cathedral Square to the north, where he and other radical Anabaptists were placed under the protection of the Bishop's old rival, Count Oldenburg. Krechting started a new movement that was taken over by David Joris, a more conservative leader. Oldenburg finally, in 1538, gave in to pressure to evict the Anabaptists, but continued to protect Krechting, who settled down and raised his two young sons, Herman and Henry. The boys, who had witnessed the events, turned out well: Herman became a successful businessman in Bremen, and his brother, after a career as the city's mayor, wrote a history of the Anabaptist kingdom that may still be read today in the city's historical archives. Their father's body lies in the graveyard of the old church near Bremen, under a crumbling stone that says "On June 28, 1580, the honorable Henry Krechting peacefully left this world."

Only Bernard Rothmann remained, as he does today, unaccounted for. The last image of him during the battle for Münster, white-robed, sword in hand, pierced in the side by a spear, is appropriately apocalyptic. When his body was not found, it began to be rumored that he had, like Krechting, escaped. He was sighted in Rostock, Lübeck, and Wismar . . . he was under the protection of a Frisian prince . . . he was behind the continuing Anabaptist raids in distant provinces of Germany. The Bishop, for his part, thought his great enemy had escaped. In 1537 a warrant circulating for Rothmann's arrest described him as a sturdy, square-shouldered man with clear eyes and straight dark hair, who often wore a Spanish cap. A physician from Arnhem who answered to this description was taken into custody; he sued for false arrest and received a settlement for his trouble.

Two questions that underline any attempt to understand past events apply with special pertinence to the rise and fall of the Anabaptist Kingdom of Münster: Why did it happen, and what does it mean? To these might be added a third and somewhat easier question: Many other more important events from this and other periods have long since been forgotten; why should Münster have persisted in claiming our attention?

The answer to the last question is dramatically visible today. Two hundred feet above the old Market Square, now called the Prinzipalmarkt, in modern, late-twentieth-century Münster, hang three iron cages, each measuring about seven feet by three feet by three feet. They are the same cages that Bishop Franz had had built nearly five centuries ago to contain the bodies of the three men executed before his eyes. The cages rest above the nave of St. Lambert's Church, over the clock. One is slightly larger than the other two and positioned above them. In each cage, between dusk and dawn, a faint light is visible from a tiny yellow bulb; the lights were placed there in 1987, a more sentimental time than 1536, "in memory of their departed souls." The tower itself, with its Gothic spires and crenellations, stands out against the night sky like an emblem of the Middle Ages. But while the cages are the same, the tower is a late-nineteenth-century neo-Gothic replacement of the original fourteenth-century tower, whose simple rounded elegance was rejected in favor of the bizarre and jagged exaggeration that characterizes the neo-Gothic style.

The cages, like the public execution of those they contained, were originally intended to frighten those who might be tempted to rebel against the state; the church was not consulted about its new decorations. The bodies were left in the hanging cages to rot, prompting artists to draw ravens descending on them to pluck out what flesh the torturers had left; the bones were not removed until half a century later. Within a century Münster and its grisly cages were famous, and nearly synonymous with each other, but it was only with the translation of Kerssenbrück's history from Latin into German in 1771 that the story began to be more widely known in its full details.

The Romantic and Victorian fascination with the Middle Ages, prompted in part by the wrenching demands of the modern period that are still with us today, impelled some visitors to Münster to try to re-create the fervor of the emotions that had ruled the little city so long ago. Instructed by Goethe in the concept of the "daemonic," which linked man's creative and destructive urges in deeds and in art, one such visitor fairly terrified himself with his reconstruction. This was Gerhart Hauptmann (1862–1946), winner of the Nobel Prize for literature in 1912. A prolific poet, novelist, and dramatist, Hauptmann had written a play about the Peasants' War, *Florian Geyer*. He visited Münster in 1900, seeing the story of the Anabaptists as packed with dramatic material; his particular interest, as a later writer explained it, was the terrible fate of the misled masses who followed their fanatical leaders and the power of religious movements when fueled by social injustice. Hauptmann stayed in the city for several days, jotting notes and reactions in his diary. One night, he wrote, he stood alone in the main square, opposite the City Hall. He began to shiver, then to sweat profusely from every pore, though it was a chilly evening. He felt a "paroxysm of angst" as he heard frightful shrieks of anguish echoing through the cobblestoned streets, sounds like those of animals being tortured to death. He had to retreat from the square, trembling; he felt then the birth amid terror and oppression of a religious destiny for himself, a deep identification with the "ecstatic religion of the people" of that earlier time, and vowed that he would one day capture and recreate those terrible days in a drama of his own making.

Hauptmann never wrote his play, but the modern visitor to Münster will still see the cages that prompted his "paroxysm of angst," because they continue to be regarded as tourist attractions and as municipal symbols, though not with unanimous local approval. In the 1880s the city decided to repair the cages, which had been damaged by rust, and to replace them on the new church tower as "not insignificant" reminders of the city's history; there they remained until November 18, 1944, when British bombs landed on the church tower. The highest cage—Jan's—fell into the street; the lower-left cage, facing the tower, fell into the organ loft; the third cage remained dangling above the huge clock. In 1948 the tower was reconstructed; the cages were repaired—the workmen commented favorably on the quality of the original construction—and put back in their original positions, again without debate.

Only recently, it seems, have some begun to question whether it is appropriate for such a display to hang from a church tower. In 1996 the foremost living authority on the Anabaptists, Karl-Heinz Kirchhoff, wrote a short book about the cages and their history in which he cites the local newspaper's letters-to-the-editor section to explain the arguments. The cages are, some say, an "unbelievably tasteless" aesthetic affront and should come down. Perhaps they are unpleasant, others respond, but they are reminders of the evils of the ruling classes in the Middle Ages and should remain (not the reaction the Bishop would have wished). The winning essays in a contest for schoolchildren said the cages should remain in place as a reminder of a "less quiet time" in the city's history.

There are other reminders of the "less quiet time." The beautiful new City Museum was finished in 1983, a few blocks from St. Lambert's Church. Its opening exhibition was a full retrospective of the Anabaptist Kingdom, including a three-hundred-page catalog, and a special permanent section remains. The visitor may see, perhaps with something of the shiver that Hauptmann felt, the huge iron tongs, black and sinister against the white wall, that were the tools of the executioners. He may touch, if he wishes, the sword that Knipperdolling used as Jan's first designated executioner, Jan's own suit of armor, and the spiked collars that held the three men to the post as they died. There are also three full-size replicas of the cages, built in the late-nineteenth century and housed for many years in the city zoo, for some time with dummies in them representing the three dead men.

Outside, in the now-needed fresh air, the modern visitor can visit the Overwater Church, still missing the tower the Anabaptists demolished, and cross the stone bridge over the river Aa to the Cathedral. Münster remains a predominantly Catholic enclave in Lutheran northern Germany, and the Cathedral, which Jan had desecrated and turned into his armory, remains at its center; Herman Kerssenbrück, the boy who lived through the early stages of the revolt and was evicted from the city by Jan Matthias, returned in the 1550s as the schoolmaster of the Cathedral and spent twenty years compiling his account in Latin. One of Kerssenbrück's major themes was that Protestantism itself, not just Luther or Jan van Leyden, was at the root of the disturbances, and he did what he could to encourage the Counter-Reformation whose effects are still visible.

The City Hall where Knipperdolling and Tilbeck were co-mayors has no memorials to the Anabaptist period; instead, it celebrates, especially during the year of my last visit, 1998, its more famous and productive history as the site of the negotiations that led to the Peace of Westphalia in 1648. This famous treaty marked the end of the Thirty Years' War and the introduction of a long period of peace and prosperity throughout Europe.

Modern Münster has a population of nearly a quarter of a million people and has spread far beyond the boundaries of Jan's small medieval city of fewer than ten thousand. As the capital of Westphalia, its major business is government and education, with the second-largest university in Germany. The river Aa has been dammed to form a beautiful small lake within an easy walk of downtown. A cruise boat takes visitors to the small zoo at the other end of the lake, and to the splendid Westphalian Museum of Natural History. Or one may choose to walk along the lake and wander through a re-created sixteenth-century farming village.

The walls and moats that once defined Münster are long gone; only the *Buddenturm* Watchtower and parts of the *Zwinger* and the bases of the stone walls remain as obvious reminders of the medieval period. In their place is a comfortable promenade, three miles long and two hundred yards wide in places; a broad pedestrian walk and a bike path are shaded by linden trees and bordered by ponds where swans and geese and ducks glide serenely past overhanging willow trees. This beautiful park, one of the loveliest in Europe, includes at its outer edges the former wasteland in which the desperate refugees from King Jan's New Zion wandered so many years ago. No trace of their desperation remains.

Similarly, in the heart of town one may sip a beer at the end of a warm July afternoon, as I did, at a table opposite the City Hall, and take pleasure in the ambience of a European city. Students, businessmen, and nuns pedaled through the square on the bicycles for which the city is now famous. Tour buses and taxis rumbled over the cobblestones, leaving lingering clouds of exhaust fumes. A Swedish band, students working their way through Europe, offered an acceptable version of Glenn Miller's "In the Mood" up the street, in front of St. Lambert's Church.

And looming over all—noxious tour buses, busy cafés, darting bicycles, energetic students—were the three cages of King Jan, Knipperdolling, and Krechting, each a perfect medieval memento mori, like the skull on the desk of Rembrandt's physician.

This macabre juxtaposition suggests why Jan's story lives on as it does. It was made tangible by the very cages that the Bishop hoped would ensure that he and his authority would be remembered, and those who opposed him recalled only as miserable wretches who deserved what they got. Without the cages, first suggested by the captured king himself, the name of Jan van Leyden would be as remote today as is that of Franz von Waldeck. With the cages, and because of them, he has continued to spark debate about what he did. Given his theatrical persona and his sense of irony, we may assume that Jan would be amused.

In the decade before Münster all Anabaptists, peacefully inclined or not, were attacked as servants of Satan, led by him "into the dark forests and woods, into caves and holes . . . [where he] gathers them only in corners, telling them to preach only in secrecy." Martin Luther saw in their "grand, wicked words" and actions "the true fruits of the devil." Another observer saw them as even more of a threat than the heathen Turks, who were then knocking on the gates of Vienna; the Turks were at least clear about their intention to destroy Christianity. But the devil who aided the Turks directly worked his way more insidiously through the Anabaptists, who "conceal and decorate their poison with such an appearance that at first glance it seems to be a good holy life, not an evil one," and "simple and foolish folk" are drawn in by this appearance.

Before Münster, it was the Anabaptists' relative subtlety and sophistication of argument and appeal, along with a certain naive honesty, that had most alarmed their opponents. But after the trouble there began to get serious, according to a recent study by Dale Grieser, the crudeness of the takeover and the rule by the two Jans and the two Bernards in Münster suggested to Martin Luther that Satan had overplayed his hand and was actually losing, not enhancing, his power. Luther mocked the New Jerusalem as the work of a "young, ABC devil or schoolgirl devil, who does not yet know how to write." After all, only the blind could fail to see that theft of property, the subversion of civil authority, polygamy, and murder were Satan's handiwork. The devil had gone insane or grown stupid, having discarded his old and clever technique of "transforming himself into an angel of light" in order to lure his victims to their doom. For Luther, the Bishop and his assorted princely allies had erred in the first place by using military force against the Anabaptists in Münster; they should rather have used "the sword of the spirit" and tried to "tear their hearts away from the devil" by preaching the true word of God. Instead, "they wrested control of the bodies away from the devil, but ceded him their hearts."

Not everyone thought Satan had lost his touch: Urbanus Rhegius "saw the devil's footprints all over Münster." He was not an apprentice devil, said Rhegius, but "the devil of a thousand arts" who was using the Anabaptists to attack "scripture, Christ, and Christianity and all faith" in order to "become a lord in Westphalia over body, soul, and goods." It was the diabolical influence of Bernard Rothmann, more than that of Jan or Knipperdolling, that shaped events in Münster, in particular his desire for personal power: rather than remain "a poor Mr. Bernard with no name" in the Catholic Church, Rhegius says, this "miserable theologian . . . talkative and proud," said to himself, "I don't want to be either Papist or Lutheran, I want to begin my own sect, so I can get some followers."

What strikes the modern reader most about all of this is the sincerity and omnipresence of the belief that Satan, incompetent or not, was to blame for what happened in Münster—not as metaphor or hyperbole but as a real and tangible presence. The difference between our own time and that of Jan and the Bishop seems profound: other than a few on the religious right, no one has argued that the devil spawned David Koresh and the Branch Davidians at Waco, the nearest modern equivalent to what happened in Münster. Rather, the causes of Waco are assigned to mental illness, crowd psychology, social conflicts, and official ineptitude, all things we believe we can understand if not cure—unlike Satan.

Madness was in fact also considered by Jan's contemporaries as a motivation for his rapid though brief success, as were the constructs of psychology and sociology as we know them now; once they identified Satan as the source of the trouble, it was still necessary to explain why a certain group of people and only they were so susceptible to his wiles. Antonius Corvinus, after his interviews with Jan and the other captured leaders, published his observations on the Anabaptists in order to prove that they were deeply irrational; the world they had created was an inversion of the real world, just as carnival season is a reversal of ordinary laws of reason and social order. The Anabaptist

Kingdom, he said, had been no more than an *Affenspiel*—an ape's game.

Corvinus was following the lead of his master, Philip of Hesse, who had earlier chided Bernard Rothmann for his indifference to logical arguments against his position and compared him to his court jester: "You act like our fool Jochim when someone says something to him that he does not like to hear. So he starts to talk about something else." Corvinus saw the inability of Rothmann and the other preachers to respond to logical argument as evidence of God's punishment for their misbehavior: He had given them "perverted minds" that put them beyond reach. Responding to Corvinus's "brotherly admonition" with "contempt, even ridicule and laughter," the Anabaptists proved to him how foolish they were, turning "everything upside down" in order to destroy it: they converted marriage into prostitution, a tailor into a king, a merchant (Knipperdolling) into a hanging judge, a preacher (Rothmann) into a political propagandist. The famous sketch of King Jan capering around the beheaded Elizabeth Wandscheer captures perfectly the mad and murderous carnival of destruction that he had created.

Certainly Jan seems to be a character ready for the psychoanalyst's couch. I am unaware of any direct commentary on him, but Ernest Jones, a colleague and follower of Sigmund Freud, provides some useful insights in his work *On the Nightmare,* in which he includes a chapter about the medieval concept of the devil. He cites as his starting point Freud's key assumption that "the Devil is certainly nothing else than the personification of the repressed, unconscious instinctual life," and goes on to note a number of points that augment those made in the earlier discussion of Luther. Of particular importance in connection with Jan is the church's link between sex and sin; the obvious association here is with Jan's polygamy, widely held to be vivid evidence of his insatiable and devilish lust. But there are less obvious details as well. The devil is sterile; Jan's later unions produced no children, a fact remarked on at the time. The devil often limps; Dusentschur did limp, in fact, while Jan did not, but in the popular literature of the day he is sometimes called the limping king. The devil is often ugly, but just as often strikingly beautiful, as in Milton's *Par-*

adise Lost; much of Jan's appeal lay in his physical grace and beauty. Finally, the most dreaded sin for the Church was incest, a particular favorite of the devil; if one subscribes to the common Freudian notion that the son wishes to kill his father and marry his mother, Jan's clever manipulation and dispatch of his older mentor Jan Matthias and his marriage to the dead Prophet's wife strongly suggest an incestuous relationship.

The rebellious but envious son's imitation and defiance of the father is at the heart of Jones's discussion of the devil, as it was of Milton in *Paradise Lost.* Jan's own father denied him and condemned him to illegitimacy. He found a father-substitute in Jan Matthias and a father-in-law in Bernard Knipperdolling, both of whom he surpassed and displaced. In the Bishop he found a churchly father who could not be displaced, and who administered his ultimate chastisement, his banishment to hell.

Jan also shares other qualities that Jones and Freud associate with the devil. He is arrogant and presumptuous, as we have clearly seen: these are the prime aspects of the devil, "the Arch-rebel; his insubordinate disobedience and final insurrection against the authority of God the Father is the very paradigma of revolution." Moreover, he has a mocking quality that is particularly infuriating to figures of authority: "The Devil mocks at the endeavours and strivings of men, derides their ambitions and makes sport of their failures. He teases, annoys and harms them out of pure enjoyment at doing so, undoes their labour and baffles all their efforts." Finally, the devil, for all his cleverness and malice, has, like children and like Jan, a naïveté that makes him easy to trick sometimes: "The tales in which the Devil, presenting at times an incredible naïveté, is easily hoodwinked form an extensive chapter in the history of demonolatry, and have furnished an important source for the later conception of clowns, buffoons, and stage fools."

Later observers rejected both Satan and madness as primary causes of Münster. For Karl Marx and his friend and collaborator Friedrich Engels, the source of evil lay in the class system, based on the exploitation of the poor working masses by their privileged idle overlords. The inequitable distribution of wealth and property was bound to lead to violent efforts to right the situation. Nine years before Mün-

ster, a renegade priest, Thomas Müntzer, had led the notorious Peasants' Revolt that resulted in the deaths of himself and one hundred
thousand farmers and artisans, as well as thousands of priests and landowners. Engels explained this insurrection as the first of a series of
modern efforts that included the French Revolution of 1789 and that
were culminating in his time with the revolutions of 1848 in Germany
and France. The admitted excesses of the rebels derived from their
long oppression.

Following Engels's lead, some later writers argued that the Anabaptist Kingdom of Münster, when seen in its proper social and historical context, was in fact a people's movement directly related to
the Peasants' Revolt. The emphasis now shifted from the evil deeds
of a maniacal brotherhood to the oppression by the ruling classes that
killed the more moderate Anabaptists and drove the rest to violent
resistance. The rebels had the right instincts: driving out the forces of
superstition represented by the established Church; heroically insisting
on the right of the individual against the tyrannical state; eliminating
class distinctions by calling all men and women brothers and sisters;
and sharing all goods and property. Knipperdolling, originally praised
as the merchant who gave up all that he owned in order to follow
Christ, becomes for later communist ideologues the model of a heroic
convert from capitalist exploiter to man of the people. Jan himself is
now at least a Savonarola, a man of courage and integrity, if a bit
excessive in his zeal, and perhaps even a new Spartacus. The Bishop,
never an admirable figure, becomes now the personification of corrupt, unyielding tyranny.

Because they lacked power to do more than mock their superiors,
at least initially, these rebels were often forced by circumstances to
turn their world upside down, to make it a *verkehrte Welt*. Typical
images of the ass playing the lyre or of the blind leading the blind in
the twelfth-century *Mirror of Fools* spoke of the past being stood on its
head by the present, which later became a formula for "the struggle
of youth over age, frivolity over seriousness, inexperience over wisdom." The contemporary philosopher Michael Bakhtin describes this
inversion in a way that sounds like a script for the Anabaptist Kingdom: the king is now a youth or a fool, or both. Wisdom and order
are replaced by license and folly. All forms of the sublime and the

mysterious are degraded and travestied. The respectable orders that purport to know and understand cosmic truths are seen to be mere sham. Thus carnival is the very image of revolution. In America during the political turmoil of the 1960s, radicals wore pig costumes in courtrooms to mock the reason, truth, and justice the system presumed to stand for. They understood that nothing is so powerfully disruptive as the idea of carnival in the courtroom. Similarly, in 1968, when France and Germany were in the midst of revolutionary turmoil led by students, there was a fringe movement in Münster dedicated to the memory of Bernard Knipperdolling as a heroic martyr in the battle against an unjust system; it included a Knipperdolling *Kneipe* (bar) and even a newsletter. The former editor of the Knipperdolling newsletter today writes *Krimis* (crime thrillers).

For Friedrich Reck-Malleczewen, a well-born Prussian Catholic writing in the 1930s about the Münster episode as an example of "mass insanity," explanations that apologized for Jan and Knipperdolling were themselves little short of madness. Reck was a staunch opponent of Hitler who would later die at Dachau for his beliefs, which were incorporated in his argument that the Anabaptist Kingdom and its leader were forerunners of Nazi Germany and of Hitler. He watched helplessly as "truth was distorted and history falsified," in the words of his widow, as good men were persecuted for their refusal to bend and as other good men did bend, thereby losing their minds and souls. One who did bend was Gerhart Hauptmann, who had been moved to a "paroxysm of angst" in Münster at the turn of the century but by the time of Hitler was sufficiently caught up in the "ecstatic religion of the people" to turn his back on the liberal Social Democrats and to remain a respected figure in the Third Reich. He was honored by Goebbels, Hitler's propaganda minister, on the occasion of his eightieth birthday in 1942.

Reck wrote about Münster in terms of its "symptoms, its ideas, its configuration" originally in the form of a novel, publishing it in the dangerous year of 1937; after the war his widow re-issued the book as a historical account, calling attention to the analogies Reck intended between Jan's kingdom and the Third Reich.

Some of the similarities between Hitler and Jan are obvious even without Reck's guidance. Both were illegitimate and raised by their mothers in poverty. Both were foreigners, Hitler coming from Austria and Jan from Holland. Both were largely self-educated and scornful of formal knowledge and received opinions. Both were rootless wanderers and apparent failures in their early years. Both were artistic, Hitler as a painter and Jan as an actor and author of dramatic sketches. Both were moved by resentment against those who had failed to acknowledge their existence, let alone their merit: fathers, churches, governments. Both had extraordinary gifts of oratory, organization and planning, and of inspiring followers to implement their visions. Both *had* visions, expressed in the same terms, of a thousand-year *Reich*. And both were psychopaths, i.e., mad or evil, or both. (Thus are we driven back to the original explanations of Martin Luther and his contemporaries!)

There are also similarities between the organizational elements of the two regimes. Both required the indoctrination of children through early education and military training; the substitution of the group for the individual and the family in terms of loyalty and obligation; the inclusion of the chosen and the exclusion of the rest; elaborate ceremonies, marches, and public gatherings; symbols and slogans; and abrupt promotions and demotions, appearances and disappearances. Most important, both required absolute, unquestioning obedience to their leader, based on faith rather than reason or law, and the penalty for disobedience was death.

The means by which such groups gain power include a gradual, step-by-step undermining of local authority. This is achieved by manipulation of the voting process through pressure tactics, cheating, and terror. An outside enemy must be found, requiring a temporary alliance with the authorities. Once the government is sufficiently infiltrated, its more moderate leaders are caught between the conservatives and the radicals and are immobilized. New dangers are found, both internal and external, requiring immediate and decisive action: the traitors within are exposed and expelled or murdered; their property is appropriated, their books and profane images piled high in the streets and burned. Resistance from former allies who balk at such tactics is mercilessly crushed: the middle ground has vanished, and those who are not with the rulers are against them. The only means for ensuring continued obedience is a greater threat from outside the regime; thus the enemy's attempts to negotiate are rejected as treachery. The stakes are constantly raised until an apocalyptic final battle (one that, in Hitler's case, Reck did not live to see to its conclusion) results in complete destruction. For the rebel forces, the destruction of the world is of little importance:"If the heavens fall," they say, "we will eat all the larks." If they lose, it is ordained, and they will return; if they win, the thousand-year kingdom will ensue.

Norman Cohn, in his book *The Pursuit of the Millennium,* describes a series of religious events and their leaders in northern Europe from about 1200 to 1550. Different though they were, all those involved shared a belief in a Millennium, "not necessarily limited to a thousand years and indeed not necessarily limited at all, in which the world would be inhabited by a humanity at once perfectly good and perfectly happy. . . . [They were] seized at least intermittently by a tense expectation of some sudden, miraculous event in which the world would be utterly transformed, some prodigious final struggle between the hosts of Christ and the hosts of Antichrist through which history would attain its fulfillment and justification."

Cohn's book, published in 1957, was prompted by the similarities he saw between the violent irrationality of the so-called "chiliastic" movements of the past and the totalitarian states of Nazi Germany and Soviet Russia. Like Friedrich Reck, Cohn sees in the Anabaptist Kingdom of Münster a forerunner of the Nazis; part of his stated aim is to show that it was not an isolated aberration but a model of its kind. Accordingly, he gives the story of Münster pride of place in his account, his final chapter, "The Egalitarian Millennium."

Cohn's account of Jan's kingdom is more temperate than Reck's, and his insights draw usefully upon the social sciences to note some important additional points in his concluding remarks. The first is that modern extremists in Germany and Russia claimed that both science and history (when properly understood and revised) supported their views, whereas their predecessors depended on religious texts for their justification. His second point is that the periods resemble each other in that "one cannot afford to ignore the psychic content of the phantasies which have inspired them," which Cohn says are essentially those of paranoia. "The megalomaniac view of oneself as the Elect, wholly good, abominably persecuted yet assured of ultimate triumph; the attribution of gigantic and demonic powers to the adversary; the refusal to accept the ineluctable limitations and imperfections of human existence, such as transience, dissension, conflict, fallibility, whether intellectual or moral; the obsession with inerrable prophecies—these attitudes are symptoms which together constitute the unmistakable syndrome of paranoia." Cohn has amply demonstrated in his narrative that the paranoia is often justified, especially in the case of the Anabaptists—people were indeed out to get them. But his third point is that the proscribed groups stubbornly fed upon their own delusions and ruthlessly imposed them on others when they could— Hitler's "final solution" to his "problem" of the Jews, extermination, is the most extreme example.

Cohn concludes that members of chiliastic groups suffer from an impaired sense of reality. The movements grow stronger during periods when other institutions are seen to fail. When their own efforts fail to change things, their followers are "overwhelmed by a sense of disorientation, frustration, impotence." The poor and the dispossessed were the likeliest prospects for membership in chiliastic groups in the Middle Ages, as in Münster, and they remain so today, according to Cohn.

Cohn was writing nearly half a century ago. Like the rest of the so-called First World nations, America in the last years of the twentieth century, prosperous and at peace, seems a poor candidate for the emergence of apocalyptic groups such as those of the past. And yet the imminence of the year 2000 has prompted much popular speculation as well as scholarly thought about the near future and the distant past. There is a Center for Millennial Studies at Boston University, with its own Web site, and books are appearing with titles like *The End of the World as We Know It: Faith, Fatalism, and Apocalypse in America* (Daniel Woyjcik, New York University Press, 1997), and Stephen Jay Gould's *Questioning the Millennium: A Rationalist's Guide to a Precisely Arbitrary Countdown* (Harmony Books, 1997). And there are college courses like the one at Agnes Scott College on "Apocalypse and Revolution" being offered around the country.

Some scholars concern themselves with current events such as the destruction of the Branch Davidians at Waco and the bombing of the

Federal building in Oklahoma City that seems to have followed as a consequence of Waco; the Heaven's Gate suicides in Rancho Bernardo; the Jim Jones disaster in Guyana; even the Million-Man March on Washington; all of which they see as symptoms of millennial frenzy. Others cast a similarly wide net over popular entertainment, examining *Dr. Strangelove, The Seventh Seal, Blade Runner, Road Warrior,* and even *Moby Dick* for their insights into the future.

Arbitrary dates of course mean very little, and most people are realistic enough to think of the future in benign terms such as grandchildren and retirement, not apocalypse, but some popular historians, hoping to impose large patterns of meaning, fall into traps of chronology. As recently as 1988, Richard Erdoes has explained that as the year 1000 approached in Europe, "[some people] were certain that the Second Coming of Christ would fall on the last day of the year 999, at the very stroke of midnight. Others were equally convinced that Armageddon would come a little earlier, on the eve of the nativity when 'the Children of Light would join in battle with Gog's army of hellish friends.' Some fixed the date on the day of the summer or winter solstice of the thousandth year after our Lord's passion . . . though people quarreled about the exact date and hour, they all agreed . . . that 'Satan will soon be unleashed because the thousand years have been completed.' " Many historians now regard this supposed panic as a myth created in the nineteenth century by Romantic historians such as Jules Michelet. Some people no doubt thought the end was near, just as some do today, but most regarded it with the skepticism that Kerssenbrück shows in his comments on the hysterical reaction to Bernard Rothmann's prediction of the imminent fall of the Overwater Church Convent.

To be sure, certain prophecies have a way of becoming self-fulfilling: the Anabaptists were correct in foretelling the end of the world in terms of their own fate. Today, sociologists have collected a host of evidence that some might interpret as signs of imminent apocalypse, whether good news or bad: the collapse of the Soviet Union and the growth of the Internet on the one hand, the spread of AIDS and of terrorism on the other. All are seen as signs or portents, just as the reflected light on the clouds above Münster looked like avenging angels to the Anabaptists.

The groups that emerge today, as the Anabaptists did in the past, have what sociologists call "totalistic" world views and charismatic leaders; they are "volatile" and inclined to violent confrontations with authorities or within the group, and hence are inherently unstable. Not the devil is to blame, but "brainwashing, "coercive persuasion," or "mind control"—"an ego-alien 'false' self" is imposed on cult victims through psychologically coercive conditioning processes and induced hypnotic states. Participation in these groups is seen from this standpoint as essentially *involuntary*." This explanation has a familiar ring (once the social-science prose is interpreted) in terms of the An- abaptist experience in Münster: both Jans were "alien," or foreign, as were many of their cadre; Knipperdolling had a "false" self imposed on his true one, perhaps; the Company of Christ were expert at co- ercive conditioning; et cetera. The editors of the text in which this approach is described disagree with it; they feel that brainwashing is less frightening than the idea that people can be persuaded to join such cults *without* such brainwashing, and prefer to attribute the appeal of cults to our "cultural fragmentation." However, the culture in Jan's time was monolithic, not fragmented, so the relatively old-fashioned view may hold best for the past.

Another familiar echo from the past is that with groups such as Jonestown and the People's Temple Movement, "[t]hemes of destruc- tion, redemption, flight and deliverance taken from the book of Isaiah were used to justify a prophecy of the destruction of the fattened nations and escape of the righteous into a new nation . . . The United States, its institutions and even its standards of beauty were portrayed as the 'beast'—totally irredeemable. Well-versed in both doctrinal and operational aspects of the opposing forces of good and evil, members of the People's Temple were prepared for sacrifice, struggle and an apocalyptic 'final showdown.' "

The most important similarity between the Anabaptists and Amer- ica's current cults is their concept of being special, or of the Elect. The definition in a recent text, though it is also cumbersome, merits quotation in full: "An elect group is specified whose members are encouraged to define their collective and personal identities in terms of absolute contrasts with radically disvalued individuals, groups, or cultures outside of and presumptively hostile to the group. The group envisions itself as an enclave of truth, purity, and virtue in a corrupt, evil, and doomed world, and it may anticipate or even welcome the world's hostility. Participants may acquire a sense of wholeness, purpose, and purity, and, moveover, *may experience relief from anxiety or depression,* which, however, may depend upon continuing loyalty to and solidarity with the movement and adherence to group beliefs."

With all of this sociological ammunition in hand, it is time to take a look, finally, at the incident that first prompted this book: the destruction of the Branch Davidians and their leader, who called himself David Koresh, in Waco, Texas, in April 1993. David Koresh, born Vernon Howell, was a talented amateur musician who had been a member of the Seventh-Day Adventists; becoming captivated by church-sponsored "Revelation Seminars," he joined an offshoot group, in itself a branch of another group, called the Branch Davidians, in 1981. He displaced the leader of that group after "various vicissitudes and altercations (including a shoot-out)," at which time he adopted the name of David Koresh. The group's property near Waco was renamed Ranch Apocalypse, in readiness for the final desperate struggle between the government, which Koresh called the Babylonians, and the Lamb, himself and his followers. The precipitating charge that brought the Federal government down on him had to do with his accumulation of unlicensed firearms; it should also be noted that he was under investigation by the state of Texas for statutory rape and child abuse while "spreading the seed of the Messiah."

The first, failed attempt of the FBI to take the compound led to a fifty-one-day standoff with the FBI; a recent study suggests that "Koresh and his subleaders may well have wished to find a peaceful solution to the confrontation. However, the shoot-out with the FBI had no doubt enhanced the salience and immediacy of Koresh's . . . apocalyptic vision. He may well have been inhibited" from surrendering "in part because his prophetic vision would be compromised if the dramatic confrontation ended 'not with a bang but with a whimper.' By definition *an apocalypse does not peter out!*" (Emphasis in original.)

The final attack by the government, with armored vehicles, tear gas, and heavy weapons, resulted in the deaths of Koresh and seventy-five other men, women, and children; the causes of death include, primarily, the terrible fire that followed the attack, but how the fires began was never determined. A continuing and major point of controversy turns around how many people died as a result of government action, and how many might have killed themselves or been murdered by Koresh and other followers.

The dissimilarities between Münster and Waco are obvious. A ranch with a few hundred people is not a city with nine thousand; the Texas group was more or less complete in itself, without large numbers of like-minded sympathizers spread around the continent; there was never any threat that Koresh and his group would cause a national disturbance; their relative power vis-à-vis the government's was so tiny that they could have been obliterated at any moment that the government chose; religious intolerance on the part of the government was not seen by anybody but Koresh's group as a reasonable charge against it. But most important is the simple fact that Koresh and his followers did not face certain death if they surrendered, as Jan most surely did.

That said, the similarities are still striking. In addition to the public drama of a prolonged standoff, we have both parties refusing to negotiate for anything other than total surrender, extensive dithering on the part of the government paralleled with increased isolation of the besieged, a final resolution that was marked by unnecessary brutality, and the deaths of many innocent people who had taken the wrong path, following the wrong man. The chief rebels, Jan van Leyden and Vernon Howell, were both self-created young men who changed their identities; both saw themselves in the form of the biblical David; both usurped the authority of the previous prophet; both lacked formal education but had a thorough knowledge of the Bible and complete recall of it; both were talented performers with a marked artistic bent; both took more wives than the law, religious or secular, allowed; both were cunning, unscrupulous, and, in Jan's case at least, murderous; and both were capable of inspiring great affection despite all that was known to be reprehensible about them.

One question remains. Why are we interested in such characters and events? After all, the Anabaptist Kingdom in Münster is far less important than the Peasants' Revolt or the Siege of Vienna, just as dozens of more important events than Waco were happening in 1993.

Is the appeal simply that it is perversely entertaining to imagine Thornton Wilder's idyllic *Our Town* turning into a hellhole, as in Shirley Jackson's "The Lottery"? Is it merely modish paranoia combined with popular entertainment, as in *The X Files*? Is it a deep sense of social malaise, of a world without purpose, design, or moral foundation? Or is the appeal, despite repeated warnings that we don't learn anything from history, to learn to recognize dangerous characters and ideas so that we can avoid repeating our mistakes?

All of these, perhaps. Or maybe, less ambitiously, these are all fascinating stories with characters and ideas that move us to a response. The story of the Anabaptists in Münster, the original apocalyptic horror story, is inherently dramatic—indeed, melodramatic in the tradition of *Grand Guignol,* Kurosawa's *Ran,* and three or four of Shakespeare's tragedies. But what, finally, to return to the question posed above, does it mean? Here are a few concluding speculations.

What it means, in the larger sense, is that Virginia Woolf was wrong when she said human nature changed in the early twentieth century. The people in Münster were recognizably like those of today—not only like those in Rancho Bernardo or Waco but like all of us, no matter how strongly we resist that idea. Who can deny, after considering human behavior past and present, the pervasive appeal of the irrational, of the desire, if only in fantasy, to wield total power over others, of furious resentment at mistreatment and resulting revenge fantasies? Who among us can read about the courage of those who defied Jan and died, or about the shifting allegiances and accommodations of those who did not, without wondering how we would have behaved? And who doubts that many people today around the world still have to make similar choices?

It means, then, that this story is not just a historical anecdote about a group of peculiar north Germans and Hollanders in the late Middle Ages but about people who may be seen as universal archetypes of heroism, villainy, aspiration, and defeat. Their own archetypes were drawn from the Bible—Hille Feyken as Judith, Jan as King David, Jan Matthias as Enoch. The modern reader, often more familiar with literary than with biblical models, may see King Lear in Knipperdolling, Iago combined with Macbeth in Jan of Leyden, and Don Quixote in Jan Matthias.

It means, finally, that there are recognizable patterns of human and social experience, many of them dismaying. Like the Nazis, the Anabaptists destroyed competing icons of worship in the churches and burned books in the public square. Like the Serbs in Sarajevo before the war in Bosnia, they dismantled a shaky though functional ecumenical community in Münster and drove the unbelievers from the city. Like the disciples of David Koresh and Jim Jones, they followed a charismatic leader to their doom.

And like all of these disparate forces of anarchy and destruction, Jan van Leyden and his Company of Christ shook the foundations of their world. What makes them worth remembering is that they were the precursors and to some degree the progenitors of the political and religious violence that have become so much a part of our world today.

Cast of Characters

This partial list of names is limited to those who appear more than once in *The Tailor-King*. The more important names are in bold type.

Melchior von Buren. Owner of the residence in Münster that King Jan makes his palace; one of the Bishop's military staff.

Charles V. Holy Roman Emperor, concerned with unrest caused by the Anabaptists in Germany, orders their ruthless suppression.

Antonius Corvinus. Catholic priest who interrogates Jan, describes his character and his death.

Ulrich von Dhaun. Commander in chief of the Bishop's forces.

Divara. Formerly a Carmelite nun, then wife of Jan Matthias, finally wife and queen of King Jan.

Johann Dusentschur. Lame goldsmith from nearby Warendorf, who crowns Jan van Leyden as king of Münster.

Hille Feyken. Fifteen-year-old Dutch girl who tries to re-enact the biblical story of Judith and Holofernes.

Dietrich Fabricius. Lutheran clergyman, formerly an associate of the Anabaptists.

Henry Graes. Anabaptist schoolmaster who is captured by the Bishop but is reportedly saved from death by an angel.

Henry Gresbeck. Young carpenter who returns to Münster to protect his mother, instrumental in King Jan's defeat; later writes a useful account of his adventures.

Jaspar Jodefeld. Lutheran co-mayor, with Herman Tilbeck, who opposes the Anabaptists take-over.

Herman Kerssenbrück. Young Latin scholar who witnesses the initial troubles in Münster and later writes the fullest contemporary account of the Anabaptist Kingdom.

Bernard Knipperdolling. Prominent local businessman who becomes Jan van Leyden's father-in-law and his chief executioner.

Bernard Krechting. King Jan's chief of staff who is with him until the end.

Henry Krechting. Brother of Bernard, King Jan's chancellor, formerly a soldier, who survives into a serene old age.

Jan van Leyden. (Jan Bockelson). Handsome young tailor's apprentice, playwright, and adventurer who becomes king of Münster.

Martin Luther. Father of the Reformation, stern opponent of the Anabaptists.

Jan Matthias. Aging Dutch baker turned Anabaptist apostle who initiates the terror in Münster.

Philip Melanchthon. German Lutheran, humanist scholar, and associate of Luther who wrote in opposition to the Anabaptists.

Dirk von Merveldt. Bailiff of the Cathedral in Münster.

Ida von Merveldt. Abbess of the Cathedral in Münster (not related to Dirk).

Henry Mollenheck. Important guild leader who organizes the only serious opposition to Jan van Leyden.

Gert von Münster. An officer in the Bishop's army who defects to the Anabaptists.

Johann Nagel. A professional soldier for the Bishop, nicknamed Hansel Eck, or little Hans in the corner, who joins the rebel Anabaptists and is instrumental in their defeat.

Philip, Landgraf (Count) of Hesse. Influential neighbor and friend of Franz von Waldeck, a moderate Lutheran who works for peace.

Bernard Rothmann. Brilliant Anabaptist preacher and rhetorician, the party intellectual and propagandist.

Herbert Rusher. A blacksmith whose early opposition to the Anabaptists causes him to become their first victim.

Wilhelm Steding. A Prussian nobleman who leads the successful final assault on the Anabaptists.

Herman Tilbeck. Co-mayor with Jaspar Jodefeld before the take-over and a secret Anabaptist who betrays his city.

Franz von Waldeck. Prince-Bishop of Münster, forced into an expensive sixteen-month-long siege by the stubborn Anabaptists.

Elizabeth Wandscheer. King Jan's favorite wife, after Divara, who challenges his inhumanity at great cost.

Gerlach von Wullen. A nobleman and soldier who joins King Jan's cause.

Friedrich von Wyck. A Lutheran Bremen attorney. Hired by the moderates in Münster to negotiate between the Bishop and the radicals, he angers both.

CHRONOLOGY

805   Bishopric of Münster founded.

1517   Martin Luther initiates Protestant Reformation in Wittenberg.

1523   Anabaptism defined and formulated by Swiss reformer Conrad Grebel.

1524–1525   Peasants' Revolt against Church and state throughout Germany leads to mass destruction and death.

1525   Münster wins independence from Church and degree of self-rule, government by council and mayor.

1527   Rome sacked and destroyed by armies of Charles V.

1529   Emperor Charles V orders wholesale extermination of "every anabaptist and rebaptized man and woman of the age of reason."

1531   Former Münster priest Bernard Rothmann becomes radical Lutheran, destroys "idols" in his former church, Saint Mauritz.

1532   **February** Prominent citizens meet to organize resistance to the Bishop; mob attacks Catholic churches.

            March New Prince-Bishop, Franz von Waldeck, assumes post. City limits Catholic freedom of worship and assembly.

May   Bishop imprisons local businessmen traveling to Lübeck.

December   Anabaptists raid Bishop's residence, capture hostages.

1533

February   Truce results in exchange of prisoners, guarantees of city independence, declarations of loyalty to Bishop.

March   Anabaptists force election of new, more radical council that nullifies treaty.

June   Melchior Hoffmann, peaceful Anabaptist leader, imprisoned in Strasbourg; Jan Matthias, Dutch convert, assumes leadership of radical sect advocating violent rebellion.

June–September   Influx of foreigners destabilizes Münster.

October   Mass conversions and re-baptisms begin.

November 4   Remaining council moderates try to evict Bernard Rothmann, now declared Anabaptist; armed standoff between Lutherans and Anabaptists follows. Moderate Lutheran Philip of Hesse brokers truce.

1534

January 4   Philip's emissary Fabricius taunted and humiliated when he opposes Rothmann publicly; Bishop later demands Rothmann's expulsion.

Mid-January   Jan Bockelson arrives from Leyden, Holland, to coordinate Anabaptist activities in Münster.

February 8–10   Anabaptists fear sell-out by Lutherans to Bishop, attack City Hall; moderates retreat to stone-walled church. First armed conflict between groups.

ca February 12   Arrival of Anabaptist Prophet Jan Matthias; new council entirely consisting of Anabaptists formed.

February 27 Catholics and moderate Lutherans driven from the city.

February 28 Bishop initiates blockade.

Mid-March City prepares for Bishop's attack; Matthias confiscates private property and wealth; Münster blacksmith murdered by Jan van Leyden for resisting.

March 27 Dutch supporters coming to Münster intercepted in Holland.

April 5, Easter Sunday Jan Matthias singly challenges Bishop's army, is killed; Jan van Leyden assumes leadership.

April 9 Church towers and steeples destroyed, remains used to shore up city walls.

ca April 10–12 Jan disbands council; twelve Elders now to rule, as in ancient Zion, with him at the head. Opponents are imprisoned or executed.

May 25 Bishop's attack fails; Jan's dominance strengthened.

Mid-June Dutch girl, Hille Feyken, leaves city on mission to assassinate Bishop Franz.

Mid-July Jan van Leyden forces Elders to decree polygamy both legal and desirable, takes Matthias's widow and ultimately fifteen other women for himself.

July 30 Rebellion prompted by resistance to polygamy crushed; scores are executed.

August 28 Bishop's second attack repulsed; he begins construction of impenetrable cordon, intends to starve city into submission.

ca. September 1 Jan becomes King, establishes court; remaining opposition punished by death, including two women beheaded for opposing polygamy.

October 23   Teams of apostles sent to neighboring cities to gather support; most are captured and executed.

November 2   Bishop's emissary allowed to visit city, reports Jan and followers determined to resist; Bishop continues to tighten siege.

1535

January   Jan's efforts to rouse support abroad intensify; opposition by Luther, moderate Anabaptists in Holland grows.

March 26   Growing hunger and fear are exacerbated by defection of prominent aide to Jan, who sends public letter denouncing him; terror increases.

April–May   Thousands flee starvation and terror, are refused succor by Bishop. Two Anabaptist guards defect, reveal plans for city's defense that aid plan for third attack.

June 22   Night attack succeeds; most Anabaptists are killed; Jan, other leaders captured.

1536

January 22   Jan and two other prominent rebels executed in Münster; bodies are placed in cages hung from church tower. City soon becomes powerful center of Catholic Counter-Reformation.

NOTES

The references are to authors listed in the "Sources" sections that follows.

CHAPTER ONE: A NEW DAWN

5–7   Market Square events: Kerssenbrück 483–84 (Löffler 18–22); Baring-Gould translation 253–60.

7–8   Rothmann warning to nuns: Kerssenbrück 480 (Löffler 13–14).

9–11   Anabaptist beliefs and origins: Williams 190–95, Cohn 274.

11–12 Melchior Hoffman: Williams 293–94.

12   The numbers of Anabaptists throughout Europe were relatively small. According to Claus Peter Clasen, there were no more than 30,000 in the vast area that includes Austria, Switzerland, and southern Germany during the long period from 1525 to 1618. *Anabaptism: A Social History*, 27.

13–14 Münster description: Karasek 14–15; Church privileges: Homann 22–24.

13–15 Rothmann background: Rammstedt 40–42; Melanchthon: Homann 34.

15–16 Rothmann activities, challenge to von Wiede: Homann 31.

16–17 Knipperdolling meeting and church attack: Homann 33–34.

17–18 Knipperdolling imprisonment and torture: Homann 20. Kirchhoff thinks it unlikely that Knipperdolling was tortured because only executioners were allowed to inflict torture and Knipperdolling was not being held or charged for a capital offense. Kirchhoff interview.

18   Von Waldeck as "brave and righteous knight": Homann 34.

18   Von Waldeck's title: According to Dr. Rolf Klötzer, von Waldeck was always identified in contemporary documents as "der Konformiert," meaning that he was elected and confirmed as a secular leader. However, Franz referred to himself as "Bischof" and so did his antagonists in Münster and all subsequent writers, so that term has been used here. Klötzer interview.

19–20   Attacks on Catholic beliefs: Homann 36–44.

20   Charles V and von Waldeck: Homann 38–39.

20–21   Summons by Bishop: Kerssenbrück 474 (Löffler 10).

21   Blockade begins: Klötzer 33; Homann 38–40.

21–22   City council seeks help: Detlef 21, Homann 41.

22   Raid: Klötzer 39; truce arranged: Krahn 135.

23   Rothmann's appeals to foreigners: Kerssenbrück 509, Cohn 280.

23–24   Council elections: Homann 56–57.

24–25   Public baptisms: Karasek 39–40, Gresbeck 11.

25   Growing antagonism between groups; von Wyck mediates truce. Homann 58–60.

25–26   Fabricius visit and hostile reception: Brandler 110, Klötzer 55. Klötzer cites an associate of Fabricius as writing to Philip that their primary disagreement with Rothmann was over child baptism, and that in other respects their doctrines were similar.

26–27   Von Waldeck's response: Kerssenbrück 478 (Löffler 12).

27   Von Waldeck turns away delegation: Kerssenbrück 479 (Löffler 13).

27–28   Convent does not fall: Kerssenbrück 483 (Löffler 14).

CHAPTER TWO: THE GODLESS EXPELLED

29–30   Attack on city council: Kerssenbrück 487–89 (Löffler 18–19).

31–32   Truce and Tilbeck role: Kerssenbrück 492–96 (Löffler 20–24).

32   Farmers' departure: Rothmann letter in Stupperich, *Schriften*, 279.

33–34   Celebrations and carnival parodies: Kerssenbrück 495–96, 509 (Löffler 25–26).

34   Krechting brothers' arrival: Kerssenbrück 503 (Löffler 25–26).

35   Von Wyck death: Kerssenbrück 512–15 (Löffler 25–26).

36   Matthias arrival: Gresbeck 6.

37   New council: Kerssenbrück 519 (Löffler 42).

37–38	Cathedral vandalism: Kerssenbrück 521–22 (Löffler 43–49).
39	Demands for expulsion, first departures: Kerssenbrück 532–53 (Löffler 52).
40	Matthias's language: Baring-Gould 273, citing Kerssenbrück 532 (Löffler 52).
40	Knipperdolling intervention: Kerssenbrück 532 (Löffler 52).
40–42	Expulsion: Kerssenbrück 534–40 (Löffler 53–56).
42	Old woman's forced conversion: Kerssenbrück 540 (Löffler 56).
42	Roll death: Kerssenbrück records Roll's capture on Feb. 14. His death did not occur in fact until the following September, in Maastricht, not Utrecht. Detmer note 1, 509. The effect on the spirits of the Anabaptists was nonetheless disturbing. The false report was probably a deliberate deception by the Bishop.

CHAPTER THREE: A MIGHTY FORTRESS

44	Bishop's commanders: Kirchhoff, *Belagerung,* 79–81.
45	Judefelder Gate: "Judefeld" was a family name, similar to that of the co-mayor Jodefeld, and does not refer to a Jewish field as it might appear. There were no Jews in Münster at this time, all of them having been expelled in the pogroms of the late-thirteenth century. Kirchoff interview.
45	Bishop's supplies: Kirchhoff, *Belagerung,* 83–84. Kirchhoff drew this and other information regarding expenses and income from the meticulously detailed and extant accounts compiled by the Bishop's "Pfenningmeister" Hägebock, among other sources. Kirchhoff interview.
45–46	Bishop's soldiers: Kirchhoff, *Belagerung,* 79–81; Rules for behavior: Kerssenbrück 527–28 (Löffler 45–46).
47	War expenses: Kirchhoff, *Belagerung,* 84–87.
47	The gold guilder (Gulden) was the currency used in the Rhine area; the Emden guilder was used in the north of Germany, along the Dutch border. The Emden guilder was worth about fifty dollars in today's American currency, the gold guilder slightly less. A typical soldier would receive three to four guilders per month, from which he had to feed and clothe himself. Karl-Heinz Kirchhoff's estimate above of 34,000 guilders

would put the Bishop's total monthly payroll costs at $1.7 million.

48–49   City defenses: Kerssenbrück 545; Barret-Gurgand 83–87; Kirchhoff, *Belagerung*, 83. Rothmann invitation: Krahn 146.

49–51   City preparations for war: Kerssenbrück 549–54 (Löffler 60–62).

51–52   Songs: Brecht 43–48.

52–53   Book-burning: Kerssenbrück 564 (Löffler 70).

53–54   Confiscation of private property: Kerssenbrück 556–61 (Löffler 64–69).

53   Rothmann on property: Cohn 289; Knipperdolling on property: Krahn 142.

53–55   Rusher resistance: Paulus 226–30.

55   Victorian phrasing: Baring-Gould 282.

56–57   Rusher death: Kerssenbrück 559–60 (Löffler 72), Gresbeck 28–31.

57   Valuables collected: Kerssenbrück 556–58 (Löffler 71), Gresbeck 32.

CHAPTER FOUR: DEATH OF A PROPHET

61   Rothmann and duty: Krahn 147–48.

61   Rothmann's invitation: Cohn 290–91.

61–62   Nakedness: Krahn 147.

62   Persecution of Anabaptists: Krahn 147–48.

63   Dutch supporters intercepted, weapons found: Stayer, *Anabaptists and the Sword,* 262; Court judgment: Krahn 147.

64   Marriage ceremony: Cornelius 38.

64–66   Matthias's vision and death: Gresbeck 38–40; Kerssenbrück 568 (Löffler 73). Kerssenbrück writes that the soldiers were particularly brutal with Matthias because they knew he was responsible for the humiliation of the revered Canon Dungel. The anecdote concerning the sexual organs of Matthias is from Kerssenbrück.

66–67   Max Weber: Reinhard Bendix, *Max Weber: An Intellectual Portrait,* 298–307.

70–71   Jan van Leyden background: "Bekenntnis [Confession of] Jan van Leyden," in Cornelius 398–03, Detmer, *Bilder,* 21–23.

71–73   Jan's speech and its success: Gresbeck 38, Kerssenbrück/Detmer 570–71, Baring-Gould 286–87.

CHAPTER FIVE: THE BISHOP AND THE MAIDEN

74–75   Insults: Gresbeck 49–50, Kerssenbrück 588 (Löffler 89–90).

75   Messages: Kerssenbrück 586 (Löffler 86–87). The text of the message in Kerssenbrück is long enough, at about six hundred words, and sufficiently tempered in tone to suggest that the soldiers who read it must have been both patient and receptive to the arguments it contained.

75–76   Church towers: Kerssenbrück 571–72 (Löffler 71–72).

76   Jan's naked run: Baring-Gould 288–89.

76–77   Elders appointed: Kerssenbrück 574 (Löffler 78–79).

77–78   Rules for Anabaptists: Kerssenbrück 577–85 (Löffler 80–86).

78–79   Bishop's preparations for attack: Kirchhoff, *Belagerung*, 89.

79–80   Letters exchanged: Barret-Gurgand 109.

80   Bishop's optimism: Kirchoff, *Belagerung*, 89.

80–81   Anabaptist victory: Kirchoff, *Belagerung*, 89, Barret-Gurgand 110–11.

81   Bast death: Kerssenbrück 589–90 (Löffler 90–91).

82–85   Judith story: "Judith and Holofernes" in *The Anchor Bible Judith: A New Translation with Introduction and Commentary by Carey A. Moore*. Doubleday: New York, 1985, 190–221. One of the so-called "apocryphal" pre-Christian books of the Bible, Judith's story is not recognized as part of the accepted canon for various reasons by Roman Catholics but is often included in English Protestant Bibles.

85–86   Hille Feyken: Gresbeck 44–46; Kobalt-Groch 65–69.

86–88   Hille's capture and death, Ramert betrayal: Homann 116; Luther: Kobalt-Groch 81; Naïveté: Reck 90. Some months later the Bishop would try to ransom one of his commanders who had fallen into Jan's hands after a battle, Caspar Marschalk. The captain had been severely wounded, Jan reported through a messenger. He would be willing to trade him for Herman Ramert. The Bishop refused, saying that Ramert had earned his protection and that he would not give him up to the Anabaptists and certain death.

89   Dürrenmatt: *Es steht geschrieben* 101.
89–90   Feminist views: Kobalt-Groch 97–104; Psalmus and Simon: Kobalt-Groch 91, 97.

CHAPTER SIX: COUNTER-REVOLUTION

91–92   Rothmann sermon: Krahn 144.
92   Anabaptist women: Williams 507.
93   Paracelsus: Williams 509.
93   New marriage rules: Gresbeck 62–64.
93–94   Objections to polygamy: Williams 513.
          Jan's demands: Dorp 238.
95–96   Jan and lustful behavior: Homann, 128.
96–97   Mollenheck and revolt: Kerssenbrück 621–21 (Löffler 108–110), Gresbeck 75–79. Gresbeck provides the basic account of this heroic effort. Most later scholars pay it surprisingly little attention; Paulus, 259–68 and 346–63, is the exception in making Mollenheck, whose first name he changes from Henry to Christian, an important sacrificial victim, and in re-creating the episode; the details of the gathering of the supporters, the method of surrender, and the nature of his death are from Paulus. A recent English novel, *The Garden of Earthly Delights,* shows the leader of the revolt, now merely a nameless saddler, being torn limb from limb before the eyes of the Jan figure, with the victim's wife and son being forced to watch (370–72). In fact, although the deaths were deplorable, there is no record of Mollenheck himself being tortured.
97   Schlachtscape captured with wives: Gresbeck 74.
98–99   Gert the Smoker: Gresbeck 58–59.
99   Mollenheck and Bishop: Paulus 357.
99–101   Mollenheck defeat: Paulus 360–62.
101   Baring Gould on Kerssenbrück: 299; Gresbeck story: 78; Dorp on deaths: 238.
101–102   Supporters' deaths: Kerssenbrück 625 (Löffler 110).

CHAPTER SEVEN: KING JAN

103   Anabaptists' lustful behavior: Kerssenbrück 625–26 (Löffler 110–11), Baring-Gould 300–01, Gresbeck 62–73.

103   Gresbeck marriage: Gresbeck 72–73.
104   Protests heeded: Gresbeck 79–80.
104   Marriages casually dissolved: Grieser 256.
104   Moat problem: Kirchhoff, *Belagerung*, 106.
105   Building of moving wall: Kirchhoff, *Belagerung*, 107.
106   Bishop's truce and messages: Homann 144.
107–109   Attack: Gresbeck 80, Barret 128–29, Homann 140–45.
109–110   Dusentschur crowns Jan king: Gresbeck 95–96, Kerssenbrück
           633–35 (Löffler 126–27); Cohn's translation of Jan's response:
           295–96.
111   Jan's court: Gresbeck 83; Reck 110.
112   Clothing, money: Gresbeck 94–95.
112–113   Entertainment: Homann 156.
           Jan's entrance on judgment days: Kerssenbrück 662–63 (Löffler
           138–42).
113   Executions: Kerssenbrück 687-688 (Löffler 143-144); Stayer,
           Anabaptists and the Sword, 258.
114–116   Knipperdolling's outburst: Kerssenbrück 690–93 (Löffler 145–
           47), Gresbeck 142–50; Political motivation: Klötzer interview;
           Epilepsy: *Encyclopedia Britannica*, 8, 1957 654–55. Surprisingly,
           none of the sources consulted for this account consider epilepsy
           as a cause for Knipperdolling's behavior.
           Peter Van Sittart, in his novel *The Siege,* represents this episode
           as imagined by one of the merchant's enemies: "mighty Knip-
           perdollink calling himself Court Fool, dancing before King and
           the Sacred Cows, kissing their hands, then announcing that he
           was the Holy Ghost" (297).
117   Daymares: Jones 27.
117   Ten Commandments: Cohn 299.

CHAPTER EIGHT: THE RETURN OF HENRY GRAES

118–119   Morning summons and gathering: Gresbeck 106–07.
120–122   Feast, apostles sent away: Kerssenbrück 703–04 (Löffler 163–
           64).
122–124   Evening meal, soldier's death: Kerssenbrück/Detmer 702–03,
           Gresbeck 114, Paulus 472–73. Detmer explains that Kerssen-
           brück's account is drawn from Dorp, who includes a detail

about "a widow who was sitting at the table and who took such pleasure in witnessing the murder that the king laughed out loud."

124   Rumors: Paulus 484.

124–125 Dusentschur: Homann 162; Paulus (484) names Dusentschur as the executed man.

125–126 Warendorf and other apostles' fates: Kerssenbrück 708–22 (Löffler 161–70).

126–129 Graes story: Kerssenbrück 722, 724–26 (Löffler 169–70, 190–92), Gresbeck 94–95, Paulus 496–98. The details of this account concerning Graes's discovery and the guards' observation as well as the conversations are found only in Paulus; the story of the angel's appearance and the other details concerning Graes's capture are in the original documents.

CHAPTER NINE: RESTITUTION AND REVENGE

130   Biblical rescues: Peter's rescue is told in Acts 12:6–9: "And when Herod would have brought him forth, the same night Peter was sleeping between two soldiers, bound with two chains: and the keepers before the door kept the prison. And behold, the angel of the Lord came upon him, and a light shined in the prison: and he smote Peter on the side, and raised him up, saying, Arise up quickly. And his chains fell off from his hands. And the angel said unto him, Gird thyself, and bind on thy sandals . . . And he went out, and followed him; and wist not that it was true which was done by the angel; but thought he saw a vision." My thanks to Prof. Dr. Alasdair Heron for this reference.

131   Graes and Bishop: Kerssenbrück 722 (Löffler 169–70).

131–132 Bishop's frustration: Kirchoff, *Belagerung,* 120.

132   Fabricius background: Krahn 355.

132–134 Fabricius visit, Jan's threat: Löffler 178–80; Fabricius's arguments and recommendations: Kirchhoff, *Belagerung,* 119–22, Karasek 124–25.

134–135 Blockhouses: Kirchhoff, *Belagerung,* 113, 128.

135–136 "Restitution" summary: Williams 378.

136   "Restitution" and Philip: Kerssenbrück 770–72 (Löffler 202–04).
136–137 Luther on Anabaptists: Baring-Gould 336–37; Martin Luther, *Collected Works,* Wittenburg, II, 367–75, "Concerning the Devilish Sect of Anabaptists in Münster."
137–138 "Revenge": Krahn 149–51.
139–140 Graes departure, report to Bishop: Gresbeck 115, Löffler 192–93; robe: Baring-Gould 306.
140–141 Graes and Wesel: Kerssenbrück 726 (Löffler 194).
141   Good Friday revelation: Barret-Gurgand 216.
141–142 Graes letter: Cornelius 296.

CHAPTER TEN: FLIGHT

143–144 Gresbeck letter: Cornelius, Introduction, 65–66.
144–145 Turban Bill: Cornelius 312: Bishop Franz letter to Landgraf Philip: Cornelius 296.
145   Executions of women: Kerssenbrück 784–90 (Löffler 207–08).
145–146 Further executions: Busch, Graes's wife: Kerssenbrück 820 (Löffler 231); Tall Albert, Northern: Gresbeck 171–72.
146–147 Starvation: Gresbeck 170, 174–79; Kerssenbrück 798–99 (Löffler 221–23).
148–149 Refugees turned back: Kerssenbrück 805 (Löffler 223–24), Kirchhoff, *Belagerung,* 137.
149   Von Dhaun and refugees: Kirchhoff, *Belagerung,* 138.
150   Soldier's demand for food: Gresbeck 193–94.
150–151 Hans Nagel: Löffler 209–10.
151–152 Gresbeck escape, capture by soldiers: Gresbeck 194–99.
154   Gresbeck's scale model, trip to moat: Gresbeck 200.
154–155 Steding on Hans: Gresbeck 202.

CHAPTER ELEVEN: ATTACK

156–157 War wagons: Description and Graes suggestion: Barret-Gurgand 207–10; Gresbeck 129–30.
157   Bishop orders executions: Kirchhoff, *Belagerung,* 139–40.

157–159   Elizabeth Wandscheer death: Kerssenbrück 823 (Löffler 232–33), Paulus 575–76. Paulus's account here is my translation.

159–160   Bishop's final offer: Motivation: Homann, 193; Response: Barret-Gurgand 245.

160   Attack preparations: Gresbeck 212.

160–161   Hansel's key, Gresbeck's manipulation of bridge: my supposition.

161   Password disclosed: Gresbeck 214.

162–163   Steding's error, attack details: Löffler 238. Barret and Gurgand (250) suggest that Steding's soldiers, thinking they would quickly overwhelm the Anabaptists, saw no reason to share the booty with the rest of their comrades and therefore closed the door themselves in order to prevent their entry.

163   Twickel on the wall: Löffler 238.

164–165   Booty division: Kirchhoff, Belagerung, 142.

164   Krechting defense: Löffler 238–39; Raesfeld gift and common background: Kirchoff interview. Kirchhoff does not think the wagons figured prominently in Krechting's defense because they would not have had time to get them ready.

165–166   Soldiers' rampage: Lilie quote: Barret-Gurgand 253; Tilbeck et al: Kerssenbrück 849 (Löffler 239–40); Sanctus: Cohn 203.

166–167   Jan capture: Niesert 237 (Löffler 239), Reck 186–87.

167–168   Knipperdolling capture: Kerssenbrück 850 (Löffler 240).

168   Divara execution: Kerssenbrück 855 (Löffler 242).

168   Women returning: Kirchhoff, Belagerung, 144.

168–169   Bishop and Jan meeting: Gresbeck 213. Emphasis added.

CHAPTER TWELVE: PUNISHMENT

170   Jan and maidens: Dorp 399; Baring-Gould 360–61.

170   Jan and cages: Kirchhoff, Die Drei Käfige, 11.

171–173   Jan interview with Corvinus: Löffler 253–56.

173–174   Archbishop of Cologne: Reck 191.

173–174   Knipperdolling, Jan responses to questioning: Cornelius 403–05, 398–03.

174–175   Kerckering death: Kerssenbrück 855 (Löffler 243). Kirchhoff, in "Christian Kercherincks Aufstieg und Fall," Auf Roher Erde, p. 24, Nov. 1968, writes that Kerckering had been born in

1498 to a noble and wealthy family that had lived for two centuries in a great house on New Bridge Street. Stubborn and wayward as a boy, in 1519 he married a neighbor who was "wellborn" but not of the nobility, against his family's wishes. By 1532 his rebellious nature had led him to side with the Lutherans in their dispute with the Catholics concerning the disposition of St. Lambert's Church. In February 1534, he was elected to the new city council that would soon allow the Anabaptists to achieve total control of the city. After Jan became king the following summer, Kerckering took charge of supervising the city's defenses. His descendants would later claim that he had been persuaded by his wife against his own inclinations to support the Anabaptists, but he chose to remain to the end when he could have left in May. Before he was executed, Kerckering left a note for his cousin Johann Kerckering, directing him to pay one hundred and ten guilders from his estate toward his debts and to pray that his soul would go to Heaven.

175–176   Melanchthon: Baring-Gould 368, citing Martin Luther *Collected Works*, 1545–51, ii, 325.

176   Criminal code: *Der Wiedertäufer in Münster: Stadtmuseum Katalog*, 212.

176–178   Sentencing, priest's visits, executions: Löffler 267–68, citing Corvinus.

177–178   Corvinus description of executions: *Die Wiedertäufer in Münster: Stadt Museum Katalog*, 213

CHAPTER THIRTEEN: THE LEGACY OF THE TAILOR-KING

179   Plunder and pay: Kirchhoff, *Belagerung*, 144–45.

179–181   Bishop's problems: Kirchhoff, *Belagerung*, 163–65.

181   Bishop's death: Baring-Gould 370.

181   Houses: Hansel Eck: Homann 201–202.

182   Henry Krechting's peaceful death: Homann 215.

182   Rothmann's supposed survival: Reck 177.

182–183   Cages and lights: Kirchhoff, *Käfige*, 3.

183–184   Hauptmann's visit: Homann 11–13. Some visitors were harder of heart than might be expected: Heinrich Heine, the great poet, who visited the city in 1842, wrote a jingle suggesting that the new Cathedral at Cologne might "follow my advice and adorn it with the three iron cages that are now hanging high above Münster from the tower of the church called St. Lambert's": "Folgt meinem Rat und steckt sie hinein/in jene drei Körbe von Eisen,/die hoch zu Münster hängen am Turm/ der Sankt Lambert geheissen." Kirchhoff, *Käfige,* 24.

184   Overwater Church. The tower had been replaced in the nineteenth century but was later destroyed in a storm, after which it was decided to leave it as it had been in 1535.

184   Cages' damage: Kirchhoff, *Käfige,* 30.

184–185 Debate over cages: Kirchhoff, *Käfige,* 41–42.

185   Peace of Westphalia: Nevertheless, the city was besieged once again in 1657 by the Austrians; it was later occupied by Napoleon's army and it was severely damaged during World War II.

187   Anabaptists and Satan: Grieser 302, 304, 308.

187   Luther: Grieser 312–15.

188   Rhegius and Rothmann: Grieser 340–41.

188–189 Corvinus: Grieser 328.

189   Philip of Hesse: Grieser 331, 332, 334.

189–190 Jan and psychoanalysis: Jones 173–80.

191–192 Carnival world: Scribner 98; Bakhtin 78.

192   Reck on Jan: Reck 26.

192–194 Reck on Anabaptist-Nazi comparisons: Reck 19.

194   Cohn on Middle Ages, Introduction, xiii.

194   Chiliasm, Nazis: Cohn 307–14.

195–196 Year 2000: Denise K. Magner, "Apocalyptic Predictions and Millennial Fervor Attract Scholarly Notice," *The Chronicle of Higher Education,* October 14, 1997.

195–196 Apocalyptic portents: See Dick Anthony and Thomas Robbins. "Religious Totalism, Exemplary Dualism, and the Waco Tragedy," in *Millennium, Messiahs, and Mayhem: Contemporary Apocalyptic Movements.* New York and London: Routledge, 1997, p. 2.

196   The year 1000: Richard Erdoes, *A.D. 1000: Living on the Brink of Apocalypse.* New York: Barnes & Noble, 1988, 2.

196   Modern groups: Anthony and Robbins 261–63.

197   Jonestown: Anthony and Robbins 267–68, citing Constance
            H. Jones, "Exemplary Dualism and Authoritarianism in Jones-
            town," in *New Religions, Mass Suicide and the Peoples Temple,*
            ed. Rebecca Moore and Fielding McGehee. Lewiston, NY:
            Edwin Mellen, 1989.

197–198   Concept of Elect: Anthony and Robbins 268.

198   Koresh background: Anthony and Robbins 272–73.

198–199   FBI at Waco: Anthony and Robbins 275.

Sources and Writings about the Anabaptists

This book draws from a variety of original and secondary sources in an effort to tell an old European story to a new American and European audience of general readers, not professional historians. Works cited about the Anabaptists are listed first, those consulted second. General works cited and consulted are similarly listed. The introductory note discusses works in English first, then those in German, and concentrates on those works in both languages that were particularly helpful.

Works in English

There are only a few detailed reference sources available in English, and all, of course, are based on sources discussed in the "Works in German" section that follows. Those that I found useful (full citations follow below in the Bibliography) include Norman Cohn's *The Pursuit of the Millennium,* which since its appearance in 1957 has been the standard point of department for English-speaking readers who are interested in learning about the more bizarre aspects of life in the Middle Ages. Cohn's narrative summary of the events in Münster is presented by him as the culmination of a series of events that began around the year 1000. I found only two works of fiction in English on the subject. A 1962 novel, *The Siege,* by Peter VanSittart, is impressionistic and colorful. It is something of a potpourri of medieval lore and superstition, in places close to the original sources and elsewhere taking advantage of the novelist's imaginative license. The 1993 novel by Nicholas Salaman, *The Garden of Earthly Delights* (London: Harper-Collins), describes the action through the eyes of a protégé of Hieronymus Bosch who ends up in Münster with his young wife, who then leaves him to become the ruler's queen. Salaman uses some recognizable sources but changes names and invents incidents to suit his fictional purposes. S. Baring-Gould, a Victorian man of letters, devotes a long chapter to Münster in his 1891 collection, *Freaks of Fanaticism and Other Strange Events,* which was helpful in providing an English perspective and a narrative overview, as well as useful, though dated, translations from the German.

American scholarly work on Münster for many years was left almost entirely to those connected with the *Mennonite Quarterly Review (MQR),* a bi-monthly journal published at Goshen College, Indiana, and devoted to issues related to the Mennonites in this country and abroad. Most of the earlier *MQR* essays on Münster have a defensive quality to their tone, concerned as they are to demonstrate that Jan and his followers were radical and unacceptable apostates from the tenets of true Anabaptism as represented by Menno Simons, after whom the Mennonites are named. Of the approximately two dozen articles in the *MQR* (excluding book reviews) over the past half century, the most important for me has been the two-part series in 1934 by John Horsch entitled "The Rise and Fall of the Anabaptists of Münster," which lays out the narrative structure, themes, and characters of the story. In his 1936 article, "Menno Simons' Attitude toward the Anabaptists of Münster," Horsch explains in further detail the basis for separating the true Anabaptists from Jan's radical splinter group.

The major North American scholar on the subject is James Stayer, whose 1972 book *Anabaptists and the Sword* explains both the repression of the Anabaptists and their sometimes violent reactions, as in Münster, to that repression. More recently, in a 1986 *MQR* article, "Was Dr. Kuehler's Conception . . . Correct?" Dr. Stayer argues that Jan van Leyden was essentially just an actor who needed to resort to outlandish antics because he lacked the authority of Jan Matthias. Like many modern scholars, he notes in order to question it the story line that Kerssenbrück set for Münster, and which Horsch adopted: a weak, traitorous council was toppled by lower-class rabble stirred up by outside agitators. Later research indicates that wealth was relatively evenly distributed among the citizens, meaning many supporters were not economically motivated; some of the immigrants who came into the city were also wealthy, though they naturally didn't bring much with them. My own account falls between these two poles but leans more toward the Kerssenbrück/Horsch interpretation.

The foremost living German expert on Münster is Karl-Heinz Kirchhoff, who is represented more fully in the German-language section. In an *MQR* article in 1970, Kirchhoff anticipates and provides support for Stayer's position, asking, rhetorically, "Was There a Peaceful Anabaptist Congregation in Münster in 1535?" He argues that it was Jan Matthias who brought the violence with him to Münster. Left to their own devices, Rothmann and the others there before him could have worked things out peacefully. I benefited greatly from Dr. Kirchhoff's many works and, as mentioned in the 'acknowledgements,' enjoyed the privilege of a fruitful and pleasant interview with him at his home in the former Bishop's seat of Wolbeck.

Two dissertations address the event in part. Mary Eleanor Bender's 1959 Indiana University study, "The Sixteenth-Century Anabaptists as a Theme in Twentieth-Century German Literature," appraises several novels, plays, and historical narratives published in this century, all in German, about Münster, including three that are noted more fully in the German section below. Dale Grieser's 1996 Harvard dissertation, "Seducers of the Simple Folk," examines the contemporary objections to the Anabaptists in popular pamphlets of the time and devotes a chapter to the "carnival in Münster," as he calls it.

Of the many works in English on Luther and the Reformation, I relied on George Huntston Williams's *The Radical Reformation* (1962) and Cornelius Krahn's *Dutch Anabaptism: Origin, Spread, Life and Thought (1450–1600)*, published in 1968. The first is widely recognized as the standard text, and I found its scattered references to the elements that made up the Münster tragedy very helpful. The second text was essential in setting the Dutch scene and in establishing the relationship between the Germans and the Dutch of this period. Biographers of Luther such as Heiko Oberman seem not to deal with Luther and Münster in any detail; more helpful was John S. Oyer's 1964 study, *Lutheran Reformers Against Anabaptists*. Oyer was a professor at the Mennonite Goshen College, and his account is intended to reveal and explain the "unremittingly hostile" attitudes of the Lutherans to the Anabaptists which have led to historical distortions in the representations of this varied group of dissidents.

WORKS IN GERMAN

My point of departure for the voluminous sources in German on the Anabaptists in Münster was the book-length city museum catalog published there in 1983 to commemorate the new museum's first large show, which was a large display of artifacts about the Anabaptist rule of the city. The volume, *Die Wiedertäufer in Münster,* includes commentary on all of the exhibits and photographs of many, as well as explanatory essays and a useful bibliography. A key source for information and of colorful narrative details since the mid-nineteenth century has been the collection of eyewitness accounts of the Anabaptist Kingdom and the full introduction and commentary on these provided by C. A. Cornelius in his *Berichte der Augenzeugen über das Münsterische Wiedertäuferreich* (Reports of Eyewitnesses Concerning the Anabaptist Kingdom in Münster). Published in 1853, this work includes the influential man-in-the-street's narrative by Henry Gresbeck, "Meister Henry Gresbeck's Bericht," the so-called confessions of Knipperdolling, Jan, and others, and letters and reports by various figures, including some of the Bishop's commanders.

Cornelius's comments on Kerssenbrück and Gresbeck are detailed and instructive. The first version of Kerssenbrück's account, and the one used by Cornelius, was the handwritten narrative done in Latin, *Anabaptist Furosis Historica Narratio.* Kerssenbrück had returned to Münster to serve as rector of the Cathedral school in 1550; by 1566 he was, according to Cornelius, a respected writer of theological works and ready to write something about what he knew about the bloody history of Münster that would be useful for future historians. He began his history of the uprising in 1566 and finished it in 1575. Although the time of the kingdom was long since past, along with most of the eyewitnesses, Kerssenbrück had a rich source of material at hand. His own memories of what he had seen as a boy were aided by what he had been told about by others. For more than twenty years he had daily intercourse with relatives, friends, and associates of the participants to augment his own memories. According to Cornelius, Kerssenbrück's sharply observant sense of the details and personalities that he observed, as well as his intimate knowledge of the city and its surroundings, let him keep the clarity of his youthful eyes as he pursued the causes and effects of what he had seen with the wisdom of his years. Additionally, he had the benefit of other published accounts before his, and he was given access to official city and state archives.

Cornelius says Kerssenbrück judged what he heard carefully, avoiding mere rumor or being carried away by the eloquence of the speaker. His style throughout is careful and selective; he likes to show his learning through mythological, literary, and historical allusions, adorning his factual narrative with tools of classical rhetoric. He even allows Knipperdolling, at the beginning of the Bishop's siege, to cite Thucydides concerning the relative strength of the two opposing parties, the Bishop's and his own. It is true, Cornelius says, that many of these observations are tedious, trivial, or tasteless; his attempts at irony and satire are often pale and silly; his reliance on astrology is laughable. For all his faults, though, Kerssenbrück's narrative ability holds the reader's attention, Cornelius says—and he is essentially reliable. It's easy to tell what he observed himself, as he says "I," "we," and "our." We see the boy as he stands in the street with his friends listening to the Anabaptists prophesying doom and demanding repentance, pointing to signs in the night sky. He peers into Knipperdolling's house and sees the Catiline of Münster, (after the Roman traitor) standing in a corner and carrying on a conversation with his heavenly Father. Caught carrying a gun belonging to his landlord, Dr. Wesseling, he has to hide from the bullets of the Anabaptists behind the charnal house in the cemetery of St. Egedi's Church, on the same day as a fellow student has been killed.

Eventually, Cornelius says, the city authorities grew tired of Kerssenbrück's insistence on recalling such an unpleasant part Münster's history. After twenty-five years as rector, he left it once again in 1575 for a similar post in the neighboring city of Paderborn, and ended his career in Osnabrück. He died in 1585. His original Latin work was translated into German in 1771. Reprinted in 1881 and in 1929 as *Geschichte der Wiedertäufer zu Münster in Westphalen,* it remains the point of departure for all later studies. However, the eighteenth-century German translation is generally regarded as inadequate. I consulted the H. Detmer 1900 edition of the Latin text and drew on Detmer's German translations in his footnotes; I also used Clemens Löffler's 1926 chronological assembly and translations of Kerssenbrück, Gresbeck, and other sources, the full title of which is listed in the Works Cited section of the Bibliography.

Cornelius also assembled the other major primary source for the kingdom of Münster, the narrative of Henry Gresbeck, from several archival sources. Written in a north-German dialect that is nearly as difficult for modern Germans as Old English is for us, it has been translated in part by various researchers but nowhere in its entirety. Cornelius helpfully translates into modern German Gresbeck's letter to (presumably) Count von Manderscheid and provides background information on the young carpenter that later scholars use. He stresses the contrast between the learned and somewhat stuffy Kerssenbrück and Gresbeck, the "lively and spirited" and independent young man, the common man who writes as he would have talked, full of slang and idioms. He sometimes reports on things he has heard but not seen, but he does not pretend to know what is beyond his own experience, such as the inner workings of Jan's mind or his council, and he is very good on details such as the city's defensive preparations and, of course, his own adventures. "We may regard his report in general, where he speaks from what he has seen and heard himself, as historical truth." It is interesting to note that since Cornelius made Gresbeck's contribution known, the young carpenter has figured largely in the imaginative reconstructions of the Anabaptist Kingdom.

Of the many relevant works by Karl-Heinz Kirchhoff, several were especially helpful. The most recent (1996) and most easily accessible is a short book on the cages that still hang from St. Lambert's Church, *Die "Wiedertäufer-Käfige" in Münster*. Kirchhoff put quote marks around "Anabaptist Cages" because he disapproves of both the term "Wiedertäufer" as one used only by their enemies, and of the word "cages," which he thinks represents the three men whose bodies they contained as less than human. His sympathy for the rebels derives in part from his study of the oppression they faced, discussed in another work, published in 1962, about the suppression of civil liberties by Bishop Franz, "Die Besetzung Warendorfs" ("The Military Occupation of Warendorf"). The siege and conquest of the city that followed as a partial result of the Bishop's own policies is described in the 1962 work, *Die Belagerung und Eroberung Münsters 1534/35*. In *Die Täufer in Münster* (The Baptists in Münster) *1534–35*, published in 1963, Kirchhoff provides an overview of the social, economic, and religious structures of the Anabaptists in Münster. A book-length summary of the events and the scholarship concerning the episode is found in Kirchhoff's *Das Phänomen des Täuferreiches zu Münster 1534/35* (The Phenomenon of the Anabaptist Kingdom of Münster), in *Der Raum Westfalen* (The Westphalian Region), VI, 1 (Münster: Aschendorff, 1989).

Other major German sources included Horst Karasek's 1977 collection of original documents and secondary commentary, edited with an East German perspective, as the title indicates: *Die Kommune der Wiedertäufer;* Ottheim Rammstedt's often-cited 1966 *Sekte und Soziale Bewegung* (Sects and Social Movements), Gerhard Brendler's 1966 account with a Marxist perspective, *Das Täuferreich zu Münster: 1534/35,* and Rolf Klötzer's recent explication (1992) of the events in Münster as driven more by social and political dynamics than apocalypticism, *Die Täuferherrschaft von Münster* (The Anabaptist Rule in Münster).

Also useful were the works by Robert Stupperich, who in 1980 collected and edited three volumes of writings for and against the Anabaptists by Lutherans, Catholics, and Anabaptists, *Die Schriften der Münsterischen Taüfer und ihrer Gegner.* In 1958 Professor Stupperich examined the current state of research and appraised earlier scholarship in *Das Münsterische Täufertum: Ergebnisse und Probleme der Neuren Forschung* (Opportunities and Problems of Current Research).

I benefited from two popular histories intended for general audiences in Germany. The title in English of Hermann Homann's 1977 short book *Aufstieg und Fall des Wiedertäuferreiches in Münster 1534–1535* (The Rise and Fall of the Anabaptist Kingdom of Münster) seems to echo both the popular American history of the Nazi period by William Shirer, *The Rise and the Fall of the Third Reich,* and perhaps Bertold Brecht's *The Rise and Fall of the City of Mahagonny.* The second work, longer and usefully detailed, is *Der König der Letzten Tage,* the German translation of a 1981 book by two French journalists, Pierre Barret and Jean-Noel Gurgand, *Le Roi des Derniers Jours.*

A number of novels and plays have taken on the challenge of the Anabaptists in Münster. In addition to the English novel, *The Siege,* there was Friedrich Reck-Malleczewen's *Bockelson* in 1946, originally published as a novel in 1937, now subtitled "An Investigation of Mass Hysteria." The limitation of Reck's book is suggested by its title; he can barely stand to refer to the subject of his book except in contemptuous and dismissive terms because he hates so much, and his passion often overcomes him. Nevertheless, Reck's work is said to have inspired the great Swiss dramatist Friedrich Dürrenmatt's first play, *It Is Written (Es steht geschrieben),* in 1947, a strange sort of existentialist comedy. Mary Eleanor Bender, in considering the literary merits of these two works, dislikes the first and praises the second. She also dislikes Helmut Paulus's

Die Tönernen Füsse (Feet of Clay). It is, admittedly, very long, nearly six hundred closely printed pages, and written entirely in the present tense. Told from as many as thirty different points of view, it lacks references to dates or places, and is often very confusing. However, Paulus was a professional librarian and seems to have drawn reliably on the original sources, and he frequently writes movingly about the things he describes; I found his book very useful and relied on it in several key instances, as acknowledged in the Notes.

Finally, a book that was not used as reference but deserves comment is Ulrike Halbe-Bauer's 1995 novel, *Propheten im Dunkel* (Prophets in the Dark). Professor Kirchhoff provides a laudatory comment on the cover of this short novel for its representation of the Anabaptists in a more favorable way than usual—the twelve-year-old girl who narrates the story presents Knipperdolling as gruff but kindly and stresses the communal joy felt by the Company of Christ. Jan van Leyden barely appears in the story.

Interest in Münster continues in Germany. In 1985 a German living in England, Alexander Goehr, wrote an opera called *Behold the Sun*; the idea came to him after he read Norman Cohn's book, *In Pursuit of the Millennium,* he said in an interview, and he was inspired in part by Jonestown and the Khomeini revolution in Iran. (There is also an earlier opera in French by Giacomo Meyerbeer, *Le Prophète,* 1849.) In 1993 there was a four-hour commercial German television production called *Der König der Letzten Tage* (The King of the Final Days) it was very loosely—"nominally" may be the better word—based on the Barret-Gurgand history described above. Knipperdolling in this version is closer to the kindly figure in Halbe-Bauer's story, guilty of nothing more than bad judgment, and Jan's atrocities are diminished in intensity and number, and by the Christ like manner of his death. The sets, costumes, and music are impressive.

BIBLIOGRAPY

I. ABOUT THE ANABAPTIST KINGDOM IN MÜNSTER

Works Cited in the Text

Baring-Gould, S. *Freaks of Fanaticism and Other Strange Events*. London, 1891.

Barret, Pierre, and Jean-Noel Gurgand, *Der König der Letzten Tage* (The King of the Last Days). Hamburg, 1982; originally published as *Le Roi des Derniers Jours*. Paris, 1981.

Brendler, Gerhard. *Das Täuferreich zu Münster 1534–35* (The Anabaptist Kingdom of Münster). Berlin, 1966.

Brecht, Martin. "Songs of the Anabaptists in Münster and Their Hymnbook." *MQR* October 1985. (Vol 59), 362–66.

Clasen, Claus Peter. *Anabaptism: A Social History*. Ithaca: Cornell University Press, 1972.

Cohn, Norman. *The Pursuit of the Millennium*. Fairlawn, New Jersey: Essential Books, 1957.

Cornelius, C. A., ed *Berichte der Augenzeugen über das Münsterische Wiedertäuferreich. Die Gesichtsquellen des Bisthums Münster*. (Eyewitness Reports of the Anabaptist Kingdom of Münster. Historical Sources of the Bishopric of Münster). Münster, 1923

Detlefs, Gerd. "Das Wiedertäuferreich in Münster 1534/35" ("The Kingdom of the Anabaptists in Münster"). In *Die Wiedertäufer in Münster*. Stadtmuseum Münster. *Katalog der Eröffnungsausstellung vom 1. Okt. 1982 bis 27. Feb. 1983*, (Opening Show Catalog, October 1, 1982 to February 27, 1983). Münster: Aschendorff, 1983.

Detmer, Henry. *Bilder aus den Religiösen und Socialen Unruhen in Münster während des 16. Jahrhunderts* (Images of Religious and Social Unrest in Münster During the Sixteenth Century). Münster: *Westfalen*, 1903.

Dorpius, Henry. *Die Wiedertäufer in Münster* (The Anabaptists in Münster). Magdeburg, 1847.

Dürrenmatt, Friedrich. *Es steht geschrieben* (It Is Written). Zurich: Arche, 1963. First published 1947.

Galen, Hans. ed. *Die Wiedertäufer in Münster.* Stadtmuseum Münster. *Katalog der Eröffnungsausstellung vom 1. Okt. 1982 bis 27. Feb. 1983* (Opening Show Catalog, October 1, 1982 to February 27, 1983). Münster: Aschendorff, 1983.

Grieser, Dale. "Seducers of the Simple Folk." Harvard University, Theology Ph.D. Dissertation, 1996.

Homann, Hermann. *Aufstieg und Fall des Wiedertäuferreiches in Münster 1534–35* (The Rise and Fall of the Anabaptist Kingdom of Münster, 1534–35). Münster: F. Coppenrath, 1977.

Karasek, Horst. *Die Kommune der Wiedertäufer* (The Commune of the Anabaptists). Berlin, 1977.

Kerssenbroch, Hermann von. *Anabaptistici furoris: monasterium inclitam westphaliae metropolim evertentis historico narratio; im Auftrage des Vereins für Vaterländische Geschichte und Altertumkunde herausgeben von H. Detmer* (Historical Narrative of the Anabaptist Uproar in the Westphalian City of Münster; commissioned by the Association of National History and Archaeology, ed. H. Detmer), 2 vols. Münster: Theissing, 1899–1900.

Kirchhoff, Karl-Heinz. *Die Belagerung und Eroberung, Münsters 1534/35* (The Siege and Conquest of Münster 1534/35). *Westfalisches Zeitschrift* 112. 1962.

———*Die "Wiedertäufer-Käfige" in Münster.* (The "Anabaptist Cages" in Münster). Münster: Aschendorff, 1996.

———Personal interview, June 22, 1998.

Klötzer, Rolf. *Die Täuferherrschaft von Münster: Stadtreformation und Welterneurung.* (Anabaptist Rule in Münster: City Reform and World Renewal). Münster: Aschendorff, 1992.

———Personal interview, June 23, 1998.

Kobelt-Groch, Marion. *Aufsässige Töchter Gottes: Frauen im Bauernkrieg und in der Täuferbewegung.* (Rebellious Daughters of God: Women During the Peasants' War and the Anabaptist Movement). Frankfurt: Campus, 1993.

Krahn, Cornelius. *Dutch Anabaptism: Origin, Spread, Life and Thought (1450–1600)*. The Hague: Martinus Nijhott, 1968.

Löffler, Clemens. *Die Wiedertäufer zu Münster 1534/35. Berichte, Aussagen, und Aktenstücke von Augenzeugen und Zeitgenossen.* (Reports, Testimony, and Documents from Eyewitnesses and Contemporaries). Jena, 1923.

Paulus, Helmut. *Die Tönernen Füsse.* (Feet of Clay). Bonn: Vink, 1953.

Rammstedt, Otthein. *Sekte und Soziale Bewegung. Soziologische Analyse der Täufer in Münster, 1534/35*: (Sects and Social Movements: A Sociological Analysis of the Anabaptists in Münster). Cologne, 1966.

Reck-Malleczewen, Friedrich Percyval. *Bockelson: Geschichte eines Massenwahns.* (The Story of a Mass Hysteria). Stuttgart: Henry Goverts, 1968 (1946); first published 1937 as a novel, *Bockelson*.

Stayer, James M. *Anabaptists and the Sword.* Lawrence, Kansas: Coronado Press, 1972.

Stupperich, Robert. *Das Münsterische Täufertum Ergebnisse und Probleme der Neuren Forschung.* (The Anabaptists in Münster: Opportunities and Problems of Current Research). Münster: Aschendorff. 1958.

———. *Die Schriften der Münsterischen Täufer und ihrer Gegner* (Writings of the Anabaptists in Münster and Their Opponents), 3 vols. Münster: Aschendorff, 1980.

VanSittart, Peter. *The Siege.* New York: Walker, 1962.

Williams, George Huntston. *The Radical Reformation.* Philadelphia: Westminster, 1962.

Works Consulted

Halbe-Bauer, Ulrike. *Propheten im Dunkel.* (Prophets in the Dark). Münster: Westfälisches Dampfboot, 1995.

Horsch, John. *Society and Religion in Münster.* New Haven, 1984 (mostly after 1535).

———"The Rise and Fall of the Anabaptists of Münster." *MQR*, IX, April and July 1935, 92–103, 129–43.

———"Menno Simons' Attitude Toward the Anabaptists of Münster." *MQR*, X, January 1936, 55–72.

Hsia, K. Po-Chia, and R. Po-Chia Hsia, eds. *The German People and the Reformation.* Ithaca, London: Cornell University Press, 1988. Contains essay by R. Po-Chia Hsia, "Münster and the Anabaptists," 51–69.

Kirchhoff, Karl-Heinz. "Die Besetzung Warendorfs" ("The Occupation of Warendorf"), *Westfalen* 40, (1962), 117–22.

——*Die Täufer im Münster 1534–35.* Münster: Aschendorff, 1973.

——"Was There a Peaceful Anabaptist Congregation in Münster in 1535?" *MQR*, 44, Oct. 70, 359–70.

Kohl, Wilhelm. "Henry Roll: Beitrage zu seiner Biographie. *Festschrift für Alois Schroer.* "Henry Roll: A Contribution Towards His Biography." *Festschrift for Alois Schroer.* Münster 1972, 185–94.

Stayer, James. "The Münsterite Rationalization of Bernhard Rothmann." *Journal of History of Ideas,* XXVII, 1967.

——"Was Dr. Kuehler's Conception of Early Dutch Anabaptism Historically Sound? The Historical Discussion of Münster 450 Years Later," *MQR*, 60 #3, July 1986, 261–68.

Stupperich, Robert. "Landgraf Philip von Hessen und das Münsterische Täufertum." *Festgaber für W. F. Dankbaar.* ("Count Philip of Hesse and the Anabaptist Rule in Münster." *A Collection in Honor of W. F. Dankbaar.*) Amsterdam, 1977, 98–115.

——"Dr. Johann von der Wyck. Ein Münsterische Staatsmann der Reformationszeit." *Westfalische Zeitschrift* 123, 1–50. ("Dr. John von der Wyck: A Statesman of Münster During the Reformation." *Westphalian Magazine* 123, 1–50.)

Warnke, Martin. "Durchbrochene Geschichte: Die Bilderstürme der Wiedertäufer in Münster 1534–35." *Bildersturm: Zerstörung der Kunstwerk.* (Destroyed History: The Attack on Art by the Anabaptists in Münster 1534–35, in *Attacks on Art: Destruction of Artworks.*) Munich, 1973, 65–98.

II. BACKGROUND STUDIES

Works Cited

Anthony, Dick, and Thomas Robbins. "Religious Totalism, Exemplary Dualism, and the Waco Tragedy," in Thomas Robbins and Susan J. Palmer, eds., *Millennium, Messiahs, and Mayhem: Contemporary Apocalyptic Movements.* New York and London: Routledge, 1997.

Bakhtin, Mikhael. *Rabelais and His World.* Cambridge, MA: 1968.

Bendix, Reinhard. *Max Weber: An Intellectual Portrait.* Anchor/Doublday, 1960–1962.

Jones, Ernest. *On the Nightmare.* New York: Liveright, 1951.

"Judith and Holofernes": *The Anchor Bible Judith: A New Translation* with Introduction and Commentary by Carey A. Moore. New York: Doubleday, 1985.

Robbins, Thomas, and Susan J. Palmer, eds. *Millennium, Messiahs, and Mayhem: Contemporary Apocalyptic Movements.* New York and London: Routledge, 1997.

Scribner, R. W. *Popular Culture and Popular Movements in Reformation Germany.* London: Hambledon Press, 1978.

III. OTHER WORKS CONSULTED

Bainton, Roland. *Christian Attitudes Toward War and Peace: A Historical Survey and Critical Re-evaluation.* Nashville: Abingdon, 1960.

Bender, Mary Eleanor. "The Sixteenth-Century Anabaptists as a Theme in Twentieth-Century German Literature." Indiana University, German Ph.D. Dissertation, 1959.

Burke, Peter. *Popular Culture in Early Modern Europe, 1500–1800.* New York: Harper, 1978.

Contamine, Philippe. *War in the Middle Ages.* Translated by Michael Jones. Oxford: Basil Blackwell, 1993.

Grosso, Michael. *The Millennium Myth: Love and Death at the End of Time.* Wheaton, Illinois: Quest Books, 1994.

Oberman, Heiko A. *Luther: Man Between God and the Devil.* New York: Doubleday Image, 1992. Berlin: Severin und Seidler, 1982. Translated by E. Walliser-Schwarzbart.

Oman, Charles. *A History of the Art of War in the Sixteenth Century.* London: Methuen, 1937.

Ozment, Steven E. *Mysticism and Dissent. Religious Ideology and Social Protest in the Sixteenth Century.* New Haven: Yale University Press, 1973.

Prinz, Joseph. "Bernd Knipperdollinck und seine Sippe." ("Bernard Knipperdolling and His Brothers.") *Westfalen* 40, 1962, 96–116.

INDEX

Aa river, 48–49, 186
adultery, 92–93
Albert, Tall, 145
Amsterdam, 138
Anabaptist Kingdom of Münster, 38–39
  contemporary views of, 187–90
  daily life in, 63–64
  defenders of, not professional soldiers, 49–53
  foreigners in, demands of, 104
  forerunner of modern totalitarian regimes, 192–94
  historical meaning of, 182
  its persistent hold on the imagination, 182–87, 200–201
  Marxist view of, 190–91
  theories on the causes of (madness, Satan, etc.), 187–90
  weapons and ammunition of, 49–51, 156–57
Anabaptists
  beliefs and practices, 2–3, 11, 13, 64
  held to be irrational, living in a topsy-turvy world, 188–89
  leadership of, 36
  morale of, 51–52
  numbers of, in Europe, 209
  origins of, 9–12
  persecution of, by contemporary rulers, 2–3, 10, 44, 60, 187, 191
  present-day descendants of, 3
  as prototypes of later revolutionaries, 3
  support for, 12–13
Anabaptists, Dutch, 42, 60
  (1534) called to Münster, 60
  (1534) rounded up and executed, 62
  (1534) trek to Münster, disrupted, 62–63
Anabaptists of Münster
  secret pact of (1532), 16–17
  survivors of, after the fall of the Anabaptist Kingdom, 181–82
apocalyptic final battle, belief in imminence of, 3, 12, 194
Arnheim, Henry von, 96, 99, 102
artillery, 45, 106, 156–57
Assola (maid), 29
authority
  Anabaptists' resistance to, 10–11
  resistance to, incited by the Protestant Reformation, 14

Bakhtin, Michael, 191
baptism
  doctrine of, 9–11, 172

baptism (*continued*)
    infant, 16, 172, 210
    mass, public, 24–25, 36, 42
Baring-Gould, S., *Freaks of Fanaticism and Other Strange Events*, 39, 223
Barret, Pierre, 228
Bast, Wilhelm, 81
Bender, Mary Eleanor, 224
Bentheim, Prince of, 45
Berg, Jurgen tom, daughter of, 7
Bevergen, 35, 44, 155
Bible, 53, 92
    Luther's translation, 14
Bill, Turban, 144–45
Bispinck, Herman, 97, 99, 102
Bockelson, Jan. *See* Leyden, Jan van
book-burnings, 17, 52–53
booty, 164–65, 179, 218
Boventorp, Johann, 166
brainwashing, 197
Branch Davidians, siege at Waco, Texas, 188, 195–96, 198–99
Brand, Clara, 168, 181
Brand, Martha, 145, 168
Brecht, Bertold, 228
Buren, Melchior von, 31, 38, 44, 202
    house of, 51, 111
Burgundy, 180
Busch, Sander, 145
Bussenmeister, Tile, 27, 50, 100, 164

cages, legend that Jan van Leyden and others were exhibited live and traveled, 170–71
cages, three iron, for displaying the bodies of Jan of Leyden, B. Knipperdolling, and B. Krechting, 171, 177, 183, 184–85, 186–87, 227
cannibalism, 146, 147
Capenberg, 47
carnival time, 33–34, 192

Catholic Church
    corruption of, by time of Luther, 1–2
    economic power and activities of, 13–14
    rituals and symbols of, mocked and desecrated by Protestants, 34, 38, 112–13
    universality of, in early modern Europe, 1–2
Catholics of Münster
    (Feb. 1534) depart from Münster, 39
    (Feb. 1534) expelled from Münster, 40–42
    forbidden to practice their beliefs, 19–20
    in modern Münster, 185
    protection of, 22
    urged to be killed by Matthias, 39–40
cats and dogs, killed for food, 146
cattle dealers, Waldeck's confiscation of (1532), 24
Center for Millennial Studies, 195
Cervantes, Miguel de, 66
charismatic rule, 67–69, 197
Charles V, Emperor, 2, 18, 47–48, 133, 175, 202
    (1529) decree against Anabaptists, 10
    (1532) warning to Münster, 20–21
chiliastic groups, 195
Christ, Second Coming of, 3, 11–12, 196
Christianity, primitive, attempted restoration of, 135
church
    authority of and duty to obey, 10–11
    primitive Christian, attempted restoration of, 135

cities, German, governments of, 12–14
Cleves, Prince of, 45, 47, 105, 180
Clevorn, Clara, 104, 144
Cloterbernd, August, 158
Coesfeld, 122, 125
Cohn, Norman, *The Pursuit of the Millennium*, 194–96, 222
Cologne, Archbishop of, 21, 45, 48, 105, 134, 173–74, 180
Communion. *See* Eucharist
Communist theorists, attracted by Münster affair, 37, 147, 190–91
Company of Christ, 9–10, 23, 26, 40, 42, 50, 51, 56, 60, 74, 78, 79, 86, 118, 121, 138, 163
    rules of, 78
    See also Anabaptist Kingdom of Münster
Constitutio Criminalis Carolina, 175–76
convents, attacks on, 7–8
Cornelius, C. A., 225
Corvinus, Antonius, 176–78, 188–89, 202
    interrogation of Jan van Leyden, 171–73
Counter-Reformation, 180–81, 185
crimes, punishable by death, 77–78, 175–76
Cruse, Cord, 57, 181
Culenberg, Jodokus, 7

daemonic, concept of, 183
David (Biblical hero), 109–10
deacons (Münster officials), 54
debts and obligations, abolition of, 54
Delft, 138
Denker, Johann, 147
Dettmar, Nicolaus, 100–101
Deventer, 138
Dhaun, Ulrich von, 148–49, 153, 157, 160, 161–63, 167–68, 180, 202

Divara, wife of Jan Matthias, later Jan van Leyden's queen, 36, 72, 95, 103, 111, 119, 145, 168, 202
Don Quixote, 66
Dostoevsky, Fyodor, *The Brothers Karamazov*, 2
Drier, Else, 145
Dungel, Johann, 41, 212
Dürer, Albrecht, 9
Dürrenmatt, Friedrich, *It Is Written (Es steht geschrieben)*, 89, 228
Dusentschur, Johann, 109–10, 118, 121–22, 124–25, 172, 189, 202
    crowns Jan van Leyden king, 110

ecstatic and orgiastic scenes, 7, 33
Elect, concept of, 194, 197–98
Engels, Friedrich, 190–91
epilepsy, 116
Erdoes, Richard, 196
Estmann, Johann, 165
Eucharist, doctrine of, 121, 172
executions, 56–57, 81, 98–99, 101–2, 113, 145, 157, 174, 176

Fabricius, Dietrich, 25–26, 202
    negotiations of, 132–34
farmers, Catholic sympathies of, 31–32
feasts and festivals, 37–38, 120–21
feudal system, 66, 67
Feyken, Hille, 82, 86–90, 92, 202
followers, relation to leaders, 68–69
fornication, 92–93
fortifications, 48–49
French revolution (1789), 3, 191
Freud, Sigmund, 189

Geelen, Jan van, 138, 139, 157, 165
Germany, lowland, linguistic and cultural similarity to the Netherlands, 59–60

Goehr, Alexander, 229
Goethe, 183
gold, silver, and jewelry, confiscation of, 57
Graes, Henry, 24, 52–53, 119, 122, 126–29, 138–43, 156–57, 181, 202
 (1534) miraculous escape of, 128–29
 (Jan. 1535) reports Jan van Leyden's plans to Waldeck, 139–41
 (March 1535) public letter denouncing Jan van Leyden, 141–42
 real reason for his escape, and offer to spy, 130
 wife of, executed, 145
Grebel, Conrad, 9, 10
Gresbeck, Henry, 55, 64, 103–4, 143–44, 149–55, 156–57, 160, 161, 181, 202, 225, 226–27
 (May 1535) reveals plans for Münster's defense, 154–55
Groningen, 138
Guelders, Duke of, 157
guilder, present-day value of, 211
guilds, 54
Gurgand, Jean-Noel, 228

Halbe-Bauer, Ulrike, *Propheten im Dunkel (Prophets in the Dark)*, 229
Hamm, Count Meinhardt von, 155
Hardwick, Reiner, 158
Hasselt, 62–63
Hauptmann, Gerhart, 183–84, 192
Heaven's Gate suicides, 196
Heine, Heinrich, 220
Hesse, 180
history, uses of, 1–4
Hitler, Adolf, similarities with Jan van Leyden, 192–94
Hobbels, Catharina, 167–68
 husband of, executed, 168

Hoenes, Anna, 145
Hoffman, Melchior, 11–12, 33, 36, 60, 61
Holland, 59–60, 134
 Anabaptists of. *See* Anabaptists, Dutch
Holschern, Elizabeth, 113
Homann, Hermann, 228
Horsch, John, 223
horses, killed for food, 146
Horst, Lenz von der, 154
human nature, hasn't changed, despite Virginia Woolf, 200–201
hunger and starvation during siege of Münster, 146–47
hymns and psalms, 52

Iburg, 128
idol-smashing, 15, 17, 38
incest, 190
Inquisition, Spanish, 2, 176
interrogations, 171–74

Jesus, as leader, 68–69
Jews, not present in Münster, 211
Jodefeld, Jaspar, 23–27, 30, 31–32, 34, 37, 202
Jones, Ernest, 117
 On the Nightmare, 189
Jones, Jim, and Jonestown, Guyana, mass suicide, 196, 197
Joris, David, 182
Judgment Day, 118–19
Judith and Holofernes tale, 82–90, 213
Jülich, Count von, 140

Karasek, Horst, 228
Kerckering, Christian, 112, 166, 174–75, 218–19
 daughter of, marries Christoph von Waldeck, 112, 166

Kerssenbrück, Herman, 41, 167, 185, 202–3
testimony of, 5–8, 225–26
Kibbenbrock, Gerd, 37, 103, 166
Kirchhoff, Karl-Heinz, 180, 184, 224, 227
Klopriss, Johann, 125–26, 132
Knipperdolling, Bernard, 6, 23, 24, 25, 27, 30, 31–32, 37, 40, 41, 51, 53, 54, 60, 71, 72, 75, 77–78, 86–87, 101, 110, 111, 113, 123, 133, 141, 145, 159, 166, 181, 190, 191, 192, 203
(1532) idol-smashing attacks of, 16–19
(July 1534) attempted overthrow of, 97–98
(June 1535) capture of, 167–68
(1535) interrogation of, 173–74
(Jan. 1536) execution of, 176–78
daughter of, married to Jan van Leyden, 71, 95
vision of, 114–17
Kobalt-Groch, Marion, 89
Kockenbeckin, Katherine, 113
Kohüs, Magnus, 165
Kolthave, Anna, 57, 181
Koresh, David, 188, 198–99
Krahn, Cornelius, 224
Krampe, Herman, 99, 100
Krechting, Bernard, 34, 111, 123, 166, 203
(Jan. 1536) execution of, 176–78
Krechting, Henry, 34, 49, 51, 55, 57, 70, 111, 113, 123, 164, 174, 181–82, 189
Krechting, Henry, II, 182
Krechting, Herman, 182

Latin, 19, 25
law, rule by, 66

leaders
relation to followers, 68–69
three types of, in Weber's scheme, 66–69
Leddanus (coppersmith), 147
Leyden, 138
Leyden, Jan van (Jan Bockelson), 6, 24, 25, 30, 32, 33, 37, 51, 52, 57, 86–87, 159–60, 203
(1533) mass baptisms of, 24–25
(March 1534) executes Herbert Rusher, 56–57
(April 1534) inherits leadership of Jan Matthias, 69–72
(July 1534) attempted overthrow of, 97–102
(Sept. 1534) crowned king, 110–13
(Oct. 1534) executes a captured soldier, 123–24
(April 1535) gives noble titles to his closest followers, 147
(June 1535) in final battle of Münster, 163
(June 1535) capture of, 166–67
(June 1535) meets Waldeck, 168–69
(June 1535) prisoner in Dülmen, 170
(1535) interrogation of, by Corvinus, 171–73
(Jan. 1536) execution of, 176–78
attitude toward women, 89–90
compared to Hitler, 192–94
compared to Satan, 189–90
court of, 110–13
early life, 70–71
famed as new David, 109–10
leadership talent of, 72–73
lust of, 95–96
marriages of, 103, 111
polygamy doctrine, 93–96
remorse of, before his execution, 176
visions of, 76

lie, the big, 73
Luther, Martin, 2, 15, 52, 88, 135–37, 172, 203
  Bible translation, 14
  excommunicated, 9
  opposition to Anabaptists, 10, 187
  support for authority, 14
  Wittenberg theses, 8–9
Lutherans of Münster, 15–16, 172
  (1532) ordered by Charles V to leave Münster, 20
  (Feb. 1534) expelled from Münster, 40–42
  radical, 24
  urged to be killed by Matthias, 39–40
Lüttich, Bishop of, 132

madness, said to be motivation of the Münster Anabaptists, 188–89
Manderscheid, Count Robert, 143–44, 153–54
Marie of Burgundy, 47, 71, 132, 133, 180
marriage, doctrine of, 91–96, 172–73
marriages in Münster
  annulled, 93, 104
  forced, 104
  polygamous, 92–96, 104, 113, 173
Marschalk, Caspar, 213
Marx, Karl, 190
Mass, mock, 112–13
Matthias, Jan, 12, 16, 33, 36–41, 52–58, 190, 203
  (Feb. 1534) summoned to Münster by Jan Bockelson, 36–37
  (April 1534) killed in "single combat" against Waldeck's army, 64–66
  opposition to, 54–56
  visions of, 64–65

Melanchthon, Philip, 7, 15, 135, 136, 203
  calls for extermination of the Anabaptists, 175
Mengerssen, Hermann von, 44
Mennonite Quarterly Review, 223
Mennonites, 3, 89, 223
mercenaries, generally, 46
mercenaries, Waldeck's
  contract with Waldeck, 46–47
  drunkenness of, causes an attack to fail, 80–81
  final pay of, 179–80
merchants of Münster, 54
Merveldt, Dirk von, 16, 38, 86–88, 203
Merveldt, Ida von, 8, 24–25, 27, 37–38, 203
Meyerbeer, Giacomo, 229
Michelet, Jules, 196
Millennium, concept of, 194
Million-Man March on Washington, 196
Milton, Paradise Lost, 190
miracles
  biblical certainty of, 130
  escape of Henry Graes, 128–29
  Jan of Leyden heals a sick girl, 70
  three suns, 33
Moer, Bernard, 147
Mollenheck, Henry, 37, 54, 77, 96, 203
  (July 1534) failed counterrevolution of, 97–102
Morrien, Eberhard von, 35, 44, 149, 181
Münster
  (1525) grant of freedom, 14
  (Feb. 1532) revolt against Catholic rule, 16–20
  (Oct. 1532) blockaded, 21–22
  (Feb. 1533) treaty with Waldeck agreed to, 22

(March 1533) radicals elected to power, 23

(Feb. 1534) Anabaptists attack Lutherans in City Hall, 29–32

(Feb. 1534) fear that Waldeck will attack, 30–31

(Feb. 1534) new radical council formed, 37

(Feb. 1534) outside supporters arrive, 34

(Feb. 1534) siege of, 43, 44–48, 74– 76, 78–90

(March 1534) invites Dutch Anabaptists to come to Münster, 60

(April 1534) council disbanded, replaced by twelve elders, 76–78

(May 1534) first attack on, fails, 80– 81

(Aug. 1534) second attack on, fails, 105–9

(Oct. 1534) apostles sent to neighboring towns to gather support, and failure of their mission, 121–30

(Nov. 1534) Fabricius tries to negotiate with Jan van Leyden, 132–34

(Nov. 1534) sealed off, 134–35

(Jan. 1535) conditions in, after prolonged siege, 139–40, 146– 48

(April 1535) refugees from, refused succor by Waldeck, 148–49

(May 1535) defectors reveal plans for city's defense, 153–55

(June 1535) final, successful attack on, 156–64

(June 1535) street fighting and conclusion of the war, 162–64

description of, 13–14

fortifications of, 48–49

later history of, after the Anabaptist reign, 180–81, 220

modern-day sights of, 184–87

predicted center of revolt for conquest of Europe, 60

predicted scene of Apocalypse and Second Coming, 3, 12

steeples and towers of, demolished by the Anabaptists, 75–76

traditional government of, 14, 48

walls and moats, 186

wealth and power of, 5–6

See also Anabaptist Kingdom of Münster; siege of Münster

Münster, Gert von, 48, 98–99, 203

Münster City Museum, 185, 225

Müntzer, Thomas, 14, 191

Nagel, Johann ("Hansel Eck"), 150– 55, 160, 161, 181, 203

nakedness, public, 61–62, 76

Nazi rule, 89

similar to Anabaptist Kingdom of Münster, 192–94

New Zion, 38–39

Niland, Master, 111, 145

1960s ethos, 192

Northorn, Claes, 145–46

Oberstein, Count, 153

Oldenburg, Count, 182

Osnabrück, 47, 122, 126–28

Overwater Church, 22, 185

Overwater Church Convent, 8, 24– 25, 26

conversion of nuns of, 92

predicted destruction of, 27–28

Oyer, John S., 224

Oykinkfeld, Johann, 96, 99, 102

Paderborn, 47

Paracelsus, 93

paranoia, and totalitarianism, 194–95
Paulus, Helmut, *Die Tönernen Füsse*
    (Feet of Clay), 54, 228–29
Peace of Westphalia, 220
Peasants' War (1525), 9, 14, 47, 54,
    183, 191
People's Temple Movement, 197,
    198
Peter, Saint, 216
Philip, Count of Hesse, 18, 45, 47,
    106, 132, 133, 136, 149, 180,
    203
    (Oct. 1532) negotiates between
        sides in Münster, 21
    (1535) delegation from, 159–60
Phillips, Obbe, 62
polygamy, 92–96, 104, 113, 173
poverty, vow of, 112
prince-bishops of Germany, role of,
    17
private property, 16
    abolition of, 53–54
    opposition to, 23
Protestantism
    beginning of, 8–9
    supposed cause of the Münster
        disturbances, 185
"Psalmus" (Peter Simons?), 89

Raesfeld, Johann von, 44, 164
Ramert, Herman, 70, 87, 88, 213
Reck-Malleczewen, Friedrich, 88–89,
    192–94
    Bockelson, 228
Redeker, Herman, 27, 34, 56–57,
    147
Revelation, Book of, 11
revolutions of 1848, 191
Rhegius, Urbanus, 188
Riemensneider, Evart, 64, 98, 166
Riemensneider, Jaspar, 166
Röchell (soldier), 166–67

Roll, Henry, 23, 25
    death of, 42
Rome, Sack of (1527), 9, 164
Rothmann, Bernard, 14–20, 24, 32–
    34, 42, 52, 77, 86, 103, 111,
    113, 123, 133, 159, 166, 188,
    189, 203
    (1533) attempted expulsion from
        Münster, 25–26
    (Feb. 1534) inveighs against
        Overwater Church Convent, 27–
        28
    (July 1534) attempted overthrow
        of, 97–98
    lively religious services of, 20
    mysterious disappearance of, 167,
        182
    preaching of, 7–8
    propaganda leaflets of, 23, 60–61
    "Restitution" (pamphlet), 135–37
    "Revenge" (pamphlet), 137–38
    sermon on marriage, 91–93
    writings of, 135–38
rule, three types of, in Weber's
    scheme, 66–69
Rusher, Herbert, 54–57, 69, 71, 96,
    203
    death of, 57
Russian revolution (1917), 3

St. Lambert's Church, 17, 20, 22, 25–
    26, 183
St. Mauritz Church, 15, 45
St. Paul's Cathedral, 13, 38, 185
Salaman, Nicholas, *The Garden of
    Earthly Delights*, 214, 222
Sanctus, Henry, 166
Satan
    Jan of Leyden compared to, 189–
        90
    said to inspire Anabaptists, 187–88
    traits of, 189

Savonarola, 66
Saxony, Prince of, 133
Schlachtscape, Herman, 97, 101
Schmalkaldic League, 40, 88, 181
Schulte, Bernard, 161
Second Coming of Christ, belief in,
    3, 11–12, 196
sex
    Anabaptist doctrines regarding, 64
    and sin, 189
    See also marriage
Shaffer, Johann, 119
Shirer, William, 228
Siburg, Johann von, 176
siege of Münster
    cost of, 47, 132, 211
    similarities to Waco siege, 198–99
sieges, 48–49
Simons, Menno, 2–3, 89, 94–95, 223
Simons, Peter, 89–90
Soest, 122, 124–25
Soviet Union, similar to Anabaptist
    Kingdom of Münster, 194
Spartacus, 66
Spieker, Otto, 127–28
state
    authority of and duty to obey, 10–
    11
    duty to punish unbelievers, 175
Stayer, James, 223
Steding, Wilhelm, 154–55, 161–65,
    167, 168, 180, 203
    final days, 181
Strasbourg, 12
Stupperich, Robert, 228
Sundermann (furrier), 39
Swerte, Bernard, 165

taxes, 47–48
Telgte, 80
    raid on (1532), 22
theocracy, 136

three iron cages, for displaying the
    bodies of Jan of Leyden, B.
    Knipperdolling, and B.
    Krechting, 171, 177, 183, 184–
    85, 186–87, 227
three suns, miracle of, 33
Tilbeck, Herman, 22, 23–25, 31–32,
    37, 56–57, 77, 99–100, 103,
    110, 111, 165–66, 203
    treachery of, in burning Waldeck's
    offer, 32
totalistic views, 197
totalitarianism
    Anabaptist Kingdom of Münster as
    forerunner of, 192–94
    means by which it gains power,
    193–94
    paranoia and, 194–95
tradesmen of Münster, 54
tradition, rule by, 66–67
Trier, Prince of, 105
truces, 106
trumpets sounding three times,
    prophecy of, 118
Trutelink (carpenter), 76
Tunneken, Margaret, 145
Turks, Anabaptists compared to, 187
Twickel, Johann von, 163

vandalism, 15, 17, 38
Van Sittart, Peter, *The Siege*, 215,
    222
Vinne, Dionysus, 127–28, 132
visions, 64–65, 76, 114–17

Waco, Texas, siege of Branch
    Davidians at, 188, 195–96, 198–
    99
    similarities to the Münster siege,
    198–99
Waldeck, Christoph von, 112, 166,
    174

Waldeck, Franz von, Prince-Bishop
    of Münster, 203
    (March 1532) succeeds to the
        prince-bishopric of Münster, 18–
        20
    (1532) warns Münster against
        rebellion, 20–21
    (March 1532) confiscates cattle of
        traders, 24
    (Oct. 1532) blockades Münster, 21–
        22
    (Jan. 1534) summons city
        councilors to a meeting, 26–27
    (Feb. 1534) orders van Wyck
        executed, 35
    (Feb. 1534) prepares attack on
        Münster, 44–48
    (May 1534) negotiations with
        Anabaptists, 79–80
    (June 1534) attempted assassination
        of, by Hille Feyken, 86–90
    (June 1535) enters Münster, 168
    (June 1535) meets Jan van Leyden,
        168–69
    (Jan. 1536) witnesses executions
        of Jan van Leyden and others, 177
    artillery of, 45, 106
    blood lust of, 157–58
    debts of, due to the siege, 179–80
    illegitimate son of, 112
    later life of, 180–81
    physical appearance of, 18–19
Wandscheer, Bernard, 158

Wandscheer, Elizabeth, 158–59, 204
    marriage to Jan van Leyden, later
        personally beheaded by him, 158–
        59
war, laws of, 164–65, 179
Warendorf, 122, 125–26
Warendorp, 21
war wagons of the Anabaptists of
    Münster, 156–57, 164
Weber, Max, 66–69
Wesel, 140–41
Wesseling, Johann, 29, 41
Wiede, Frederick von, Prince-
    Bishop, 14, 16–18
Williams, George H., 91, 224
Wolbeck, 44, 79
women, Anabaptist, 91–92
Woolf, Virginia, 200
world upside down (verkehrte Welt),
    188–89, 191–92
Worms, 180
Wullen, Gerlach von, 120, 166, 174,
    204
Wyck, Friedrich von, 21, 25, 26–27,
    30, 204
    flees Münster but is executed by
        Waldeck, 34–36

year 2000 studies, 195

Zwinger (gun tower), 48
Zwingli, Ulrich, 135
    opposition to Anabaptists, 10–11